Monstrous Liminality;

Or, The Uncanny Strangers of Secularized Modernity

Robert G. Beghetto

]u[

ubiquity press
London

Published by
Ubiquity Press Ltd.
Unit 322–323
Whitechapel Technology Centre
75 Whitechapel Road
London E1 1DU
www.ubiquitypress.com

Text © Robert G. Beghetto, 2022

First published 2022

Cover art by Odilon Redo.
Image provided with permission by National Gallery of Art, licensed under CC0.

Print and digital versions typeset by Siliconchips Services Ltd.

ISBN (Paperback): 978-1-914481-12-3
ISBN (PDF): 978-1-914481-13-0
ISBN (EPUB): 978-1-914481-14-7
ISBN (Mobi): 978-1-914481-15-4

DOI: https://doi.org/10.5334/bcp

This work is licensed under the Creative Commons Attribution-NonCommercial 4.0 International License (unless stated otherwise within the content of the work). To view a copy of this license, visit https://creativecommons.org/licenses/by-nc/4.0/ or send a letter to Creative Commons, 444 Castro Street, Suite 900, Mountain View, California, 94041, USA. This license allows sharing and copying any part of the work for personal use, providing author attribution is clearly stated. This license prohibits commercial use of the material.

The full text of this book has been peer-reviewed to ensure high academic standards. For full review policies, see http://www.ubiquitypress.com/

Suggested citation:
Beghetto, R. G. 2022. *Monstrous Liminality; Or, The Uncanny Strangers Of Secularized Modernity*. London: Ubiquity Press. DOI: https://doi.org/10.5334/bcp. License: CC-BY-NC

To read the free, open access version of this book online, visit https://doi.org/10.5334/bcp or scan this QR code with your mobile device:

Contents

Acknowledgements … v

Introduction … 1
   The Secular, The Sacred, and Resacralization … 7
   Modernity, Liminality, and The Uncanny … 9
   The Modern Stranger … 13
   Modern Monsters and Haunting Spectres … 16
   Chapter Summary … 17
   Notes: Introduction … 19

I: Frankenstein and the "Birth" of Secularized Modernity … 21
   Frankenstein and Secularization … 24
   The Historical Shift of the Monstrous … 29
   Modernity's Monstrous Secret … 32
   The End of the Natural and the Beginning of Artificial Reality … 35
   The Uncanny Stranger in a Secular Void … 39
   Notes: Chapter I … 43

II: Leopardi and Baudelaire: Kindred Spirits of the Modern Stranger … 47
   The Monstrosity of the Liminalizing Space of Secular Modernity … 50
   The Modern Dantes: Wanderers of a Modern and Liminalizing Hell … 55
   A Rupture in History and the Illusion of Progress … 62
   Battling the Storm that is Modernity in the Streets of Paris … 66
   Notes: Chapter II … 70

III: Violence, The Great War, and The Modern Stranger … 75
   The Great War, Irony, & Dark Utopias … 78
   The Stranger in No Man's Land … 83
   Trenches, Violence, and The City … 86
   Sickness and Irony: Zeno's Ironic Utopia … 92
   Divine Violence & Messianic Time in Miller's *Leibowitz* … 98
   Notes: Chapter III … 102

IV: Boredom – An Infinite Epilogue to the Modern Stranger — 103
- The Difficult Task of Defining Boredom — 105
- The (In)Action Films of Michelangelo Antonioni — 109
- Digital Boredom — 113
- A Heroic Lack of Attunement — 117
- Notes: Chapter IV — 122

V: The Sacredness of Digital Liminality — 123
- Hybrid Religions of Cyberpunk — 130
- God is (In) Cyberspace — 134
- Strangers in Cyberspace — 137
- Cyberspace: Heaven or Hell? — 139
- Notes: Chapter V — 142

VI: Strange Gender and Post-Humanism — 145
- From Shelley's 'Hideous Progeny' to Haraway's Cyborg — 149
- A Spiral Dance in the Abyss — 153
- Cyborgs, Dogs, and Abortions: The Abject of Gender in Kathy Acker's Don Quixote and Empire of the Senseless — 157
- Acker's Resacralization of the Symbolic — 160
- Notes: Chapter VI — 165

Conclusion: Spectral Monsters and Modern Strangers — 169
- Spectres and Monsters — 169
- Spectres and Phantoms — 172
- Addressing the Monster in the Spectral Room — 174
- Adaptation and the Future of the Modern Stranger—A Coda — 175
- Notes: Conclusion — 177

References — 179

Index — 205

Acknowledgements

I would like to thank Markus Reisenleitner, for his consistent support and guidance during the writing of this manuscript. Furthermore, I would also like to express my gratitude to Susan Ingram and John Dwyer for their added guidance and assistance. I would also like to thank Jody McCutcheon for assisting during the editorial process. Lastly, I would like to send a special thank you to Carlos Torres, Sadaf Etemad-Rezaie, and my parents for their unconditional support during this writing period.

Introduction

An age or society would then be secular or not, in virtue of the conditions of experience of and search for the spiritual.
—Charles Taylor, *A Secular Age*

We are unknown to ourselves, we men of knowledge—and with good reason. We have never sought ourselves—how could it happen that we should ever find ourselves? It has rightly been said: "Where your treasure is, there will your heart be also" ... So we are necessarily strangers to ourselves, we do not comprehend ourselves, we have to misunderstand ourselves, for us the law "Each is furthest from himself applies to all eternity—we are not "men of knowledge" with respect to ourselves.
—Friedrich Nietzsche, *On the Genealogy of Morals*

The monster ensures in time, and for our theoretical knowledge, a continuity that, for our everyday experience, floods, volcanoes, and subsiding continents confuse in space. The other consequence is that the signs of continuity throughout such a history can no longer be of any order other than that of resemblance ... Thus, against the background of the continuum, the monster provides an account, as though in caricature, of the genesis of differences, and the fossil recalls, in the uncertainty of its resemblances, the first buddings of identity.
—Michel Foucault, *The Order of Things*

At almost every point, I have to stand between alternative possibilities of existence, to be completely at home in neither and to take no definitive stand against either. Since thinking presupposes receptiveness to new possibilities, this position is fruitful for thought; but it is difficult and dangerous in life, which again and again demands decisions and thus the exclusion of alternatives.
—Paul Tillich, *On the Boundary*

Prior to his death, Walter Benjamin penned an essay entitled "Theses on the Philosophy of History" (1940/2007) that presents a theory of history as being defined by a continuous series of disruptions that alter the past and future through the rapturous present, what he claims 'as a model of Messianic time' that 'comprises the entire history of mankind in an enormous abridgment' (69). Created from the ruins of such an event—namely the French Revolution—19th-century European society was forced to deal with the idea of the modern (the *now*) in an entirely new and secularized fashion. The process of transformation was anything but fluid as the ideas of the previous "non-modern" world still endured, despite being juxtaposed with the influx of new social, political, and personal thought that was sweeping across Europe. As modernity began to rapidly change and influence European culture, many 19th- and 20th-century writers and intellectuals struggled to identify themselves with this modern paradoxical context. As a result, the modern stranger was conjured up out of the uncanny depths of secularized modernity.

Many of the writings during this period focused on the contrasts and paradoxes that contributed to the creation and evolution of the modern stranger. Although a subject whose makeup is continually shifting, the modern stranger still exists as a strong allegory for what I refer to as secularized modernity, particularly because of its unsolidified and liminal characteristics. My book assesses the transformation of the figure of the modern stranger in the literature of the modern age in terms of liminality. Along with its *doppelgänger* the monster, the stranger reflects not only uncanny otherness but the horrors and anxiety of realizing the potential imperfections and weaknesses of the individual, society, and their utopian imaginings. It must be mentioned that the modern stranger is not merely a marginalized figure. In continuing with its liminal nature, the modern stranger is also a privileged character. Just as its alienating experiences vary, so does its privilege, ranging from gender to race to class and geography: the privilege of knowledge, the privilege of opportunity, the privilege to blend in and out of society at will, to wrestle with freedom, secularism and the sacred, or simply the privilege to be bored. Yet the circumnavigating of these two paradoxical perspectives, of privilege and marginalization, once again allows the stranger during modernity to be an individual that goes beyond binary classifications, while paradoxically being caught in them, thereby being both inside and outside modernity, both remote and included. In my readings, I show the explanatory potential of focusing on the resacralizing—in a paradoxical and liminal manner—of traditionally sacred concepts such as messianic time and the utopian, and the conflicts that emerged as a result of secularized modernity's denial of its own hybridization. I understand resacralization as the movement, or dance, between the secularizing and sacralizing facets of modernity, which ultimately keep it in a liminal state.

This approach to modern literature shows how the modern stranger deals with the dangers of failing to be re-assimilated into mainstream society, instead being caught in a fixed or permanent state of liminality, a state that can ultimately lead to boredom, alienation, nihilism, and failure. These "monstrous" aspects of liminality can also be rewarding in that they confront both traditional and contemporary viewpoints, enabling new and fresh perspectives suspended between imagination and reality, past and future, that make the uncanny stranger an important figure in secularized modernity. As a "spectral monster" that has a paradoxical and liminal relationship with both the sacred and the secular, the figure of the modern stranger has played a role in both adapting and shaping a culturally determined understanding of the self and the other. With the advent of modernity, the stranger, the monster, and the spectre became interconnected. Haunting the edges of reason while also being absorbed into "normal" society, all three, together with the cyborg, manifest the vulnerability of an age that is fearful of the return of the repressed. Yet these figures can also become reappropriated as positive symbols, able to navigate between the dangerous and chaotic elements that threaten society while serving as precarious and ironic symbols of hope or sustainability.

In modernity, the sacred and the profane are no longer understood as binaries, but are liminal and constituted in a playful, nuanced, and increasingly non-dialectical relationship with each other. As a result of this liminal outlook, my book investigates the paradoxical, utopian, and negative-utopian makeup of the modern stranger as an outcome of secularizing and modernizing changes in what is typically regarded as Western, predominantly European, Judeo-Christian culture and history, beginning with the advent of modernity. I understand that terms such as *the West* and *Judeo-Christian culture*[1] can be problematic and tautological concepts, especially in regard to defining modernity, culture, and the socio-political, particularly since both consist of various and distinct societies and interpretations. Cultural theorist and philosopher Kwame Anthony Appiah points out in his fascinating article 'There is no such thing as western civilisation' (2016) that the term *the West* has had multiple meanings and connotations throughout history. As a result, establishing an essence of western culture or civilization on the basis of a false set of collective characteristics and qualities is highly problematic, as accepting such a term allocates a certain superiority that 'can look simply like a euphemism for white' (Appiah). While I do agree with Appiah's argument that there is no such thing as 'a precious golden nugget' that links ancient civilizations such as Greece and Rome to contemporary Europe and North America, I argue that the term *the West*, as erroneous as it is to define it as a certain homogeneous entity, is still a useful term when discussing 19th-century imperial and technological knowledge creation, and consequently my project. Most notably, Appiah states that the notion of *the West* does not emerge until the late 19th century, expanding during the 20th century under the guidance of imperialism (to which I would add technological and secular advancements), a time frame that ultimately coincides with the advent of secularized modernity in the early 19th century.

It may well be that it was during this time that, beginning with Europe, the West first established itself as a sort of collective entity, which simply looked to a deceitful Hegelian-like lineage in order to establish itself as a historical movement of progress and liberalism founded on Christian ethics and a belief in individual rights of agency and freedom. And while Appiah is accurate in stating that it was not just Christianity that moulded Europe, but also a combination of multiple cultural and religious societies such as paganism and Islam, Christendom has dominated what many regard as the West in recent history.

Thus, a binary essentialism of the West, as either a founder of 'exalted intellectual and artistic achievements' or a dispraising term reflecting an 'arsenic' nugget of racism, imperialism, and subjugation (Appiah 2016), ultimately created the idea of the West, whether artificial or not. Thus, the removal of the concept becomes as problematic as its implantation, for as Stefan Kubiak writes, by removing the term, '[t]he subjugation and colonization of the African, Asian and American peoples and imposing foreign control upon them suddenly loses the agent,' while simultaneously ignoring that European and American societies have eventually established 'certain cultural codes that readers educated in a particular culture are able to decipher immediately' (2017) amongst themselves.

Moreover, concepts such as secular and secularism are also not exclusively Western, despite many seeing secularism as an originary and defining characteristic of Western societies. Even Charles Taylor, who is one of the more recent scholars to advocate a direct connection between Christianity and secularism, argues that although 'there is truth in the claim that secularism has Christian roots ... it is wrong to think that this limits the application of its formulae to post-Christian societies' (1998: 31). Secularism has become a defining, even misconstrued, concept that has been used to separate what is largely considered as Europe and the Americas from the rest of the world, in order to maintain the division of self and other, while many of these "others," such as the religious challengers of secularism in the Middle East, use the same differentiation to solidify the same problematic binary on their own terms (Asad 2003: 2). Secularism, as with the notion of the West, has never lost its colonial origins in the Muslim world (Nasr 2003: 69). Nonetheless, at the same time, it would be unwise to overlook the direct cultural significance and influence that both secularism and modernity play in what I have described as secularized modernity. In this regard, I am not examining the idea of secularism through a political sense, as in the separation of church and state, but rather as a philosophical or existential mood that is distinctly connected with modernity. As a result, the focus of this project will be on what is commonly considered historically Christian societies' complex connection with secularism rather than a discussion of the concept itself. I do not examine Christianity in a theological lens, but rather as a cultural category that has had a profound influence on western traditions, norms, and symbols, and equally, its effect on paradoxically deconstructing those very same representations.

Beginning with 19th-century Europe, I explore the conflicts and paradoxes of a secular culture created from the liminal spirit of modernity's own "empty" space and its uncanny interrelation with the modern stranger. By arguing that an outsider criticizes modernity from within modernity's own liminal space, I will show: 1) how the concept of the modern stranger emerged in the late 18th and early 19th centuries, as a result of the liminality created by secularized modernity, where technological possibilities and secular reinterpretations begin to overtake traditionally held sacred realms; 2) how the modern stranger moved from being a confined member of the social underground to becoming a more prominent figure of alterity that has slowly spread into the mainstream; 3) the impact the modern stranger has had on cultural identity and the concepts of self and other within social environments, from the modern metropolis to more liminal contemporary arenas, such as social media and communities where identities become further fragmented; 4) the potential of resacralizing sacred and utopian elements and the tensions that arise through this paradoxical and secular reinterpretation of sacred concepts such as the messianic and utopian; and finally, 5) the modern stranger and secularized modernity's relationship with the monstrous that is found in both its utopian and anti-utopian origins. I examine how these secular/sacred binaries engage in a dialectical, yet non-essential, connection with one another by investigating the ways in which the modern stranger addresses the process of secularization, and how the stranger's situation in liminal space can be seen as a form of resacralization in the modern world.

I contend that, in reference to the modern stranger, defining or essentializing the figure could result in the creation of other sets of binaries, dissolving the purpose and productiveness of liminality, even the commonly used negative concepts of boredom and alienation, which themselves could be viewed as constructive elements of change. Furthermore, my book will tackle the potential triumphs and difficulties that arise with a concept of utopia that is based on ideas of lack, estrangement, boredom, and abjection. Modern alienation and disillusionment, which was a main focal point of early and late modernism, has not vanished in current society and still creates further fragmentation between the self and other, especially as a result of technological advancements in social interactions. In a world that has seen many social movements, subcultures, and what Victor Turner calls anti-structures, the question of how the modern stranger inhabits itself within these 'anti-structural communities' becomes increasingly important in the development of identity, or non-identity, in the contemporary world. The term *anti-structure community* is derived from Turner's work and describes communities that challenge the dominant structural order of society. As Turner argues, these communities break 'in through the interstices of structure, in liminality; at the edges of structure, in marginality; and from beneath structure, in inferiority.' Although secular and temporal movements, these anti-structures retain a sacred element: '[i]t is almost everywhere held to be sacred or "holy," possibly because it transgresses or dissolves the norms that govern structured and institutionalized relationships and is accompanied by experiences of unprecedented potency' (Turner 1969/1995: 128). Nonetheless, once these communities become established in and of themselves, they 'return to structure revitalized by their experience of *communitas*' (ibid. 129). Both the structure/anti-structure and secular/resacralized practices are relevant in my study of modernity and its paradoxical and liminal quality of going beyond yet retaining its limitations.

My book is located in an interdisciplinary field of humanities research that I described as Secularized Modernity and is grounded in a combination of modern cultural history and literary criticism. It is predominantly situated in a transhumanist/posthumanist approach to socio-cultural anthropology, sociology, history, critical theory, psychoanalysis, theology, and most importantly, literary analysis, which will allow me to critically assess traditional beliefs about faith, identity, and truths commonly held in modern Western cultural and social history. Although I use the term posthuman throughout the book, I do not entirely advocate a definition based on posthumanism's materialist-centred and antihumanist foundations, nor do I completely reject transhumanism's emphasis on humanism and the individual, but rather as the liminal space intersecting between them, especially considering that antihumanism and posthumanism are still based on 'intrinsic humanist discursive values' (Braidotti 2013: 29). While the multiple strands create many paradoxes and contradictions within posthumanism, Rosi Braidotti's statement that '[t]he posthuman condition urges us to think critically and creatively about who and what we are actually in the process of becoming' (ibid. 12), in my opinion is the main aspect of posthumanism that connects the many strands together.[2]

This perspective allows for a discourse in liminality that can oscillate more broadly between socially constructed binaries, criticisms, and strategies linking culture and literature. At its core, this book is structured around literary criticism and analysis, since the modern stranger first emerged in the world through modernist literature, and also because, as François Cusset (2003/2008) indicates in his historical account of the rise of the American English department, literature is often regarded as the best medium in gaining a perspective of the other and, likewise, the perfect vehicle to integrate multiple fields together. Through the exploration of the human condition, literature helps us to make sense of the ambiguities of the modern world, while often illuminating 'the complex cultural, social, and representational issues tied up with conceptual shifts and technological innovations' (Hayles 1999: 24). Accordingly, this book will explore the effects the secular and the sacred have on the stranger by means of modern literary fiction. Paul Tillich argues that in order to express the complex relationship between the sacred and secularized modernity, 'we must first point to the places where the awareness of the predicament ... in our period is most sharply expressed. These places are the great art, literature, and partly at least, the philosophy of our time' (1988: 5-6). The importance of literature goes beyond an examination of the stranger within the art form, seeking to understand how literature helped change or shape liminality in modern culture and society.

The Secular, The Sacred, and Resacralization

In order to understand the socio-cultural climate in which the modern stranger finds itself, it is necessary to uncover a process of secularization in modernity, which I position around a Weberian concept of secularization as a result of disillusionment or disenchantment. More recently, secularization is no longer seen as a straightforward process, nor is the secular viewed as necessarily being a binary to the religious. Prominent secular or post-secular scholars (Asad 2001, 2003; Casanova 2010; Connolly 2010; Taylor 2007) argue, in one form or another, that the secular seems to have a strong relationship with religion and especially the sacred. Originally, the secular/religious dichotomy, advocated and popularized by thinkers such as sociologist Émile Durkheim (1912/1975), conceived of the profane sphere as completely separate from religious influence. However, more recently, are no longer understood as binaries, but are liminal and constituted in a playful, nuanced, and increasingly non-dialectical relationship with each other. For instance, anthropologist Talal Asad goes beyond the typical dichotomies such as sacred/profane, reason/imagination, and symbol/allegory that 'pervade modern secular discourse' (2003: 26). Asad claims that the secular is not a substitute or 'a mask for religion' (ibid.), and yet is also not independent from it; or, in other words, the secular is the 'Siamese twin' of religion (2001: 221). As he maintains, since 'the secular is so much part of our modern life, it is not easy to grasp it directly,' and therefore 'best pursued through its shadows' (2003: 16). Even for Mircea Eliade, who argues more along the lines of the profane and sacred as opposites, the two are not purely caught in their contrasting binaries, at least in terms of lived experience, since the behaviour of the religious individual and that of the non-religious individual are similarly based upon myth and symbolism (1957/1959: 204).

Although religion as a practice does require ritual and tradition, there is still a cognitive, psychological, or existential essence to it that cannot be removed in the modern age. Charles Taylor (2007) famously argues that in our secular age, God has become marginalized, distant, and absent, resulting in a more liminal "providential deism" and the "disenfleshment" of religion. The modern secular, especially in traditionally Judeo-Christian societies, tends to push the sacred into the internal world of the individual. Although resulting in somewhat different conclusions, both Giorgio Agamben (2005) and Alain Badiou (2003) talk of a fracture with Jewish history in the writings of Saint Paul, creating a path for modern humanism. To some critics, Paul's reading of the Old Testament makes him possibly history's first deconstructionist (Hart in Manolopoulos 2009: 75; Weisberg 1984: xvi), while the deconstruction of Christianity is simply part of the continuation of its own movement (Nancy 2005/2008), resulting from its own self-distortion. When debating the idea of secularism as an early beginning of disenfleshment, scholars often overlook this separation that St. Paul created in *Galatians*. The removal of historical rituals that stand between God's covenant and humanity created a rupture in what Eliade argues is the passageway or bridge between the profane and sacred, God and human (Eliade 1959: 182) in Christian societies. Eliade says that the desacralization of modern humanity is a result of the Judeo-Christian secularization process, which became epitomized by Friedrich Nietzsche's proclamation that 'God is dead':

> Nietzsche's proclamation was new for the Western, Judeo-Christian world, but the death of God is an extremely old phenomenon in the history of religions—of course, with this difference: that the disappearance of the High God gives birth to a more vivid and more dramatic, though inferior, pantheon—whereas in Nietzsche's conception, after the death of the Judeo-Christian God, man has to live by himself—alone, in a radically desacralized world (Eliade 2013: 48).

However, there seems to be no final step to this process that Eliade mentions. Although it seems society is desacralizing, historically secularization has led to new forms of religious organizations, as with the Protestant Reformation; but more importantly to this study, secularisation has also allowed for a resacralisation of secular space, opening up new possibilities of the sacred that are centred more on an individual's personally constructed morals and tenets than on dogmatic tradition. No longer are traditionally and religiously established rituals necessary to directly connect with the sacred; rather, faith develops internally, personally, yet at the same time is still grounded in historical and cultural remnants. The secularizing of modernity seems to routinely create a new or resacralizing practice within its inherent liminal space, and therefore the act of desacralizing is misleading.

Asad suggests that this epistemological turn is a result of post-Enlightenment European thought, in which the sacred and faith both 'came to be constituted as a mysterious, mythic thing, the focus of moral and administrative disciplines' (2003: 33) resulting in the removal of any kind of habitual character. Therefore, this notion of religion aided by Enlightenment thought helped to establish a classification of religion later asserted by Tillich: '[b]eing religious means asking passionately the question of meaning of our existence and being willing to receive answers, even if the answers hurt ... it is the state of being concerned about one's own being and being universally' (1988: 1). Taking this explanation into consideration, the idea of being religious has shifted in Western modernity to something essential, universal, and beyond tradition, which seems to be only a way of expressing one's religious spirit. The notion that the religious is something everyone experiences regardless of practice or belief is analogous with Julia Kristeva's psychoanalytical thesis in *This Incredible Need to Believe*: religion is not an illusory practice, but rather the place where one forms one's own identity through a natural and psychological need to believe. By way of the secular, the psychoanalytic examination of the inner self for Kristeva allows for 'the *access to the sacred* that Christianity made possible' (2006/2009: ix).

The tension between the idea of the sacred as a form of cultural ritual and tradition versus that of an existential and universal psychological desire for faith has opened up a liminal space between traditional ritualistic and cultural aspects of the religious and secularized modernity, thus creating a more ambiguous cognitive and metaphysical outlook on faith. To be clear, what I refer to as resacralization is not exclusively sacred, at least in a traditional sense, but rather a simultaneous process or dance between the secularizing and sacralizing facets of modernity, which ultimately keeps it in a liminal state. Moreover, unlike most understandings of post-secularism,[3] resacralization does not operate in solidifying binaries of religious and secular; rather, it is a process of blurring binaries. At least in terms popularized by Jürgen Habermas (2005/2008), post-secular societies are ones in which religious individuals and nonbelievers engage in a practice of 'complementary learning,' while resacralization is not necessarily about religion but rather about the sacred.[4]

Modernity, Liminality, and The Uncanny

Like the term *secular, modernity* itself is an ambiguous term and defining it can be equally as challenging. Generally, it is thought of as either an ongoing project (Bauman 1991; Giddens 1990; Habermas 1985/1990) or an age that concluded in the mid- to late-20th century, defined by ideology, its pursuit of progress, and ultimately its failure to deliver (Baudrillard 1976/1993; Lyotard 1984). Nonetheless, in order to consolidate my focus in defining modernity, I shall go back to Baudelaire's original and paradoxical meaning of *modernité*, coined in "The Painter of Modern Life," as a fleeting and ephemeral experience or strange feeling of modern life that is in flux with 'the eternal and the immutable,' (Baudelaire 1863/2010: 12–13) and how this sensation has had a profound effect on the relationship between past, present, and future. As Michel Foucault intones, 'Baudelairean modernity is an exercise in which extreme attention to what is real is confronted with the practice of a liberty that simultaneously respects this reality and violates it' (1984: 41). Modernity is much more than a time period characterized by rational discourse, rapid industrialization, and technological advancement. It is an investigational yet tentative attitude that facilitates a certain sense of freedom, only obtained through a transformation formed in uncanny or liminal space. Yet as the postmoderns correctly argued, it was likewise a monstrous age of imperialism, systematic violence, racism, hubris, patriarchy, and many false utopian promises disguised as unfortunate consequences in modernity's unquenchable thirst for progress and innovation. However, the critique of modernity is not postmodern in essence, but was born with modernity itself; therefore, modernity cannot be simply generalized as an age of rationalism and contemporization, since a focus on irrationality and absurdity was developed at the same time. As Zygmunt Bauman contends, 'postmodernism is modernity coming to terms with its own impossibility' (1991: 272), a sentiment I share and develop by arguing that the characteristics of postmodernity are in fact fashioned in modernity, especially in regard to the perspective of the modern stranger.

For Anthony Giddens, one of the most crucial aspects of modernity is the *disembedding* of time and space, meaning 'the 'lifting out' of social relations from local contexts of interaction and their restructuring across indefinite spans of time-space' (1990: 21). Accordingly, modernity's delicate and liminal character not only distinguishes it from any preceding age, but allows it to linger perhaps even beyond its own culmination. Linda Hutcheon develops this relationship further than does Giddens, using a more liminal and uncanny interpretation. For her, postmodernism's connection with modernity is paradoxical in that it is 'neither a simple and radical break from it nor a straightforward continuity with it: it is both and neither' (Hutcheon 2003: 18). Likewise, I also use the term *postmodern* in certain instances in this book. Since modernity is a continuing process, what has been labeled as postmodernity possesses its own developed characteristics. Similarly, in respect to postmodernism, I essentially agree with Arthur Asa Berger's claim that '[p]ostmodernism has the essential double meaning: the continuation of modernism and its transcendence' (2003: 58), though even this view links it to modernity's secularization/resacralization practice. Whether modernity has continued or been replaced by postmodernity, or whether the binary of modern/postmodern itself has been exhausted, one of modernity's main enduring contributions is its liminal and uncanny spirit.

Based on these arguments, my central premise of modernity is that its liminal makeup and lingering characteristics result in an age where space and time no longer coincide or are confined by boundaries, thereby leaving modernity to be defined by an uncanny and liminal structure. While it was Arnold van Gennep (1909/1960) who first introduced the concept of liminality, Turner focuses and expands on van Gennep's "sacred" middle state located between the phases of separation and reaggregation within a ritual passage. Turner refers to the liminal as a state of being "in between," or a "threshold" and a point of limit. It is a temporal state of marginalization and ambiguity, located between the profane and sacred, in which one's identity dissolves but also remains in a state of 'becoming' (Turner 1967/2011: 94). For Turner, liminality is a highly important aspect of the ritual process, not just for the individual but in 'all phases of decisive cultural change' (1978: 2), for it is during the liminal phase that the individual must prepare for an uncertain future.

However, there is a possibility that a person fails to be re-assimilated into normal society and instead is caught in a fixed state of liminality (Turner 1975: 261). Here, Turner focuses on religious vocations such as the Christian monastic life or the notion of pilgrimages that are shared by many of the world's religions, where the religious or sacred passage is a spiritual or symbolic state that continues throughout one's life:

> "The Christian is a stranger to the world, a pilgrim, a traveller, with no place to rest his head." Transition has here become a permanent condition. Nowhere has this institutionalization of liminality been more clearly marked and defined than in the monastic and mendicant states in the great world religions (1995: 107).

This notion of a permanent state of liminality that once seemed to be a condition of the strictly religious or sacred realm is now seen as a secular condition, which has become a consequence of modernity itself (Szakolczai 2000). As secularized modernity continues to push us further into liminal space, it runs the risk of also leaving us in a fixed or permanent state of liminality (Turner 1975: 261). The liminal personae are either involuntary or voluntary, existentially or physically, set 'apart from the behavior of status-occupying, role-playing members of that system' (ibid., 233). However, this fixed state is problematic: if everything is constantly in flux, then constant change itself remains the same, and the source of excitement in liminal space becomes a boring routine in and of itself. 'Individuals are forced to invent more and more sophisticated and ultimately perverse forms of entertainment in a mad search after experience, in the wish to surpass in excitement the boredom of the hectic existence in a permanent state of liminality' (Szakolczai 2000: 229).

I examine liminality in a secularized modern context in comparison to the classical anthropological understanding found in the works of Turner, in an attempt to understand how the concept changes with modernity and if it still contains a sacred element in a secularized world, as it did in small tribal societies. Most importantly, a discussion of liminality's positive and negative elements in modern society and its strangers, liminal figures themselves, is germane to my work. In this regard, Agnes Horvath, going beyond Turner's definition—which strictly focuses on small tribal societies—notes that liminality is in fact a strong aspect of the modern age and that 'the term can be applied to concrete historical events, and *should* be applied, as offering a vital means for historical and sociological understandings' (2013: 2). Like Szakolczai, Horvath has a pessimistic view towards the liminal, arguing that the liminal in modern society is an extremely dangerous and problematic concept that destroys unity, order, and a 'reversal of the self-evidence of reality' (ibid. 4). Although the skepticism that both Szakolczai and Horvath share of modern society becoming too liminal, and thereby too chaotic and unstable, is understandable, these "dangerous" aspects of liminality can also be rewarding, in that they confront traditional and commonly held viewpoints, enabling new and fresh perspectives suspended between imagination and reality.

Turner's liminal phase between the seen and unseen evokes an unsettling eeriness of something strange but familiar. It is here that Sigmund Freud's concept of the uncanny has a direct link to liminality, since it operates in the same sphere of limits, abnormality, and strangeness, often associated with liminal experiences or marginality and thresholds (Royle 2003: vii). As stated by Turner, in this state the entity is

> betwixt and between the positions assigned and arrayed by law, custom, convention, and ceremonial. As such, their ambiguous and indeterminate attributes are expressed by a rich variety of symbols in the many societies that ritualize social and cultural transitions. Thus, liminality is frequently likened to death, to being in the womb, to invisibility, to darkness, to bisexuality, to the wilderness, and to an eclipse of the sun or moon (1995: 95).

In his essay "*Das Unheimliche*" ("The Uncanny"), Sigmund Freud (1919/1955) expands on Ernst Jentsch's use of the term *unheimlich*, of being a product of intellectual uncertainty. Fear and anxiety arise when the person is confronted with something strange or alien. Freud, on the other hand, defines the *unheimlich* as something that is familiar and agreeable, yet also unfamiliar and hidden. According to Freud, the reason the uncanny terrifies is because it brings to light the fears and anxieties that we have previously come into contact with but have repressed. Being both familiar and alien, the uncanny leaves an impression of discomfort and anxiety in the subject due to the paradoxical feeling of being simultaneously fascinated and repulsed. Since the uncanny is what 'ought to have remained hidden and secret, and yet comes to light' (ibid. 130), this cognitive dissonance is a result of the "other" being contained within the self, thus dissolving the subject-object distinction. By referencing Mary Douglas' *Purity and Danger* (1966), Turner has shown that the liminal *persona* is 'regarded as polluting to those who have never been 'inoculated' against them' (Turner 2011: 97). Thus, liminal figures represent an uncanny fear or danger of polluting normal society.

Moreover, the uncanny seems to be a by-product of a teleological, secularized modern world. Terry Castle (1995), Mladen Dolar (1991), and Anthony Vidler (1992) all argue that the rise of the uncanny is directly related to both secularization and modernity. According to Dolar, prior to modernity, the pre-modern uncanny, if we can call it that, was something that existed solely for the world of religion and spirituality, 'largely covered (and veiled) by the area of the sacred and untouchable' (1991: 7); however, it is secularized in the modern age, becoming the paradoxical mark of modernity by encompassing the ambiguity and uncertainty entrenched in the modern mind. The uncanny arose from the Enlightenment and modernity's 'psychic and cultural transformations,' its 'aggressively rationalist imperatives ... [which] also produced, like a kind of toxic side effect, a new human experience of strangeness, anxiety, bafflement, and intellectual impasse' (Castle 1995: 8). As with liminal space, the uncanny is not unified or harmonious, but rather a continuous alienated and ambiguous state caught in a tension between the boundaries of self and other.

The Modern Stranger

By the 19th century, many critical observers were left in a state of bedlam, disenchantment and alienation, which led to the rise of the hyperconscious stranger or outsider, an individual who was simultaneously modern and anti-modern. Western modernity had altered the perception of the stranger, as Georg Simmel first argues, as 'someone who is able to leave as quickly as he arrived, and replaced … with someone who was able to exist and function among the rest of society' (1908/1964: 402). Immersed in the paradoxes of modernity but also critical of its rational limitations, the stranger challenged the laws of society, nature, and the so-called objective truths coupled with instrumental reason (ibid. 403–405). With the ascent of the modern stranger, the paradoxical role of being both immersed in and removed from society allowed contemporary individuals to confront the issues that were related to secularism, modernity, and urbanization and also critique the normalization of modern city life. The modern stranger was a member of society because it lived in and was absorbed by the everyday banality of city life, not simply contributing to the population but even social amd economic aspects of modern life. However, it was removed or felt socially removed from society because its thoughts or ideologies (or lack thereof) were contrary to those of the majority, or it was marginalized by its otherness.The modern stranger, therefore, crosses borders which are not geographical, but liminal, metaphysical, emotional, and psychological.

Zygmunt Bauman, in *Modernity and Ambivalence* (1991), reasons that modernity, which he deems to have originated during 17th-century Europe but which now has become globalized, is a social construct that looks to impose intellectual, social, and political order through rationality. However, when society becomes fashioned into familiar and manageable classes and structures, Bauman claims that there are always individuals and subcultures that cannot be managed or controlled. The result, then, is not a world of chaos and terror, but instead one of ambivalence and alienation, as the notion of "strangerhood" becomes a universal condition of modernity and individuality. Modernity's attempt to remove all uncertainty and ambivalence in society through rational thought seems to have a reverse effect. Echoing Theodore Adorno and Max Horkheimer's thesis in *Dialectic of Enlightenment* (1944/1982), which contends that rationality's attempt to overcome nature and mythology only led back into a world of mythology, Bauman states that ambivalence and alienation seem to lie at modernity's core. Extending the work of Simmel and Jacques Derrida, Bauman introduces the metaphorical subject of the stranger. Accordingly, the stranger, or society's 'undecidables' (appropriating Derrida's term), are monstrous, uncanny, and 'the true hybrids' that are 'unclassifiable' within society (Bauman 1991: 58). By being someone who is present yet removed, or familiar and at the same time unfamiliar, the stranger 'does not fall into society's social order by living outside of social borders' and 'therefore becomes an object of fear and a threat to society' (ibid. 60). As a result, '[t]he stranger undermines the spatial ordering of the world' and 'disturbs the resonance between physical and psychical distance ... he is *physically close* while remaining *spiritually remote*' (ibid.). Moreover, the stranger is perpetually liminal figure for '[u]nlike an alien or foreigner' Bauman argues that the stranger is not a figure 'temporarily out of place' but 'an *eternal wanderer*, homeless always and everywhere, without hope of ever 'arriving' (ibid. 79).

Although I base much of my work on Bauman's analysis, I critically deviate from his thesis by arguing that the modern stranger is not necessarily '*spiritually remote*,' as Bauman argues, but rather finds ways to uncannily resacralize itself within the liminality of secularized modernity. John D. Caputo argues in "Hospitality and the Trouble With God" that there is an explicit connection between the stranger and God in that '[t]he stranger is both a venerable figure and dangerous. The stranger is maddening, like God. Undecidable, like God' (2011: 86). I agree with Caputo's assessment of a God who goes against 'the tendency of theology to think in terms of the divine order, and of God as the source of order' (ibid. 83). Caputo's concept of God is rather 'something out of order ... trouble, as a source of disruption and interruption', a God that is 'the source of irregularity, of disordered and displaced orders...' (ibid. 83–84). However, I consider this concept of God—as 'something out of order'—directly tied to both the unleashing of the uncanny in secularism and secularized modernity itself, in which humanity must accept its liminal role as both creator/created and where God is made from our image rather than we from His.

In *Strangers to Ourselves*, Julia Kristeva's notion of the stranger being contained within the self, 'the hidden face of our identity' (1988/1991: 1), is another important aspect in linking the stranger and the uncanny. She argues that through the other, we are able to see our own otherness since, according to her, we are all strangers to ourselves. Here, Kristeva applies what she claims is Christianity's greatest legacy of self-questioning (2009: viii-ix) to the idea of the stranger. By recognizing each other through our weakness, our own strangerhood, we thereby remove the uncanny fear of the foreigner. With Kristeva's argument, we can see the uncanniness of the other invading the self, as the way we feel towards a stranger reflects what we unconsciously feel about ourselves. In this sense, Kristeva points out the modern shift of the psychoanalytic stranger, which encompasses everyone, as becoming a liminal experience of both encountering, and likewise being, a stranger. It is this paradoxical and liminal situation that has allowed for a new perspective of strangeness, where the self is not solidified or established by the other, or foreigner, but rather by self-estrangement. By doing so, Kristeva (1991) argues that the ingrained negative attitude towards strangers and foreigners is removed in favour of a more fluid and ambiguous understanding of the terms:

> Let us not seek to solidify, to turn the otherness of the foreigner into a thing. Let us merely touch it, brush by it, without giving it permanent structure. Simply sketching out its perpetual motion through some of its variegated aspects spread out before our eyes today, even some of its former, changing representations scattered throughout history. Let us also lighten that otherness by constantly coming back to it—but more and more swiftly. Let us escape its hatred, its burden, fleeing them not through leveling and forgetting, but through the *harmonious* repetition of the differences it implies and spreads (3).

Through maintaining a 'fleeing eternity or … perpetual transience' (ibid. 4), the stranger resides in a place of liminality that allows for both the linking together and presenting of differences, which subsequently leads to a strange form of freedom or happiness.

As a danger to social structures, the stranger paradoxically becomes the central figure of utopian thought. A major portion of this book, which is tied to the sacred and the secular, is the idea of the messianic, or messianic time, and its relationship with utopia. Based on the work of Ernst Bloch (1918/2000), I show how the undecidability of the stranger can become a form of resacralization and itself a utopian element for social change, even among anti-structures. In an attempt to remove the negative connotations that come with a blueprint understanding of utopia, Bloch's understanding of the term is never static. It is not a final ending place but a dialectical process or "spirit" that manifests itself out of the darkness of the present world (2000: 201). Utopia, according to Bloch, is inherent in the unhappiness, despair, and frustration in the present world, in which '[h]ope is in the darkness itself' (ibid.). Bloch's use of utopia is imperative for our culture, as the notion of alienation and disillusionment is not absent from our current society, especially since the struggle concerning religion and secularization has created its own outsiders, not from a Marxist perspective. I will focus on ways through which, if possible, the modern stranger can use alienation as a positive force, comparable to the way Deleuze and Guattari (1972/1983, 1980/1987) have taken a similar tactic with Jacques Lacan's (1977) definition of desire as a lack. Alienation, like desire, has the possibility to be utopian, productive, and even courageous. The "tragic joy" that Nietzsche (1888/1911a) discussed is a necessary tool for the stranger. It could be used as a weapon to fight the boredom of life, purity, or social structure, albeit paradoxically, since one can only experience this beauty by submersing oneself in the mundane horror and unclean liminal space in order to experience the beauty of the sacred aspects that are found within it.

Modern Monsters and Haunting Spectres

Notions of liminality, the uncanny, and the modern stranger are all directly tied to the concept of monstrosity, and therefore represent a central theme of this book. An etymological study of the word *monster* exposes a double meaning: one strain derives from the Latin (to reveal or show), and the other is *monstrum* (to warn), which traditionally has been viewed as representing a divine omen or portent of an unexpected misfortune (Biles 2007: 3; Frueh 2001: 26). As with the stranger, the uncanny shift of the monster from the Middle Ages to modernity is a movement towards liminality. The monster transforms from being outside the borders of what is traditionally regarded as human to a presence that is located at its threshold, and as a result, it challenges what we consider to be human, along with our notions of what is monstrous, impure, ugly. As such, it is a compelling representation of both the natural/artificial divide of posthuman gender blurring, and particularly as symbolic of the abject female body, which, like the monster, violates boundaries and threatens social stability (Kristeva 1980/1982). To this effect, Braidotti appropriately emphasizes the monster's liminal character, describing it as representative of 'the in-between, the mixed, the ambivalent,' located 'between the sacred and the profane. The peculiarity of the organic monster is that she is both Same and Other. The monster is neither a total stranger nor completely familiar. He exists in an in-between zone' (2011: 216). By representing what is both liminal and structural to human identity, the monstrous other for Braidotti 'helps us understand the paradox of "difference"' (ibid.). Braidotti not only acknowledges a sacred/profane element to the liminal monster, but also a gender transgressive symbol, where the altering of pronouns is a result of seeing the monster as 'a process without a stable object' (ibid. 243).

With secularized modernity, the monstrous becomes a symbol of the loss of both spirituality and traditional values in the new technological age, and likewise a representation of our existential displacement in such a morally ambiguous and liminal universe. Although the monster is conjured up in early modernity in order to differentiate a world of progress from a world of superstition, the modern form of the monstrous is ultimately found in secularized modernity itself, in its notions of progress: 'The monster ... threatens modernity, in that it originates in modernity, but reflects the limits of it' (Scott 2007: 2). The monster of modernity shows the vulnerability of an age that is fearful of the return of the repressed, and as a result, the monstrous has also become a reappropriated positive symbol within modernity, one that goes beyond the dangerous representation of chaos and peril that threatens society, to a precarious and ironic symbol of hope and even sustainability.

In relation to monstrosity, the notion of the spectre also gains new significance during modernity, especially through the hauntological work of Derrida (1993/2007). While also haunting us on the edges of reason, the spectre becomes ever closer to the theme of monstrosity the more the fragmented self recedes further away from the physical world and body, making monster and spectre almost interchangeable in modernity's liminal space. The liminal metaphor of the spectre is a haunting image of the present that also disrupts time. While the spectre foreshadows through haunting repetition, limiting our knowable future, it also sideshadows by offering us numerous presents. In writing, sideshadowing is used to produce a sensation of the 'something else'. Unlike foreshadowing that comes from the future, sideshadowing 'casts a shadow "from the side" ... from other possibilities ... Sideshadows conjure the ghostly presence of might-have-beens or might-bes' (Morson 1994: 118). In light of this, as with the monster, the spectre acts as a warning through foreshadowing, but also acts as a messianic and divine spirit of utopian potential.

Chapter Summary

The opening chapter of my book argues that Mary Shelley's *Frankenstein* (1818/1999) is the ideal text in outlining secularized modernity and the monstrosity that lurks within it, demonstrating the paradoxes and ambivalences of modernity that have challenged us ever since its publication. Through this reading, I trace how the novel constitutes a change and development of the modern uncanny and liminal stranger from the Gothic tradition, as a response to the dissolving of collective binaries in the secularizing Western world and ever-increasing fragmentation of modern society, from its once strongly held morals to the deconstruction of the internal and external self. *Frankenstein* portrays the rise of a paradoxical world where, although humanity is given the freedom to create with autonomous and enthusiastic purposefulness, in actuality our existence contains no real plan or blueprint. I argue that *Frankenstein* portrays the exemplar of the modern stranger and the liminal condition that the modern individual has endured, and therefore acts as a foundation to the philosophy and ideas found in the following chapters.

The second chapter examines two of the most influential philosopher-poets of secularized modernity, Charles Baudelaire and Giacomo Leopardi, who helped define and influence our views of the modern condition through the expansion of the notion of the monstrous that was laid out in *Frankenstein*. Through the poetry and philosophical writings of Baudelaire and Leopardi, I examine the rise of nihilism and boredom in an intensifying urban age and the beginning of a resacralization process that created a secularized modern form of the sacred from the ashes of the mythos of Christology. Leopardi and Baudelaire looked for meaning in the ashes and ruins of the previous age, while simultaneously being cautious of the terrifying new epoch of the secular "hell" that was forming around them.

Chapter three focuses on the historical event of the First World War that brought the liminality, absurdity, and most importantly, the violence of modern warfare into the lives of everyday individuals, resulting in the modern stranger becoming a figure more grounded in everyday life. Here, the monster of modernity is transformed into an incurable sickness that has infected society but also resulted in an ironic and paradoxical form of utopia. Together with Ernst Bloch's iconoclastic utopian theory, I examine anthropologist Maurice Bloch's re-evaluation of liminality, which states that two different thresholds of violence define one's rite of passage. As a result, I focus on modernist works such as Italo Svevo's *Zeno's Conscience* (1923/2003, Robert Musil's *The Man Without Qualities* (1978/1995), Fritz Lang's *M* (1931/2004), and Walter M. Miller's *The Canticle of Leibowitz* (1959/2007), in order to show how both the modern stranger and modern monster are thrust back into postwar society.

The fourth chapter propels us into the post-WWII age of the spectacle of social media. I link the liminal concept of boredom to the continuing effects of secularized modernity. More so than previous eras, the modern age generates a significant amount of ambiguity and fragmentation in its comprehension of boredom. By examining various forms of boredom through the films of Michelangelo Antonioni, the writings of author Tao Lin, and the philosophical works of Sara Ahmed, I explore how these different kinds of boredom tend to blend into one another when outlining the modern experience of the stranger, with the concepts of mood and boredom working to redefine the modern stranger for contemporary modernity.

In chapter five I look at the tensions of self and other through online communities and social media, and how this is creating new forms of fragmentation. The internet is a new form of liminal or Third Space[5] created in virtual environments and is quickly becoming the preferred means of social interaction, yet also has many interesting philosophical and existential implications, which can result in certain resacralizing or utopian elements. This chapter focuses on early literary and film depictions of cyberspace found in the science fiction genre of cyberpunk, most notably in William Gibson's novels and Mamoru Oshii's anime series *Ghost in the Shell*. While also examining Dave Eggers' novel *The Circle* (2013), I discuss how the notion of cyberspace has changed as this technology has become more entrenched in our lives. I explore the changing landscape of identity as the lines between human and machine become more obscured, with both therapeutic and threatening consequences that accompany an increasing production of, and reliance on, online identities in social media.

The final chapter looks at the modern stranger in regard to gender and transhumanism/posthumanism. Gender binaries have been used throughout history to establish a male-dominated and patriarchal society, tackling the uncanny fear of self and other. This chapter returns to Shelley's *Frankenstein* and shows its influence on Donna Haraway's cyborgian feminism, and Hélène Cixous' reimagining of the mythical figure of Medusa in relation to ideas such as gender, sexuality, the monstrous, and abyssal resacralization. In addition to these theorists, I examine the novels *Don Quixote: Which Was a Dream* (1986) and *Empire of the Senseless* (1988) by Kathy Acker, in her attempt to deconstruct gender binaries and the language that upholds them through the feminist act of writing herself, while simultaneously and paradoxically acknowledging that she is still liminally confined to these binaries.

The intention of this book is to examine the liminal sphere located between the secular and sacred that I argue has characterized modernity itself. This space has consequently altered the makeup of the stranger from something external into a figure far more liminal, which is forced to traverse this uncanny space, in an attempt to find new meaning for an age that is struggling to maintain any. In many ways, the modern stranger as a figure of literature and cultural imagination has become more complicated and challenging in the contemporary age, going beyond people who are psychological or even spiritual inable to blend in and out of society. However, while the stranger may be changing once again, I contend that defining or essentializing the figure could result in the creation of other sets of binaries, and thereby dissolve the purpose and productiveness of both strangeness and liminality.

Notes: Introduction

[1] While the concept of a Judeo-Christian tradition is highly contested and debated (see *Is there a Judeo-Christian Tradition?: A European Perspective* (2016) for both a historical account of the term's origin and an extensive discussion of relativeness), a strong underlining link not often discussed is the effect secularism has had on—and its resulting complex relationship with—these two religious traditions.

[2] The essential, although simplified, difference between transhumanism and posthumanism is that transhumanism is 'an intensification of humanism, a type of hyper-humanism' as a result of advanced technology, whereas posthumanism represents a complete break with humanism (Ranisch and Sorgner 2014: 8). However, I argue that as with postmodernism and modernity, the break between the two is not entirely complete.

[3] Many scholars (Bader 2012; Beckford 2012; McLennan 2009) have questioned both the meaning and usefulness of the term.

[4] In differentiating between the sacred and religion, I follow Kristeva's understanding of the sacred being '[n]ot religion or its opposite, atheistic negation, but the experience that beliefs both shelter and exploit, at the crossroads of sexuality and thought, body and meaning' (Clément and Kristeva 2001: 1).

[5] The term "Third Space" was first introduced by cultural and post-colonial theorist Homi Bhabha. According to Bhabha, the Third Space is a liminal

space of cultural hybridity, 'which gives rise to something different, something new and unrecognizable, a new area of negotiation of meaning and representation' (Rutherford 1990: 211). While the term is largely used in post-colonial studies, the concept is largely missing from studies on internet and cyberculture. According to Masoud Kosari and Abbas Amoori however, the term does have a place in studies of cyberspace, since it 'necessitates redefining society and social interactions,' while '[t]he increasing expansion of the borderline spaces, better called *interpenetration*, necessitates further complications of the mental and conceptual spaces' (2018: 185).

Frankenstein and the "Birth" of Secularized Modernity

"There is something at work in my soul which I do not understand."
　　　　　　　　　　　　—Mary Shelley, *Frankenstein* (2003)

The spirit, the specter are not the same thing, and we will have to sharpen this difference; but as for what they have in common, one does not know what it is, what it is presently—This Thing is absent.
　　　　　　　　　　　　—Jacques Derrida, *Specter of Marx*

The sight of the burning tree inspires a vision of the majesty of the day which lights the world without setting fire to it at the same time.
　—Max Horkheimer & Theodor W. Adorno, *Dialectic of Enlightenment*

Just as primitive man believed himself to stand face to face with demons and believed that could he but know their names he would become their master, so is contemporary man faced by this incomprehensible, which disorders his calculations. "If I can but grasp it, if I can but cognise it", so he thinks, "I can make it my servant."
　　　　　　　　　　　　—Karl Jaspers, *Man In the Modern Age*

The beginning of the 19th century was a significant period of transition within Europe, as the accruing of contemporary history's revolutionary, secular, and modernizing ideals were beginning to be integrated into quotidian life. The signature distinction of this time is essentially tied to the implementation of the dominant modern principles of reason, progress, and social change, which were all grounded in a consciousness or "soul" of individualism and autonomy. Yet this amalgam of modern, and often opposing, principles produced a problematic and paradoxical condition for many modern individuals who were caught between two existing worlds: that of the traditional past and the

---

How to cite this book chapter:
Beghetto, R. G. 2022. *Monstrous Liminality; Or, The Uncanny Strangers Of Secularized Modernity*. Pp. 21–46. London: Ubiquity Press. DOI: https://doi.org/10.5334/bcp.b. License: CC-BY-NC

modern one that was being implemented. It was this conflicted and tumultuous age that was the backdrop to Mary Shelley's *Frankenstein, or the Modern Prometheus*,[1] a novel that primarily lays out the psychological and spiritual paradigm of not only the emerging modern and secular world during the early 19th century, but also one that lingers and continues to uncannily haunt modernity. From the incessant "Frankenstein complex" to our tensions between ambiguity and knowledge; from our uncanny fear of self and other to the concept of the stranger increasingly alienated from society, nature, and a silent God, Shelley's novel illuminates a shadowy interweaving counterpart to the prevailing ideals of the early modern epoch—a "monster" of modernity that should not exist, but nonetheless does, throwing a shadow and haunting humanity along its journey of progress. Due to Shelley's interpretation of these modern struggles and by being one of the first illustrations of modernity's abject space, a liminal zone encompassing both fascination and repulsion, the rising questions and complications of secularized modernity were epitomized within the pages of Shelley's seminal novel.

It should be noted that this is not just another reading of *Frankenstein*, a novel that has been analyzed in academic circles for countless years, but an analysis that contextualizes *Frankenstein* within the imminent rational and secularizing modern world as an indicator of the paradoxes and ambivalences of modernity. Through this reading, that the novel constitutes the literary emergence and development of the modern, uncanny, and liminal stranger caught in the intensifying malaise of secularized modernity. Nonetheless, important scholarly work on the subject is highly relevant to my own writings on the topic and will be used to support this claim. For example, Fred Botting's deconstructive analysis of Shelley's novel in *Making Monstrous: Frankenstein, Criticism Theory* is essential in showing the novel's multiplicitous spirit, arguing that every textual interpretation that tries to centralize or unify the novel's meaning ultimately fails or contradicts itself. Botting's reading of *Frankenstein* is situated in the extremes between Victor Frankenstein and his Creature; the former stands for a fixed identity, totalitarianism, and authority, while the Creature represents an unstable difference and otherness (1991: 139). While I agree with Botting that these two representations of identity exist within the novel, I do not feel that a dualistic separation between the characters is justified, but rather that both simultaneously represent fixed and fluid identities in their own right. The Creature can be as demanding and totalitarian as its creator, while Victor's hope of progress places him in an undertaking of discovering unfixed possibilities, a mission that David Foster Wallace describes as 'selfless' and 'messianic' (2013: 133). Another important aspect of Botting's work is his interpretation of the monstrous as a manifestation of the turbulent political climate of the time, commencing with the French Revolution. While this is a significant aspect of the book, I expand on this idea by arguing the French Revolution was just as essential to the secularization process and the age's religious and spiritual discontent as it was to the political spectrum, culminating in the novel's ambiguous and liminal stance in both areas.

Lee Sterrenburg's work is similarly important in that it also looks at the political and psychological fallout that the French Revolution had on Shelley's work. In "Mary Shelley's Monster: Politics and Psyche in *Frankenstein*" (1979), Sterrenburg argues that despite her dedication of the novel to her father, Shelley mainly critiques and parodies William Godwin's radical utopian politics. Originally influenced by her father and husband Percy Shelley's contemporary radical and utopian political ideals, Shelley slowly abandons these in favour of a more anti-revolutionary position, culminating in the political ambivalence that exists within the novel. This theory goes against Anne K. Mellor's claim that the two editions show a radical change between them. Mellor's *Mary Shelley: Her Life, Her Fiction, Her Monsters* is a biographical and feminist analysis of Shelley's work that explores how the all-male creation myth highlights the 'hierarchical power-systems both within the nuclear family and in the society at large,' the real monsters of the story (1988: 217). Although Mellor's study details the way that Shelley's life influences the majority of her work and presents many compelling arguments regarding hierarchical power-systems, her analysis of *Frankenstein* at times undermines the novel's premise regarding the ambiguity encompassed within modernity and the fear that comes with contesting that ambiguity, particularly when concerning Mellor's study of the edited novel's ending over that of Mary Shelley's unpublished original.

Mellor's main argument in the chapter "Revising Frankenstein" is that Shelley altered the meaning and spiritual core of the novel in the 1831 edition to coincide with her radically new philosophical and political views at the time, views that had become far more pessimistic and melancholic once she 'had lost faith in the possibility that a generous, loving, and nurturant response to both human and physical nature might create a world without monsters' (ibid. 176). However, the attempt, even if futile, to suppress the uncanny at the end of the novel and the inevitability of a modern world *with* monsters exists in both editions. The two editions should not be seen as distinctive or opposites, but instead more like shadows of one another. They both ask the question of whether secular knowledge and agency are able to steer human history consciously towards scientific and linear progress, or whether freedom has simply left us in a world dictated by chaos and chance. If we examine the two editions of *Frankenstein* together, Shelley seems to argue that both chance and fate are somewhat paradoxically interlocked with one another.

Frankenstein is by no means an outdated tale representing an early modern and transitional society that no longer exists. As with modernity, our current age's fragmented identity is symbolically tied to the Creature's physical façade of scattered limbs assembled together. Society in late modernity continues to be caught within a social narrative which stems from multiple storytellers, perspectives, and sources of knowledge, and which still resembles a hybrid creature uncannily akin to the one Victor Frankenstein created in the darkest corners of his laboratory. As Richard J. Dunn argues, '*Frankenstein* is concerned with a fragmenting society in which communication remains incomplete' (1974: 416). More importantly, reaching a multitude of theories such as Marxism (Michie 1990; Moretti 1982), along with disciplines such as environmental studies (Curtin 2005; Hammond 2004), psychoanalysis (J. Berman 1990; Marsh 2009), and especially regarding racial (Malchow, 1993; Piper 2007; Young 2008), feminist (Hoeveler 2003; Yousef 2002), and gender studies (Mellor 1988; Thornburg 1987), *Frankenstein* remains not only a prophetic warning, but a modern myth that relentlessly renews its influence in our disjointed and continuously becoming artificial-reality. As Jon Turney argues in *Frankenstein's Footsteps: Science, Genetics and Popular Culture*, Shelley's 'story about finding the secret of life became one of the most important myths of modernity,' adding that 'now that the secrets of life are ours for the taking we need to ask what role that myth will play in the collective debate about how to make use of them' (1998: 2–3). In this regard, *Frankenstein* seriously encompasses Marshall Berman's paradoxical disposition of modernism, 'to be fully modern is to be anti-modern' (1982/1988: 14), in such a highly developed and felicitous manner. Shelley's modern Prometheus[2] has become the creation story of the modern era, our mythos that captures and illuminates our modern experience of struggling to belong in a secular and alienating world where responsibility ultimately rests with the individual. Yet *Frankenstein* is an uncanny or paradoxical creation myth, since the apocalyptic end to the older, traditional world is entirely intertwined with the birth of the new, monstrous one, and as a result, provides us with a prototype of the modern stranger that encapsulates a world that creates far more questions than answers.

Frankenstein and Secularization

Mary Shelley's *Frankenstein* points to a problematic and paradoxical characteristic of modernity: with the arrival of the French Revolution, humanity's attempt to free itself from destiny still leaves it in the hands of chance, where human control outside the hands of God is no more realistic.[3] By 1818, the enthusiasm of the French Revolution was slowly subsiding, while its most famous original critique, Edmund Burke's *Reflections on the Revolution in France* (1790/1999), was gaining popularity outside of conservative circles with freethinking individuals like Mary Shelley, who began to side with Burke's reproach of reason as a universal and objective standard (Sterrenburg 1979). Caught within this tension, Shelley's novel takes a liminal stance as it 'seems to both construct and undermine the possibility of authority: it operates within but subverts and leaves open the binary limits it confronts' (Botting 1991: 152). *Frankenstein* simultaneously builds and deconstructs the teleological narrative of modernity by addressing the ambiguous situation of its age, which was caught between a 'monster of a constitution' (Burke 1999: 196) in anarchy and destruction and the utopian spirit of humanity's ability to ambitiously change the world for the better. The novel's moral and socio-political stance is a liminal hybrid positioned within this void, between two contrasting views of utopian and revolutionary change: one of fear, and one of optimism. Yet despite the growing criticism of romanticizing the historic event as utopian, Burke's attack on the French Revolution was unable to stop the lasting ideological, social, and spiritual effects the French Revolution had upon European society.

As Albert Camus claims in *The Rebel*, after the storming of the Bastille and the subsequent 'guillotining [of] God on January 21, 1793' (1951/1991: 39), freedom and progress have taken over the area of the sacred by reducing God 'to the theoretical existence of a moral principle' (ibid. 132), thereby making the newly acquired values of nation, liberty, and reason the new authoritative religious forces on earth. The French Revolution and ensuing destruction of the monarchy created a gap or void between God and humanity with the killing of the King, God's voice or bridge from earth to heaven, leaving the Republic on its own without any of God's moral laws (ibid. 39). The violent Jacobin chapter of the French Revolution aspired to serve as 'the bearer of the messianic mission of the hopes of the moderns' (Cristaudo 2012: 256), making it the defining moment when Jacob's ladder would be deconstructed and rebuilt, no longer as a passage between heaven and earth, but between humanity and its ambitions. Located within this unsettled social, political, and spiritual environment, unable to situate itself amongst contrasting ideologies, *Frankenstein* 'molds them into a unique third' and 'asks what it is like to be labeled, defined, and even physically distorted by a political stereotype' (Sterrenburg 1979: 166).

This move towards secularized modernity leads not only to an unnerving political and moral malaise, but also to a spiritual void that begins to accumulate due to a state of fleeting impulses and a blurring of traditionally held dualities previously cemented into the social and cultural structure. This thrusts certain modern individuals, exemplified in the novel by both Frankenstein and the Creature, into a state of liminality and strangerhood, not merely due to the political situation but also because of the spiritual and moral traditions that were upheld by the strict and hierarchical structure of the great chain of being. Shelley's world of *Frankenstein* lacks a God, at least one that is pure or omnipotent; it is also noteworthy to mention that in a text where creator and created play such a significant role, in both editions God's name is usually uttered in reaction to horrible acts[4] (Shelley 2003: 26, 58, 74, 195, 199), while Justine's unbreakable faith simply results in her tragic yet forgotten death. The Frankensteins' servant is accused of and executed for the murder of Victor's younger brother William—the Creature's first victim—and once arrested, confesses to a crime she did not commit out of fear of being excommunicated from the Church and the possibility of going to Hell. Justine suffers from the 'misery of innocence' (ibid. 89), and her sentencing further exemplifies the novel's ambiguity concerning corruption, justice, purity, chance, and fate. God is nowhere to help an innocent person who becomes a victim of a series of events over which she has no control or even knowledge.

However, the irreligious stance of the novel does not come from a removal of religion or sacredness, but instead from the secularizing/resacralizing process that lies in modernity. The novel secularizes, yet retains, the mythos of Christianity, though the allegorical aspects of the religion are blurred, inverted, or distorted. While in the creation story of Genesis, in which Adam and Eve lose their innocence from their acquired ability to recognize the difference between good and evil, Shelley on the other hand reverses this by bestowing the loss of innocence on Frankenstein and the Creature, and subsequently the reader, as a result of the removal or blurring of good and evil, where one cannot distinguish between the two, especially since this problematic binary can no longer be attributed to the mysterious plan of God. Yet, in neither story can the protagonists return to their familiar "Edens" of innocence and ignorance; instead, they are propelled into the future without the parental protection of their creator. *Frankenstein* takes this even further: the shock of animation supersedes, via modernity's shadowy secret of bland ugliness and powerlessness, the omnibenevolence and omnipotence of a creator. With *Frankenstein*, Shelley secularizes the question of theodicy. The responsibilities formerly attributed to God now lie on humanity's shoulders, yet she reminds us that the question of evil can no longer be circumvented with answers of divine mystery, since humanity has taken command of the course of history. The future that Shelley formed in her imagination, and foreshadowed in reality, is one in which God has abandoned humanity in the same way the Creature was abandoned by his 'natural lord and king' (Shelley 2003: 102–103). By abandoning the Creature, Frankenstein simply lives up to his role as creator and leaves his creation to its own devices.

To be fair, as original as *Frankenstein* is, it borrows considerably from the secularizing literary devices of the Romantic and Gothic novels that preceded it, exemplifying the seeds of modernity that both traditions began to cultivate. Not only did it continue the Gothic genre's aesthetic of dark and mysterious atmospheric tales of suspense and supernatural terror; more notably, concerning its socio-cultural and psychological effects, the novel renews the Gothic and Romantic modern and liminal ritual of secularizing the sacred into the uncanny, a phenomenon that manifests itself in modernity from the ashes of religion. In *Unquiet Things: Secularism In The Romantic Age*, Colin Jager challenges the notion that as modernity secularizes, the presence or 'noise' of religion is eliminated. Instead, Jager claims that the secular 'silence' is unable to completely remove the 'residue or ghost' of religion and the sacred (2015: 4), and that 'within the static, the ambient noise, the alternative frequency … we can hear the particular kind of unquiet …' (ibid. 9). These noises and disturbances in secular space have often been characterized by moments of the uncanny. In *Gothic Riffs: Secularizing the Uncanny in the European Imaginary, 1780–1820* (2010), Diane Long Hoeveler, using Charles Taylor's secularizing process outlined in *A Secular Age* (2007),[5] focuses on the Gothic as a cultural practice designed not necessarily as a reaction against secularism, 'but as part of the ambivalent secularizing process itself' that was 'invented to instantiate the rise of secularism' (Hoeveler 2010: 6). According to Hoeveler, '[a]s a major component of the secularizing process, the gothic aesthetic anxiously looked both backward and forward at the same time, torn between reifying the past and anxiously embracing a future it could not quite envision' (ibid. xvii). Due to this position of being caught in the ambiguous modernizing attempts of society (although a society where myth and magic still hold power over the social imaginary), the uncanny originates with the Gothic tradition (ibid. 30). The Janus-faced genre stands between a feudal and religious past and a contemporary world being established on the rational principles brought forth from both the Protestant reformation and the subsequent Age of Enlightenment. Yet what essentially makes the Gothic genre modern, according to Hoeveler, is its preoccupation with the 'just now' or the moment of immediacy, reflected in its fascination with death, the apocalypse, and alienation (ibid. 11). Due to what Hoeveler identifies as gothic 'riffs,' the Gothic represents 'the first truly modern discourses in which individuals stand in sort of existential alienation in a universe of their own largely imaginary making' (ibid. 15).

If, from its earliest inception, the Gothic was itself a modern genre that drew out the uncanny through the secularization of the sacred, and likewise emphasized the concept of the wandering, alienated, and liminal individual, then why should we begin secularized modernity with Shelley's novel, which many critics argue was simply part of the Gothic tradition, or at the very least, immensely influenced by Romantic, Gothic literature, and even established folklore (Haggerty 1989; Kilgour 1995; Tichelaar 2012)? It must also be stated that, although the Gothic genre has many similar literary devices and tropes as a whole, it cannot be classified in any exclusive way, since the essence of what ties the genre together is vague or 'mutable' (Goddu 1997: 266), and its meanings or interpretations fluctuate in accordance with the historical, cultural, and ideological environment in which they were created and understood (Botting 2001: 1).

That being said, there are multiple reasons for beginning the advent of secularized modernity and the modern stranger with Shelley's celebrated novel. First of all, despite its clear influences from and affiliations with Gothic literary conventions, it would be deceptive to simply categorize Shelley's masterpiece as part of the Gothic tradition. *Frankenstein* is a difficult novel to classify in any single genre, even transformative ones like Romantic and Gothic, for it stands in a textual liminal space in and of itself as it redefines or goes beyond previous, commonly used Gothic and horror elements, twisting and blurring commonly held dichotomies, such as myth and reality, good and evil, light and dark, villain and hero, real and artificial, and even representations of the double or *doppelgänger*—far beyond any novel before it.

However, what truly distinguishes *Frankenstein* from previous Gothic novels, and what makes it a forbearer of modernism and science fiction (Botting 2005; Donawerth 1997; McMahon 2007; Reichardt 1994; Stableford 1995),[6] is that it is not merely concerned with the past or simply the 'just now,' but instead with our paradoxical future of what is becoming. The reason why Gothic literature was 'anxiously embracing a future it could not quite envision,' as Hoeveler argues, had to do with its adherence to past traditional dichotomies it was trying to reject, such as Catholicism, while championing a more rationalist view of Christianity that ultimately upheld the same binaries.[7] On the other hand, by looking towards a prophetic future, *Frankenstein* is curious about and troubled by the uncertain society that is forming, perhaps more so than the one it is leaving behind. It is first to envision a world where science, technology, and secular knowledge look towards, and succeed in, replacing ancient beliefs, customs, and previously held social constructs. Whereas the supernatural undertaking of the Gothic was still reliant on the recognizable characteristics, symbols, and dualities found in Christianity, *Frankenstein* borrows but blurs the lines of these universally recognized moral symbols. The supernatural and the uncanny are no longer located in the feudal and religious past but instead in the conceptualization of secular knowledge and a scientific view of progress that gave humanity its hegemonic belief that the future can be moulded and controlled. Published at the cusp of the Gothic tradition, *Frankenstein* reconstructs the liminal text or bridge between the secular uncanny of the early Gothic and the rising modernist tradition, caught in a battle between the artificial and natural which would endure well into the 20th century. The novel does not contemplate the past while standing in the present as the Gothic genre, but rather resides in the modern liminal state where past, present, and future collide with one another, leaving the stranger in an ambiguous position of struggling to find meaning or any remnant of the sacred in the intensifying cold and calculated world.

The future God in *Frankenstein* is not an omnipotent being removed from our society but, instead, the ambitious man, symbolized by Victor Frankenstein, who is immersed in, though detached from, society. Frankenstein's secularized and liminal stance of creator and created is furthered by the act of secrecy. Whether Frankenstein should have shared his creation, his secret, with the rest of humanity, and whether his silence demonstrates an abuse of power, are questions that have lingered throughout the history of the novel. His whole experiment is shrouded in mystery and secrecy from beginning to end as one secret consequently leads to another—at first to hide his controversial research and maintain his authority and power over unearthing science's 'unknown powers' and 'deepest mysteries' (Shelley 2003: 49), but then continuing in order to protect his family and, more importantly, modern secular society. If we examine the Augustinian understanding of secrecy, it paradoxically shifts from a divine element to one of sin, divided by the sacred/profane binary, in which 'God brings about this sudden conversion away from worldly values by acting on and through the hidden, concealed depths of man's corruption' (Vance 2014: 13). Consequently, the paradox of secrecy goes beyond a sacred and profane perspective and encompasses the idea itself, since in order for a secret to be recognized, there also must be knowledge of the concealment by another person, which simultaneously reveals and conceals the unknown information (Bellman 4–7).

Nonetheless, secrecy opens up the opportunity of two different worlds. The secret world actively affects the 'obvious world' (Simmel 1964: 462). The second world of ambiguity that Victor witnesses through the Creature's eyes puts Simmel's 'obvious world,' based on science and linear progress, into serious doubt. Modernity's secret now becomes Victor's once he becomes creator: that of a liminal future that cannot be controlled by humanity even though it now has gained agency in its own history. The responsibility of secrecy falls upon Frankenstein, which forces him into concealing his creation in order to protect himself and those he loves, even though in the end it ironically leads to his and his family's downfall. The novel's narrative is structured around what Freud stated as the modern and 'the secular advance of repression in the emotional life of mankind' (1900/1965: 298); the more religion wanes in everyday life, the more repressed we become.[8] Frankenstein is burdened by a secret that cannot be revealed: 'I avoided explanation, and maintained a continual silence concerning the wretch I had created. I had a feeling that I should be supposed mad, and this forever chained my tongue, when I would have given the whole world to have confided the fatal secret' (Shelley 2003: 190). The Creature is kept secret because Victor does not know what he has created, opening up modernity's Pandora's box. Frankenstein understands that the second liminal world hidden within modernity has a detrimental effect on the ideals that will supposedly take human history towards a utopia here on earth, where the world is no longer believed to be mysterious or subjected to fate, but instead controlled by the human quest for utopian perfection. In the end, the real secret Frankenstein is trying to protect is that human creation is no better than God's, when modern science promised so much more.

The Historical Shift of the Monstrous

For most of history, monsters have been represented as symbolic and liminal beings, often connected to both gods and strangers, as 'figures of Otherness [that] occupy the frontier zone where reason falters and fantasies flourish' (Kearney 2003: 3). The monster has always been a representational being that transcends the borders of sacred/profane, and in turn, as a representation of chaos, irrationality, and disorder, acts as a warning for both the individual and society at large. However, as liminal creatures, monsters simultaneously (and paradoxically) become symbols of a return to order once they are defeated at the hands of a heroic figure. The slaying of the monster in most quest fiction completes the rite of passage for the hero's journey, representing a move from the liminal phase to the phase of inclusion that ultimately restores order for both hero and society, as well as the realms of the sacred and profane. During the Middle Ages, the monster's sacred/profane relationship was strengthened, as was its function of exemplifying divine admonition, in which its death reinforced the glory and sacredness of God and the Catholic Church. Outside the oral tradition of fairy tales, monster lore during the Middle Ages did not really exist in literary popular culture and was predominantly controlled by the 'learned classes' (Smith 1986: 16). It was largely the saints and clergymen that took up the heroic mantle of monster slayers in medieval literature, as much of the literature and folklore of the time looked to reinterpret classic monsters symbolically through a Biblical and Christian lens (Bovey 2002: 27; Huet 1993: 89; Kearney 2003: 29). Even the early oral Latin fairy and folk tales were shaped by the themes of Christian doctrine, morality, and ethics (Zipes 2013: 8–9), while the presence of God was usually found in the background of most medieval fables (JM Ziolkowski 2010: 196).

Beginning with the Renaissance, monsters slowly began to be categorized much more scientifically, often seen as abnormalities surviving outside the laws and course of nature, although initially still co-existing with earlier theological constructions (Ghadessi 2018: 19). It was Fortunio Liceti (1634) who began the long secularization process of the monster that moved it away from its divine origins as 'portentous heavenly signs' (Ghadessi 2018: 21), grounding it in more of a physical and medical teratological classification, away from the religious, supernatural, and metaphysical realms of the Middle Ages. As European history shifted to the early modern period and the Enlightenment, the fear of monsters had transformed into curiosity, creating a far more relaxed outlook towards them as the Age of Reason began to take hold over society (Hagner 1999: 175). However, the monster—and the supernatural as a whole—seems to return to popular culture during the 18th century with the rise of the Romantic and Gothic literary movements. Although it kept the monster as a secularized figure, the Romantic and Gothic movements challenged reason not through religious means, but rather through an examination of excess emotions and desires. Gothic fiction frequently employed monsters as symbols of the inability to control or suppress these desires, as well as a means of critiquing the "monstrous" superstition that many Protestants argued Catholicism had attached to Christianity, and in doing so, these movements maintain the monster's symbolic nature as a warning. Nonetheless, one significant change is that the borders the monster traverses no longer exist in faraway lands the hero must travel to, but instead are located in the shadows of the modern city and the human psyche. As with the stranger, as society approaches the modern age, the monster's topographical location is far closer than it previously had been.

Despite this, the monster still retains its liminal character of being both a symbol of chaos and a return to order. Originally, Gothic literature was generally expressed through two subgenres.⁹ In Gothic terror, which was popularized by Ann Radcliffe in novels such as *The Mysteries of Udolpho* (1794/ 1987) and *The Italian Or, the Confessional of the Black Penitents* (1797/1968), the monster—and all supernatural occurrences, for that matter—is not slain by the hero, but nonetheless a return to order is achieved through its elimination. Instead of the hero defeating the monster with strength and courage, the tools of reason and rationality are used to dispel the monster as an element of superstition, and thereby continue the symbolic representation of the monster's demise leading to a restoring of order. Gothic horror, originally manifesting in Matthew Gregory Lewis' *The Monk* (1796/2004), broke away from Radcliffe's dispelling of the supernatural through reason. Although retaining the trope of monstrosity as a characteristic of Catholicism and the human psyche, the supernatural instances in Lewis' work go unexplained. The supernatural for Lewis was an extension of reality, and although he himself was a skeptic, the monsters and the supernatural as a whole in his stories reflected the hysteria, irrationality, and superstition of the many people who did believe in them (2000: 198). Lewis' horror novels went beyond the stories of terror, as they were not only a critique of Catholic mania but likened the same hysteria to the French Revolution, social change, and the ensuing chaos it would bring. Although containing a much more tragic ending than novels in the terror genre, Lewis' *The Monk* still restores a sense of order and normalcy at the novel's conclusion (Haggerty 2015: 131).

The recognition of the Creature as something real, an emphasis on violence, and its apparent anti-Jacobin stance may seem to link Shelley's *Frankenstein* firmly with the horror classification of Gothic fiction; however, as with its treatment of the uncanny and the Gothic genre in general, *Frankenstein* transcends these labels by borrowing but also subverting these classifications, residing in between both definitions of horror and terror. Shelley displays both by exercising many common horror tropes but still applying overarching senses of uncertainty and terror through the anxiety of an unknown future, which dictates the story's use of fear. More importantly, unlike previous Gothic fiction, *Frankenstein* is reluctant to restore order with the novel's conclusion. Victor Frankenstein may well be the first 'hero' who is unable to restore order, since he fails to tame or slay the monster he created; nor can he use reason to dispel the notion that the Creature is illusionary, since it was created through scientific reason itself, leaving us to contemplate a liminal and unknown future. While these reasons do separate Shelley's handling of the monster from previous Gothic fiction, her most significant act is giving the Creature its own conscience, desires, emotions, and most importantly, voice. It is the first monster that is allowed to speak, to tell its own story, and as a result, the first monster that readers truly sympathize with. With the birth of Frankenstein's creature, Shelley begins to distance monstrosity from an interpretation that simply sees it as an extension of evil, instead producing a reading that is far more indefinite. With

Frankenstein, the monstrosity contained in humans is not restricted to specific evil people or demons, but instead is something ubiquitous that lives within human, or rather male, excess and hubris.

Modernity's Monstrous Secret

In her introduction to the 1831 edition, Shelley declares a fear 'of any human endeavour to mock the stupendous mechanism of the Creator of the world' (2003: 9), solidifying the novel's discernible warning against an unrelenting thirst for knowledge and human progress in divergence of God's perfect creation. However, her anxiety continues with the terrifying thought of the mocker's success in achieving God's work (ibid.), which seems to build a sense of dread more from an uncanny fear of the monstrous achievement than from any attempt, or "failure," at playing God. The novel's sense of uncanny fear comes from Victor's triumph, for it brings to light the anxieties surfacing as a result of humanity's progress in the modern world. The imagination, agency, and thirst for knowledge that surges through Frankenstein during the process of creation and discovery vanishes once he is triumphant in creating life through artificial means. The originally beautiful physical image of the Creature alters only when it is finally animated, resulting in an uncanny terror that illuminates itself afterwards through reflection, and not during the process: '...now that I had finished, the beauty of the dream vanished, and breathless horror and disgust filled my heart' (ibid. 58). The perspective of the Creature's physical appearance changes when Victor gazes into its horrible 'watery, clouded eyes' (ibid. 186); since the eyes are traditionally known as a gateway to soul,[10] the soul of humanity is no longer masked by its physical beauty, but rather exposed through eyes that reveal a horrific truth. It is through the action of reanimated life that the internal horror has projected and manifested itself onto the physical appearance of the Creature.[11]

Here again, Shelley reverses the typical dichotomy of dark (evil) and light (good). In *Frankenstein*, light symbolizes knowledge, birth, and Enlightenment ideals, yet it becomes a threatening aspect to our existence. The Creature's eyes blend into the whiteness of the sockets, giving a lack of contrast and a terrifying sense of ambiguity. As Slavoj Žižek writes of this scene; '[t]he nontransparent, 'depthless' eye blocks out our access to the 'soul,' to the infinite abyss of the 'person,' thus turning it into a soulless monster: not simply a nonsubjective machine, but rather an uncanny subject that has not yet been submitted to the process of 'subjectivization' which confers upon it the depth of 'personality'"(1993: 240, n2). In this instance, the eyes are rendered malevolent not because of the typically dark/light juxtaposition that would historically define evil and good, but due to a liminal and abject character that subsequently reveals an uncertain truth of the contemporary secularized world controlled by modern man. It is through the eyes of the modern creation that the manifestation of the uncanny unveils the absurdity of modernity's belief in linear progress: they reveal nothing except an ambiguous future in which human agency does not translate into control. The abject Creature or monster therefore becomes the symbolic representation of this lack of control.

Shelley brought to light the anxious modern feeling of being simultaneously fascinated and repulsed by the world forming before her eyes. Once light is cast upon secular knowledge and human potential, how can it ever remain hidden from humanity again, regardless of how horrifying it may be? The modern terror witnessed during the artificial creation of life comes from a 'success' that can be neither prevented nor actively controlled, rendering Shelley's warning against the act of playing God futile. The concept of her story emphasizes both her fear of and fascination with science and progress, as she was simultaneously attracted to and disgusted with the world that was forming,[12] a sentiment that appears in both the "rebellious" 1818 edition and the "conservative" 1831 edition.[13] Shelley herself alluded to this when addressing the many alterations in her introduction to the 1831 edition, stating that she has 'changed no portion of the story, nor introduced any new ideas or circumstances ... leaving the core and substance of it untouched' (2003: 10). However, according to Mellor, Shelley's announcement is simply a lie that, as with Victor, disclaims any responsibility to her creation, itself a victim of fate (1988: 176).

Although Mellor is correct in arguing that the sense of agency and moral choice does essentially evaporate in 1831, I do agree with Shelley's statement that the essence of the novel, especially regarding its uncertain moral stance and problem of agency, does not necessarily change; the ambiguity of agency simply becomes more transparent in the later edition. The free will Victor evidently nurses in the first edition is virtually illusory, not necessarily in terms of his ability to make individual actions or choices, but rather in that the consequences of these choices are left purely to chance. Later in the 20th century, Jacques Monod argued that the scientific pursuit of knowledge disengaged the connection between humans and nature, subsequently leaving us all in the hands of chance and a world without intrinsic meaning. Prior to modern thought, 'our ancestors ... perceived the strangeness of their condition only very dimly. They did not have the reasons we have today for feeling themselves strangers in a universe upon which they opened their eyes' (1970/1972: 29). Despite what the group Monod refers to as the *animists* believed, encompassing religions to theorists such as Hegel and Marx, for Monod the world does not contain a teleonomic principle, plan, or a harmonious construction but rather that '[p]ure chance, absolutely free but blind, ... is today the *sole* conceivable hypothesis' (ibid. 112-113). The novel *Frankenstein* seems to predict this same existential theory for modern individuals as a result of the ascent of the scientific pursuit, which creates the modern stranger and propels it into the chaos of liminal uncertainty.

Despite Frankenstein's experiment coming to fruition, he is nonetheless subjected to a world of chance, as the modern world is still doomed to proceed towards a world governed by the principles of scientific rationalism. Victor, as a representation of modern humanity,[14] essentially has no choice but to proceed forward, as if it is both his and humanity's Fate to accelerate civilization to its fullest potential. Frankenstein may regret certain actions he has committed, but does not regret his vigor and passion for scientific discovery. At the end of the novel, when addressing Walton's men (who wish to abandon their captain as his expedition has become extremely dangerous), Frankenstein seems to once again locate the 'reveries while the work was incomplete' (Shelley 2003: 214), which he was unable to recall after his experiment was completed, and once again defends a scientific pursuit of knowledge and discovery despite being conscious of the consequences of his own experiments:

> Are you then so easily turned from your design? Did you not call this a glorious expedition? and wherefore was it glorious? Not because the way was smooth and placid as a southern sea, but because it was full of dangers and terror; because, at every new incident, your fortitude was to be called forth, and your courage exhibited; because danger and death surrounded, and these dangers you were to brave and overcome. For this was it a glorious, for this was it an honourable undertaking. You were hereafter to be hailed as the benefactors of your species; your name adored, as belonging to brave men who encountered death for honour and the benefit of mankind ... ye need not have come thus far, and dragged your captain to the shame of a defeat, merely to prove yourselves cowards. Be steady to your purposes, and firm as a rock (ibid. 217).

Frankenstein, like the modern world, is unable to go or look back towards the past, regardless of the consequences or the mistakes he has made. For Frankenstein, and many other moderns, the idea of progress is dependent on the severing of a past founded on myths, while focusing on the truths of the objective world, regardless of how ugly those truths may turn out to be.

Nonetheless, once Frankenstein's eyes lock upon modernity's monstrosity, no matter how hard he tries to ignore it, it haunts him until his death.. Similar to what Shelly said of her inability to get rid of the 'hideous phantom' (ibid. 9) that haunted her after the first inkling of her story came to her in a dream, the novel's ending ultimately leads to the lingering of modern liminality. *Frankenstein* has become the modern socio-cultural spectre that has haunted us ever since its publication. In *Specters of Marx*, Jacques Derrida describes the spectre as 'a kind of ghost who comes back or who still risks coming back *post mortem*' (59). Derrida's description of the spectre is extremely reminiscent of Frankenstein's Creature, a liminal figure that 'is a paradoxical incorporation, the becoming-body, a certain phenomenal and carnal form of the spirit. It becomes, rather, some "thing" that remains difficult to name: neither soul nor body, and both one and the other' (ibid. 5).

If we examine Mary Shelley's original ending,[15] in which the Creature is 'pushing himself off,' rather than the passive 'borne away' found in the final version, the Creature's sense of agency still leads it to 'be carried away by the waves' and ultimately ends with same outcome. Mellor argues that Percy Shelley's revision in the original, the change from Captain Walton losing sight of the Creature to the Creature being 'lost in darkness and distance,' is 'a defensive maneuver to ward off anxiety and assert final authorial control over his wife's subversive creation,' in an attempt to postulate 'a comforting reassurance' (1988: 68). However, the revised ending reflects the liminal and existential condition of modernity to a much greater degree, and also emphasizes and links both Walton and the Creature's sense of alienated perspective in one sentence. What also makes the Creature an uncanny spectre is that it is still becoming, unnamed and 'lost in darkness and distance,' encompassing a shadowy secret within those depthless and watery eyes.

More importantly, the ending's apparent 'comforting reassurance' leads us to an uncanny and false sense of security. As Freud writes, the author of the uncanny is 'betraying us to the superstitiousness which we have ostensibly surmounted; he deceives by promising to give us the sober truth, and then after all overstepping it' (1955: 250). The novel's ending lulls the reader into a false sense of security when the Creature states that it will take its own life and thereby remove itself from society, repressing the uncanny beyond the border of darkness; however, the novel has already established what 'ought to have been kept concealed but which has nevertheless come to light' (ibid. 14). Therefore, placing the Creature back into the security of darkness is ineffective as a comforting outcome, especially since the story lives on to haunt us, underlining one of the main premises of the novel: the impossibility of repressing the uncanny into darkness once it has come into light. Examining the ending of Freud's essay,[16] Nicholas Royle argues that the uncanny has a paradoxical role where it not only manifests itself in light but also remains uncanny within darkness, as 'something constantly destined to return' (2003: 109); and similar to the ending of *Frankenstein*, it is darkness 'which finally haunts his project' (ibid. 110). If the Creature is uncanny because it initially represents the 'return of the repressed' in creation, it remains uncanny in its dissolution back into darkness, in the miscarried attempt to once again repress the repressed and return us to a dissipated past.

The End of the Natural and the Beginning of Artificial Reality

The spectre in Shelley's novel is not a supernatural entity from the past, but rather a hybrid being that represents an ambiguous future, one that moves away from nature towards a new and artificial reality. In *Frankenstein*, the uncanny spectre materializes into a cyborg-like entity, a physical and tangible specimen signifying the transition of the spiritual and supernatural to the material, scientific, and disenchanted world. This evolution away from the supernatural does not necessarily lead to the arrival of the purely natural, nor does it remove itself from myth. It essentially means that a movement towards disenchantment or secularization paradoxically leaves us on an oscillating liminal path towards re-enchantment or resacralization. As David Ketterer explains, 'although Frankenstein supposedly eschews the supernatural, magic, or alchemy in favor of modern science as a means of instilling life into dead tissue, the distinction between natural magic and alchemy on the one hand and natural philosophy and chemistry on the other, and that between religion and science, is blurred at every surviving stage of the text' (1997: 61). Before Max Horkheimer and Theodor Adorno wrote of the mythological reverberation of the Age of Enlightenment in *Dialectic of Enlightenment*, Shelley explored the same themes in *Frankenstein*, in which the ideals that looked to dispel myth simply produced their own. Here, myth is no longer allocated or represented by a feudal or even natural world, but rather falls into the space of science and rationality.

The Newtonian Laws of Nature were seen as 'exemplars of Reason' (Smith 1986: 41), and although they were permanent and represented God's perfection, they also exemplified a contrasting 'Christian acceptance of human imperfection, manifested in sin and suffering, disease and death, with a presumptuous conviction that nature's imperfections could be made perfect by human genius' (ibid. 53). Victor, by way of modern science, looks to reverse Nature's fixed state and advance the refinement of man by perfecting nature. Shelley explicates this premise through Professor Waldman's speech, which allows Frankenstein to apprehend his 'chimeras of boundless grandeur' (Shelley 2003: 48) within a modern reality, something he realizes, although reluctantly, that he is unable to do through the ancient proto-science of alchemy:

> 'The ancient teachers of this science,' said he, 'promised impossibilities, and performed nothing. The modern masters promise very little; they know that metals cannot be transmuted, and that the elixir of life is a chimera. But these philosophers, whose hands seem only made to dabble in dirt, and their eyes to pour over the microscope or crucible, have indeed performed miracles. They penetrate into the recesses of nature, and show how she works in her hiding places. They ascend into the heavens; they have discovered how the blood circulates, and the nature of the air we breathe. They have acquired new and almost unlimited powers; they can command the thunders of heaven, mimic the earthquake, and even mock the invisible world with its own shadows' (ibid. 49).

Here, the power of controlling nature lies in replicating or mimicking it. The 'unlimited powers' modern scientists possess come not from original creation, but through artificial reproduction. *Frankenstein* examines the equivocal boundaries between natural and artificial, machine and human, in such a way that its 'brilliance … is not so much to point out that artificial life and intelligence are possible, but that human life *already is this artificial* intelligence' (Morton 2002: 47). It is the imaginative potential to dream and realize the unknown or the not-yet that distinguishes humans from animals.

By presenting us with a negation or lack (what currently does not exist), our imagination tends to lead us to a utilitarian belief in changing the world for the better by giving us alternative worlds we can strive for (Dahlbom 2013: 89). *Frankenstein* unearths and examines the artificial nature of human beings, through Frankenstein's drive for progress and also doubled through the hybrid Creature. However, our artificial potential is threatened by the natural process of life and death; by creating life through scientific means, Frankenstein attempts to overcome the natural course of existence by cheating death: 'but what glory would attend the discovery, if I could banish disease from the human frame, and render man invulnerable to any but a violent death!' (Shelley 2003: 42). Having lost his mother at an early age, Frankenstein is overwhelmed with the anxiety of mortality and attempts to conquer his existential unease in order to create a new path towards a better future for humanity. Unwilling to be confined to Mother Nature's course, or the decaying prison of the human body, Frankenstein tries to replace or assume her function of giving birth, while at the same time initiating a process that still lives with us today[17]: the possibility of cheating death.

> Life and death appeared to me ideal bounds, which I should first break through, and pour a torrent of light into our dark world. A new species would bless me as its creator and source; many happy and excellent natures would owe their being to me. No father could claim the gratitude of his child so completely as I should deserve theirs. Pursuing these reflections, I thought, that if I could bestow animation upon lifeless matter, I might in process of time … renew life where death had apparently devoted the body to corruption (ibid. 55).

Frankenstein's desire to 'break through' the 'ideal bounds' of the human body, and Nature itself, is driven by his struggle to cheat or deny death, which ultimately becomes his downfall. With the removal of God, the birth of a new being, and 'a torrent of light' (ibid.) crashing through traditional ignorance, Frankenstein must come to terms with the resulting amputation of an afterlife from the new modern human consciousness. Death, the modern world's ultimate finality, leaves us with an existential void or emptiness that Frankenstein looks to refute through a complete denial of death itself (McMahon 2007). However, Frankenstein's attempt to end the uncertainty that comes with death ironically leads to more, once again displaying a lack of control that human agency is unable to subvert.

Victor Frankenstein, however, is not a one-dimensional individual, and does not fully abandon nature for scientific pursuit. Principally a paradoxical character, he is as much of a Romantic as he is a "mad" scientist. In fact, his fascination for and complete reliance on science and nature mirror one another. Victor's connections to both science and nature become obsessions, which he uses to abjure himself from humanity and his family. His view of his father is disheartening: 'I see him now, excellent and venerable old man! His eyes wandered in vacancy, for they had lost their charm and their delight' (Shelley 2003: 201); Frankenstein looks to nature's cold immortality for comfort far more than he looks to the eyes of his father, which simply speak of death. Even after the death of Elizabeth, Victor attempts only to find a sanctuary in nature, which, as do his scientific pursuits, ultimately fails him:

> What then became of me? I know not; I lost sensation, and chains and darkness were the only objects that pressed upon me. Sometimes, indeed, I dreamt that I wandered in flowery meadows and pleasant vales with the friends of my youth, but I awoke and found myself in a dungeon. Melancholy followed, but by degrees I gained a clear conception of my miseries and situation and was then released from my prison. For they had called me mad, and during many months, as I understood, a solitary cell had been my habitation (ibid. 202).

Nature, which in many respects replaced God for many Romantics of the time, is extremely indifferent towards Victor. Similarly to how the Creature searches for its identity and meaning in relation to its creator, Victor Frankenstein positions his sense of meaning and sacredness in something that is completely detached from him. God, nature, and Victor are all connected by virtue of being silent creators; and while we know that of those three, Victor is definitely not indifferent, he still is rendered helpless, since he stands or oscillates within a liminal position of creator/created, Satan/God, or rebel/lord. It is also no coincidence that the Romantic elements, especially in regard to Frankenstein's experiences with nature and love, become much more problematic as the novel progresses, juxtaposing the scientific warning with one of Romantic excess. Victor represents the nightmare of both scientific and Romantic uncontrolled idealism.

Through the birth of Frankenstein's Creature, this idealism is potentially superseded in the modern world with a liminal cross between the two. The "artificial" Creature is depicted as more passionate, more human, than Frankenstein, making the formerly distinguishable binary of artificial and natural much more complicated, giving way to an uncanny world where "artificiality" has become the new "natural." While modernity attempts to categorize everything into binaries such as natural and artificial, Shelley shows us that it uncannily subverts these very same binaries. Freud argues the uncanny 'is created when there is intellectual uncertainty whether an object is alive or not, and when an inanimate object becomes too much like an animate one'

(1955: 233). By the early 19th century, Shelley was able to prophesize what Donna Haraway argued in the late 20th century: that 'machines have made thoroughly ambiguous the difference between natural and artificial, mind and body, self-developing and externally designed, and many other distinctions that used to apply to organisms and machines' (1985/2004: 11).[18] Monod suggests that the differences between the natural and artificial have always been misleading and that the two can no longer be regarded as opposites, as it is impossible to differentiate between natural or artificial characteristics, even in human beings. What distinguishes the natural from the artificial is that the natural contains, in and of itself, what it needs to develop, while the artificial depends on external influences and is designed for a purpose (Monod 1972: 3–4). However, what blurs this distinction for Monod is that the teleonomy, or the apparent internal purposefulness, recognizes no difference between living and non-living organisms. Therefore, natural things are as dependent as artificial things on external forces and 'endowed *with a purpose or project*, which at the same time they exhibit in their structure and carry out through their performances' (ibid. 9). Taking this into account, what *Frankenstein* claims is not that modern society leaves us dislocated from nature, which itself is alienating, but rather that what is in fact alienating is our inability to accept both our isolation, unnaturalness, and strangeness: 'man must at last wake out of his millenary dream; and in doing so wake to his total solitude, his fundamental isolation. Now does he at last realize that, like a gypsy, he lives at the boundary of an alien world. A world that is deaf to his music, just as indifferent to his hopes as to his suffering or his crimes' (ibid. 172–173). However, although Shelley seems to acknowledge the connection between nature and the artificial, the novel still seems to try to not necessarily deny, but nonetheless internalize this knowledge, putting it back into the uncanny darkness from which it came.

The Uncanny Stranger in a Secular Void

As I have argued, *Frankenstein* resides in the modern liminal state where past, present, and future become something far more uncertain, leaving the stranger in a very lonely and unclear position of trying to find importance in life. The freedom given to or forced onto the Creature emulates the newfound independence that humanity must face, forcing the Creature to contemplate its existence: 'I was dependent on none, and related to none. "The path of my departure was free", and there was none to lament my annihilation. My person was hideous, and my stature gigantic: what did this mean? Who was I? What was I? Whence did I come? What was my destination? These questions continually recurred, but I was unable to solve them' (Shelley 2003: 131). As Northrop Frye notably states, Shelley's novel 'is a precursor ... of the existential thriller, as such a book as Camus's *L'Étranger*. The whole point about the monster is not a machine, but an ordinary human being isolated from mankind by extreme ugliness' (2005: 122). Looking back, it is possible to see the Creature as simply "ordinary," with society becoming much more oriented around the liminal; but at the time it was something entirely new: it was the birth of the modern stranger, and it continues to preoccupy our existence today. Unlike Victor, whose existential crisis revolves around the ominous cloud of death, the Creature's existential malaise is situated within the menacing idea of modern life. The Creature is an uncanny representation of the modern individual born with the burden of freedom, lacking any form of established identity and tradition to which to tie oneself. With no nation, community, or family to belong to, the Creature is forced into a series of newfound questions it struggles to find answers for. Marginalized from society, the Creature as stranger must become a voyeur, a fly on the wall that observes without being seen but nonetheless is there. Being a modern liminal figure, Victor's *doppelgänger* cannot be fully absent and must exist. As the Creature explains to Frankenstein, 'I admired virtue and good feelings and loved the gentle manners and amiable qualities of my cottagers, but I was shut out from intercourse with them, except through means which I obtained by stealth, when I was unseen and unknown, and which rather increased than satisfied the desire I had of becoming one among my fellows' (Shelley 2003: 124). Like a plague, the Creature's melancholic alienation infects the people around him. In the moment before Frankenstein confronts the Creature on the mountain for the first time since its creation in the laboratory, the path up the mountain becomes lonely and desolate as Shelley links the Creature and Frankenstein by painting the estranged spirit of the modern condition:

> The ascent is precipitous, but the path is cut into continual and short windings, which enable you to surmount the perpendicularity of the mountain. It is a scene terrifically desolate. In a thousand spots the traces of the winter avalanche may be perceived, where trees lie broken and strewed on the ground, some entirely destroyed, others bent, leaning upon the jutting rocks of the mountain or transversely upon other trees. The path, as you ascend higher, is intersected by ravines of snow, down which stones continually roll from above; one of them is particularly dangerous, as the slightest sound, such as even speaking in a loud voice, produces a concussion of air sufficient to draw destruction upon the head of the speaker. The pines are not tall or luxuriant, but they are sombre and add an air of severity to the scene. I looked on the valley beneath; vast mists were rising from the rivers which ran through it and curling in thick wreaths around the opposite mountains, whose summits were hid in the uniform clouds, while rain poured from the dark sky and added to the melancholy impression I received from the objects around me. Alas! Why does man boast of sensibilities superior to those apparent in the brute; it only renders them more necessary beings. If our impulses were confined to hunger, thirst, and desire, we might be nearly

free; but now we are moved by every wind that blows and a chance word or scene that that word may convey to us (ibid. 100).

Although both Frankenstein and the Creature are stuck between the realms of chance and fate, the main difference between their liminal positions is that Frankenstein oscillates between the either/or extremes of science and nature, compliance and rebellion, while the Creature is a product of them and subsequently trapped between them, unable to move, continuously inhabiting the space between both states, where even a correlation with John Milton's rebellious Satan is lost: 'Satan has his companions, fellow-devils, to admire and encourage him; but I am solitary and abhorred' (ibid. 133).[19] Even the allusions to Christ ultimately fail, as the Creature, "God's favourite son," neither is redeemed nor does he save anyone at the end of the novel. For Jerrold E. Hogle, the Creature represents 'the *absolutely* Other,' the other's other, or more specifically a more liminal other, repositioning the Creature from the uncanny towards the abject:

> The creature is a 'monster' in that it/he embodies and distances all that a society refuses to name—all the betwixt-and-between, even ambisexual, cross-class, and cross-cultural conditions of life that Western culture "abjects", as Kristeva would put it— ... It/he is "*the absolutely* Other" ... pointing immediately, as we have just seen, to intermixed and repressed states of being, the divisibility of the body, 'thrown-down' social groups, class struggles, gender-confusions, birth-moments, and death-drives ... as well as to a cacophony of ideological and intertextual differences. All the while, though, he/it both represents each of these alterities and keeps them at a great remove by being quasi-human yet strictly artificial (1998: 185–187).

Interrelated with the uncanny, as both concepts revolve around the paradoxical, the liminal, and the confrontation with the other, the abject is distinct in that it is 'more violent' than the uncanny and 'is elaborated through a failure to recognize its kin; nothing is familiar, not even the shadow of a memory' (Kristeva 1982: 5).[20] According to Hogle, abjection becomes a more significant characteristic after the publication of *Frankenstein* due to the fact that the 18th-century Gothic 'provides the symbolic means for that very construction of "self" versus "archaic other' (1998: 179), while "*Frankenstein* offers the Gothic ghost of the counterfeit in its most achieved, complex, and influential form up to 1818, using what is most fundamental in the Gothic to alter and deepen (rather than simply reverse) it" (ibid. 203). Frankenstein's Creature is uncanny because it can be considered a non-human, but nonetheless indicates a monstrous familiarity with the human subject: 'God, in pity, made man beautiful and alluring, after his own image; but my form is a filthy type of yours, more horrid even from the very resemblance' (Shelley 2003: 133); however, the

Creature paradoxically also embodies the abject since it is inauthentic, genderless,[21] and leads to disgust and horror. Like the abject, the Creature 'disturbs identity, system, order' and 'does not respect borders, positions, rules' (Kristeva 1982: 4). It is a symbol of a world 'where meaning collapses' (ibid. 2) and results in the creation of the modern secularized stranger, a liminal character that, unlike the rebel who is at odds with society, is an individual that was born displaced from both rebellion and submission.

Another way in which *Frankenstein* distinctively separates itself from previous literature, especially of the Gothic genre, is by creating far more existential and moral ambiguity between the protagonist and its *doppelgänger*. Although Frankenstein's *doppelgänger* represents the monstrosity within him and human nature, he does not necessarily represent the naturally evil, dark aspect of the self, but rather a secularized and ambiguous un-evil monstrosity, one that lies between the binaries of good and bad, which is found in humanity, modernity, and the quest for secular knowledge. This absence of value judgment, in turn, raises more questions than answers, such as the infamous and unresolvable question that has resonated with the tale up to today: 'Who is in fact the real monster?' Yet to choose one entirely misses the point of the novel. As Reichardt maintains, 'only a human being or humanoid can be a true monster … the essential condition for a monster is that the human characteristics it possesses must not be changed too far' (1994: 139). This goes as much for the monstrous attributes as it does for the benevolent ones, making Victor as much the Creature's double as the Creature is Frankenstein's. As much as its monstrosity, the humanism displayed by the Creature shows that the dialectical essence of humanity wavers between our experiences and actions. Therefore, the projection of blame cannot fall solely on the shoulders of Frankenstein, for the Creature is rejected by everyone in the novel, not just Victor. The responsibility lies with everyone, including the De Lacey family and even the Creature itself.

Moreover, the character of Captain Walton, allows *Frankenstein* transcends the dualistic nature of *doppelgänger* concept. By adding a third "double" to the story, Shelley creates a universality of the shadow motif, which further envelops the other into the self. In addition to all three characters being explorers, wanderers, and isolated individuals in their own right, both the Creature and Frankenstein can only reveal their stories and secrets to Walton, who in turn channels these modern feelings of uneasiness to others through his writings. Through Captain Walton's letters, the modern and liminal spectre lives on to haunt society, resulting in the inevitability of truth becoming myth and vice versa. As Lee Sterrenburg contends, beginning with *Frankenstein*,

> … we are presented with the confessional of isolated protagonists who are, at least symbolically, reenacting heroic and messianic quests from a previous revolutionary age. Political themes are translated into private and psychological terms. The messianic struggles of the hero are presented subjectively, in an autobiographical confession we cannot

fully trust, and surrounded by equally subjective editors, interlocutors, and interpreters, whose presence further complicates our hope of finding a simple ideological meaning. The identity of the demonic forces is no longer clear. The specter haunting Europe is no longer the monster Jacobin. The messianic impulse remains, but its political content has been called into question (1979: 145–146).

Despite the progressive uncertainty of the messianic spectre, we still can learn from it; we can learn from what is haunting us. Walton abandons his quest because he was able to see the uncanny and abject horror of his pursuit through Victor's story and through the manifestation of the Creature itself. Although Walton's abandonment of his North Pole exploration does not end modern history's relentless pursuit of secular knowledge and discovery, it still advances an optimistic perspective because it allows us to, if not correct our mistakes, at the very least realize them. Yet even in in this regard, the liminal essence of *Frankenstein* holds power, for Shelley is unwilling to lay all the cards on the table, as the story once again ends ambiguously. Regardless of the fact that Walton saves himself and his crew from the unknown, will his sister Margaret, and subsequently the reader, heed the warning and believe his story or will it be simply dismissed as nonsensical science fiction?

Notes: Chapter I

[1] Although originally published in 1818 (1999), Mary Shelley revised the novel in 1831 (2003). There are several delicate, yet significant, differences between these two editions in regard to style, structure, and plot, the most prominent being Victor's apparent ability to exercise freewill and agency in the 1818 edition, while in the 1831 edition he seems to be a victim of fate and chance. All citations where the text is the same will be from the 1831 edition. For a detailed and interesting study on the differences between the two editions, see Anne K. Mellor, "Revising Frankenstein" in *Mary Shelley: Her Life, Her Fiction, Her Monsters* (1988).

[2] The symbol of Prometheus as both the modern individual and myth is not only used in *Frankenstein*. Mary Shelley's husband, Percy Shelley, published *Prometheus Unbound* in 1820. Despite the reactionary failures of the French Revolution, Percy's Prometheus personifies the ideal spirit of rebellion and heroic struggle, contrasting Mary Shelley's ambiguous usage of the Greek myth with a more optimistic view of human progress. Franz Kafka's parable "Prometheus" uses the myth to address the problematic question of existence. After outlining the four different versions of the myth, he writes, '[t]here remains the inexplicable mass of rock. The legend tries to explain the inexplicable. As it comes out of the substratum of truth it has in turn to end in the inexplicable' (1918/1971: 432). In a similar absurdist vein, Giacamo

Leopardi's take on the Prometheus myth, "The Wager of Prometheus" (1824/1983) in *Moral Tales*, shows Prometheus as a gambler and troublemaker. In Leopardi's tale, Prometheus takes a contest between the gods for the greatest creation too seriously, only to eventually give up on humanity after witnessing its destructive nature. Although both Leopardi and Mary Shelley portray Prometheus as a risk taker, the distinctions between the two Prometheuses highlight the differences between both writers' philosophies, which shall be further outlined in the next chapter.

3 Although the outcomes may be similar, fate and destiny are not the same as chance. As Saxena and Dixit point out, fate and destiny imply 'something foreordained or a predetermined course of events', whereas '[c]hance means something that happens unpredictably without discernable human intention or observable cause' (2001: 36).

4 The most notable being when Victor first realizes the "ugliness" of his creation: 'Beautiful!—Great God! His yellow skin scarcely covered the work of muscles and arteries beneath; his hair was of a lustrous black, and flowing; his teeth of a pearly whiteness; but these luxuriances only formed a more horrid contrast with his watery eyes, that seemed almost of the same colour as the dun white sockets in which they were set, his shriveled complexion, and straight black lips' (Shelley 2003: 58).

5 Although working around Taylor's framework, Hoeveler does not agree with his argument that during the late 18th century there existed two binary subjectivities: the porous self, who was unprotected from the 'anima' or spiritual world, and the skepticism of the 'buffered' self, who effectively removed any need of the supernatural. Hoeveler rejects this binary, arguing instead of an 'interaction' or 'oscillation' between these subjectivities (2010: 16–17).

6 Shelley was influenced by the science of her age as much as by Gothic and Romantic literature. Jasia Reichardt argues that the novel 'is not a story about alchemy and magic but science, or more precisely, about natural philosophy, chemistry and galvanism' (1994: 136–137).

7 As Hoeveler explains, although most Gothic literature was a result of Protestantism's attempt to remove the irrational elements found within medieval Catholicism, the otherness of Catholicism was still an intrinsic and uncanny component within Protestantism, leaving Gothic literature fractured between a thirst for the modern and nostalgia for the early Catholic traditions. As a result, the Gothic attempt to secularize the uncanny is a 'hazy one,' since these earlier beliefs hold as much power as the rational ones that looked to eliminate them (2010: 30–31).

8 To further the relationship between secularization and neurosis, Freud argues '[y]ou cannot exaggerate the intensity of man's inner resolution and craving for authority. The extraordinary increase in the neuroses since the power of religion has waned may give you some indication of it' (1959: 290).

9 In her essay "On the Supernatural in Poetry," Ann Radcliffe first distinguishes between horror and terror. Horror is the fear of something tangible,

exhibited through repulsion, shock, and violence, while terror is channeled through anxiety, a fear of the unknown, characterized, according to Radcliffe, as 'uncertainty and obscurity' (1826: 150). Radcliffe saw horror as inferior, unable to conjure up a sense of the sublime: 'Terror and horror are so far opposite, that the first expands the soul, and awakens the faculties to a high degree of life; the other contracts, freezes, and nearly annihilates them' (ibid.).

10 'The eye is the lamp of the body. So if your eye is healthy, your whole body will be full of light. But if your eye is evil, your whole body will be full of darkness. Therefore, if the light within you has turned into darkness, how great is that darkness!' (Matthew 6: 22–23).

11 Illustrated by Theodor Richard Edward von Holst, the 1831 edition contained the first image of the Creature approved by Shelley. An early review of the 1831 edition acknowledges that the image, depicting the Creature after animation, does not really portray the Creature as having any monstrous features outside of its large stature: 'The room and the accessories are good; but the figure is more gigantic than frightful, and the face is deficient in that supernatural hideousness on which the author so especially dwells' (cited in Moreno & Moreno 2018: 229 (*The London Literary Gazette*, 19 November 1831: 740)).

12 As Julia Kristeva explains in *Powers of Horror*, '[o]ne thus understands why so many victims of the abject are its fascinated victims—if not its submissive and willing ones. We may call it a border; abjection is above all ambiguity. Because, while releasing a hold, it does not radically cut off the subject from what threatens it—on the contrary, abjection acknowledges it to be in perpetual danger' (1982: 9). Furthermore, in terms of abject literature, 'as the sense of abjection is both the abject's judge and accomplice, this is also true of the literature that confronts it' (ibid. 16).

13 Anne Mellor attributes this pessimistic transformation to the turmoil that Shelley experienced in her personal life between both publications (1988: 170–176).

14 To be clear, Shelley sees humanity as a patriarchal society dominated by male ambitions. This topic will be examined further in Chapter 7.

15 The final lines of the novel are some of the many revisions Percy Shelley contributed to the novel before its initial publication. The original:

> He sprung from the cabin window as he said this upon an ice raft that lay close to the vessel & pushing himself off he was carried away by the waves and I soon lost sight of him in the darkness and distance (qtd. in Mellor 1988: 68).

Percy Shelley's revision:

> He sprang from the cabin window as he said this, upon the ice raft which lay close to the vessel. He was borne away by the waves and lost in darkness and distance (ibid.).

16. 'Concerning the factors of silence, solitude and darkness, we can only say that they are actually elements in the production of that infantile anxiety from which the majority of human beings have never become quite free' (Freud 1955: 252).
17. With companies such as Alcor Life Extension Foundation and The Cryonics Institute, people have started to seriously believe in the idea of immortality through the scientific methods of cryonic suspension (http://www.theglobeandmail.com/life/health-and-fitness/health/can-cryonic-therapy-literal-brain-freeze-allow-people-to-live-forever/article26703024/).
18. The relationship between *Frankenstein* and Haraway's work will be further examined in Chapter 7.
19. 1818 edition: 'Yet even that enemy of God and man had friends and associates in his desolation; I am quite alone' (Shelley 1999: 242).
20. Although Julia Kristeva (1982) argues that abjection is '[e]ssentially different from "uncanniness,"' (5), there is a strong correlation in terms of their connection to modernity and the secular. With Christianity, the abjection of the self, the 'recognition of the want' (ibid.), was absorbed by religious sacred rite and the 'ultimate proof of humility before God' (ibid.). While religious abjection solidifies or 'purifies' (ibid. 7) the subject at one point, border, or limit, the secular abject places the subject in a place of ambiguity or liminality, further breaking down the binary distinctions between self and other. Similarly, the uncanny seems to be a byproduct of a teleological and secularized modern world. Terry Castle (1995), Mladen Dolar (1991), and Anthony Vidler (1992) all argue that the invention of the uncanny is directly related to secularization and modernity. Prior to modernity, the supernatural was something that existed solely in the world of religion and spirituality; however, this spectrality becomes secularized in the modern age and transforms into the uncanny, becoming the paradoxical mark of modernity by encompassing the ambiguity and uncertainty entrenched in the modern mind. The uncanny arose from the Enlightenment and modernity's 'psychic and cultural transformations', its 'aggressively rationalist imperatives ... [which] also produced, like a kind of toxic side effect, a new human experience of strangeness, anxiety, bafflement, and intellectual impasse' (Castle 1995: 8). As with liminal or abject space, the uncanny also is not unified or harmonious, but is a continuous alienated and ambiguous state caught in a tension with the boundaries of self and other.
21. The concept of abjection in relation to *Frankenstein* and gender will be discussed in Chapter 6.

II

Leopardi and Baudelaire: Kindred Spirits of the Modern Stranger

The ancient covenant is in pieces; man knows at last that he is alone in the universe's unfeeling immensity, out of which he emerged only by chance. His destiny is nowhere spelled out, nor is his duty. The kingdom above or the darkness below: it is for him to choose.
—Jacques Monod, *Chance and Necessity*

Ah! qu'aimes-tu donc, extraordinaire étranger?
J'aime les nuages ... les nuages qui passent ... là-bas ... là-bas ... les merveilleux nuages!
(Well then! What do you love, extraordinary stranger?
I love the clouds ... the passing clouds ... over there ... over there ... the marvelous clouds!)
—Charles Baudelaire, "*L'Étranger*" ("The Stranger")

Che fai tu, luna, in ciel? dimmi, che fai,
Silenziosa luna?
Sorgi la sera, e vai,
Contemplando i deserti; indi ti posi.
Ancor non sei tu paga
Di riandare i sempiterni calli?
(What are you doing, moon, up in the sky;
What are you doing, tell me, silent moon?
You rise at night and go,
observing the deserts. Then you set.
Aren't you tired
Of plying eternal byways?)

—Giacomo Leopardi, "*Canto notturno di un pastore errante dell'Asia*" ("Night Song of A Wandering Sheppard in Asia")

How to cite this book chapter:
Beghetto, R. G. 2022. *Monstrous Liminality; Or, The Uncanny Strangers Of Secularized Modernity.* Pp. 47–74. London: Ubiquity Press. DOI: https: //doi.org/10.5334 /bcp.c. License: CC-BY-NC

> *I'm a pessimist because of intelligence, but an optimist because of will.*
> —Antonio Gramsci, *Prison Letters*

While *Frankenstein* was being published in London in 1818, miles away in the provincial Italian town of Recanati, located in the central province of Macerata, the Italian poet, philologist, and literary critic Giacomo Leopardi was developing his own related, although unique, opinions regarding the monster of modernity. Although they never met, Shelley herself resided in various parts of Italy between 1818 and 1823, continuing to focus on the premise of the dark and problematic side of imagination and desire explored in *Frankenstein* with her second novel, the historical romance *Valperga: or, The Life and Adventures of Castruccio, Prince of Lucca* (1923/1997).[1] Unlike in *Frankenstein*, the 'monster' of *Valperga* is no longer ambiguous in nature, but is clearly destructive with no utopian character (Blumberg 1993: 76). In a sense, Shelley's second novel restores morality to its dualistic beginnings of good and evil that her first novel infamously challenged. What Leopardi, and shortly thereafter French poet Charles Baudelaire, brought to the prevailing modern conundrum is a deeper plunge into the uncanny nature of modernity, in an effort to truly understand its paradoxes and alienating factors in its most complex and contradictory aspects, thereby advancing the liminalization of the dialectical binaries that were thought to structure and unify morality, time, and the character of modernity itself.

There is no longer an attempt to repress the uncanny monster; the poets believed that one must now heroically stare directly into its ambiguous eyes and not run away in horror, as Victor Frankenstein had while struggling to shove the idea of cosmicism[2] back into the void he had let it escape from. By confronting this cosmic horror directly, Leopardi and Baudelaire believed it was the only genuine, although paradoxical, way to locate any remnants of beauty or meaning contained within a calculating and unsympathetic modern world. They chose to seek meaning in the modern void rather than foster resentment toward any real or imaginary creators of humanity's predicament. This chapter, which centres on the philosopher-poets Leopardi and his kindred spirit Baudelaire, examines the advancing secularization of modern life, in which the mystery and myth of modernity, founded on a reliance of reason that was examined in *Frankenstein*, recedes further into the hellish realm of monstrosity, illusion, and artificiality.

In *Frankenstein*, Mary Shelley presented to the world a difficult question regarding the idea of progress, whereas Baudelaire and Leopardi tried to provide a difficult answer. What we see in Leopardi and Baudelaire is that the battle between nature and the spirit, and the effects of this struggle, led them to step beyond the scientific aspect of secularized modernity. Their emphasis is not on a menacing though preventable science-based future, but rather on the repetitive and cyclical past and present that have already become our future. The modern situation forces them to explore the pains of unhappiness that come with existential boredom, the problem of desire as a secular form of hell, a complete renunciation of the myth of progress, and moreover, the poet or artist's role within secularized modernity. Consequently, Leopardi and Baudelaire were two of the most truly original thinkers of the modern era. There is also a shift in regard to the alienating factors of modernity: the Creature's existential anguish came from being removed from society, whereas for Leopardi and Baudelaire, anguish no longer originates in being detached from society, but from being immersed in it.

Originally, Leopardi became famous (or infamous) for his pessimism,[3] a label obtained through the anti-philosophical ideas found in his Operette Morali (Moral Tales) (1824/1983) and in the various aphorisms found in the Pensieri (Thoughts) (1845/1981). The neo-Marxist theorist Antonio Gramsci argued that Leopardi was in a continuous state of uncertainty because of his inability to transcend his pessimism (1988: 236). Nonetheless, in spite of, or even due to, Leopardi's nihilism, Gramsci recognized the liminal and modern character of Leopardi's work, arguing that '[i]n Leopardi one finds, in an extremely dramatic form, the crisis of transition towards modern man; the critical abandonment of the old transcendental conception but not as yet the finding of the new moral and intellectual ubi consistam which would give the same certainty as the jettisoned faith' (ibid. 236). To be certain, Leopardi's writings are crowded with cynical and melancholic opinions and observations. However, more recently, scholars have been reluctant to label Leopardi as an outright pessimist and are beginning to see a certain optimism in the Italian's work, even in regard to his later, more negative writings. Cesare Luporini, who categorized Leopardi as a nihilist, was nonetheless one of the first to argue strongly in favour of a progressive reading of Leopardi's work that saw the Italian poet as a moralist thinker whose ideas were closer to the socio-political ideals of the French Revolution than originally perceived (1947/1993: 48–49).

Luporini's progressive and rationalist reading of Leopardi induced a more positive view of Leopardi, as in the analyses of Walter Binni (1947/1978) and Antonio Negri (1985/2010, 1987/2015). Nonetheless, although Negri follows Luporini and Binni in not identifying Leopardi as a pessimist, he does go against their notion of Leopardi as a progressive thinker. According to Negri, Leopardi "is not really a progressive but a libertarian in flight. Leopardi builds on disenchantment with progress and on the joy of liberation" (2010: 26). Negri restrains himself from bestowing the progressive label because it advocates a dialectical movement that contrasts both Leopardi's anti-dialectical and anti-idealist arguments and, likewise, his notion of time. Living within the untimely or crisis of modernity, Negri's Leopardi provides a new path or alternative response to it, thereby giving the Italian poet an atemporal and paradoxical messianic character in his writing that makes them still significant in our own contemporary modernity.

Likewise, despite the pigeonholing of Baudelaire into an either/or classification by some academics,[4] Baudelaire is nonetheless widely known as the poet who encompasses all the complexities of modernity, whether interpreted through an allegorical, historical, or psychoanalytic reading of his work. However, as Joseph Acquisto points out, an exclusive reading of Baudelaire that focuses on modernity largely misses the 'theologico-esthetic worldview' (2015: 57) of the French poet. Likewise, classifying Benjamin's analysis of Baudelaire as purely materialist misses the theological aspect of Benjamin's own work.

Ulrich Baer also argues for a synthesis of the metaphysical and materialist assessment of modernity in Baudelaire's work, due to his synching of the disparity between immaturity and sophistication that allows the linking of the modern poet and modern stranger within a liminal space outside of meaning, yet dependent on locating meaning. As Baer contends, Baudelaire's "L'Étranger" ("The Stranger") is a poem about searching for new beginnings, 'freedom and disinterestedness' (ibid. 57). It is a poem containing 'neither a story nor an argument' (ibid. 58), but is comprised of a stranger that represents 'the prototypical modern poet who resists the logic of exchange and profit without pretending that art remains wholly outside that logic' (ibid. 59). For Baer, Baudelaire is the first modern poet to capture the shock-like trauma and experience of modernity (2000: 4). As argued by Michel Foucault, 'Baudelairean modernity is an exercise in which extreme attention to what is real is confronted with the practice of a liberty that simultaneously respects this reality and violates it' (1984: 41). He continues: '[m]odern man, for Baudelaire, is not the man who goes off to discover himself, his secrets, and his hidden truth; he is the man who tries to invent himself. This modernity ... compels him to face the task of producing himself' (ibid. 42). This rupture that has occurred in history forces the individual not to find a historical self within past illusions, but instead to create or cultivate oneself, what Foucault calls 'heroization' (ibid.), which becomes the prevailing new form of resacralization for the modern world. While Leopardi is slightly detached from the advent of modernity (since he lived in rural Italy for much of his life), acting essentially as a pansophical modern stranger, Baudelaire pushes these ideas into the modern urban streets of Paris, to which the modern stranger must escape in order to live and breathe. With Baudelaire, the stranger no longer removes itself from society but instead plummets into it, bringing us closer to Simmel's definition of the stranger as someone 'who comes today and stays tomorrow' (1964: 402).

The Monstrosity of the Liminalizing Space of Secular Modernity

Leopardi's unceasing shift in his philosophy began with his correspondence with the liberal intellectual Pietro Giordani. This correspondence resulted in a political and religious break from his family's conservative ideals that in turn led to Leopardi's unsuccessful attempt to flee Recanati and his father's domineering character in 1818. The following year, Leopardi contracted a severe eye disease from extensive reading that would alter the way he viewed the world (Rosengarten 2012: 121); together with a development of scoliosis, these physical ailments seemed to push him towards seeing the hidden dark shadow of instrumental reason. Many of his contemporary critics, including Alessandro Manzoni and Niccolò Tommaseo, believed his pessimistic thoughts were simply a reaction to his diseases, famously epitomized as 'I am hunchbacked, therefore there is no God' (Origo 1999: 222), which Leopardi considered highly offensive to his philosophical work.[5] What these critics neglected to understand was that, like Frankenstein's Creature, Leopardi's "monstrosity" and his strangeness allowed him to see past the utopian images of progress that modernity and its adherents promised. He acknowledged the monstrosity found within modernity. In fact, Leopardi actually regards the monster as a liminal essence that balances the 'perfection' of the human spirit. Fabio Frosini claims that

> ... the notion of monster/monstrous is the chain that links 'real' and 'imaginary' because on the one hand it is the 'image' of a real error—mankind's abandonment of nature—and, on the other, the result of a miscalculation that makes a mere partial viewpoint absolute. If the second moment is applied to the comprehension of the first, the result is that every monster must be considered as something *perfect*, including the 'monstrous' separation of human race from nature. The institution of what is 'relative' thus corresponds with the origin of history, and monstrosity appears as (and therefore is) the identification mark of humanity" (2016: 1).

Therefore we see how, for Leopardi, the monstrous is contained within modernity since it abhors nature, but also for maintaining certain habits and ideas that contradict any modern or progressive thinking and governing. In Leopardi's writings, the idea of the monster or the monstrous became a recurring theme that, according to Frosini, represented a 'paradox of existence' (ibid. 113) containing a twofold meaning. The monstrous was seen by Leopardi first as an aberration of nature, and second as something that reflects foreign values and principles that belong to a different era or place (ibid. 107). Leopardi's liminal view of the monstrous therefore encompasses both the rising modern world that deviates from nature and the ideals that no longer have a place in the contemporary age but which still exist (ibid.).

For Leopardi, monstrosity as an essential product of human nature and evolution: 'L'esistenza, per sua natura ed essenza propria e generale, è un'imperfezione, un'irregolarità, una mostruosità' (1983: 1095) (\[e]xistence, by its nature and essence and generally, is an imperfection, an irregularity, a monstrosity') (2013: 1822). While humans are perfect specimens in nature, it is because of this perfection that humanity is allowed to become imperfect and monstrous 'come quelle macchine o quei lavorii compitissimi e perfettissimi, che per esser tali, sono minutamente lavorati, e quindi delicatissimi, e per la somma delicatezza più facilmente degli altri si guastano, e perdono l'essere e l'uso loro' (1983: 829) ('like those most refined and perfect machines or devices which, in order for them to be such, are intricately tooled, and hence most delicate, and on account of their supreme delicacy more easily break down than others, and lose their essence and use') (2013: 1201). As Victor Frankenstein realizes after creating his Creature, outside of nature, our quest for perfection, our messianic insistence that the future is utopian, paradoxically makes us imperfect and monstrous. Moreover, our desire to cheat death and remove human suffering, to go beyond nature, is what ultimately forces or allows us to acknowledge our monstrosity.

As with Leopardi, in Baudelaire's poetry there is no spiritual journey upwards to a better place, just as there is no discernable progress of modernity. Instead, his poetry contains images portrayed as a fragmented journey of repetition, memories, boredom, wonders, fleeting dreams, and endless nightmares. His hell is not a future place seen only when one dies, but a present one in which death becomes more of an escape than the beginning of a horrific afterlife. In his introductory poem in *The Flowers of Evil*, entitled "Au Lecteur" ("To the Reader"), Baudelaire criticizes his audience as hypocrites (2008: 6), willing to accept false illusions of progress and perfection, and unwilling to accept their (our) status as mere puppets, as '[c]'est le Diable qui tient les fils qui nous remuent!/ Aux objets répugnants nous trouvons des appas;/Chaque jour vers l'Enfer nous descendons d'un pas,/ Sans horreur, à travers des ténèbres qui puent' ('the Devil pulls on all our strings!/ In most repugnant objects we find charms; Each day we're one step further into Hell,/ Content to move across the sinking pit') (ibid. 4–5). However, as Jonathan Culler argues of the poem "L'Irrémédiable" ("The Irremediable"), Baudelaire casts doubt on the notion of Satan being an external entity that controls our actions: 'Emblèmes nets, tableau parfait/D'une fortune irremediable/Qui donne à penser que le Diable/Fait toujours bien tout ce qu'il fait!' ('Pure emblems, a perfect tableau/ Of an irremediable evil,/ Which makes us think that the Devil/ Does what he chooses to do!') (2008: 160–161). Culler argues that the phrase "makes us think" creates ambiguity around what is truly responsible for this evil (ibid. xxxiv). In both the Christian tradition and in *The Flowers of Evil*, the Devil is 'an agent or personification whose ability to act is essential' (ibid. xxxvi), though for Baudelaire, acting out our "evil" temptations is a manifestation of our psychological and uncanny desires (ibid. xxxvii). For Baudelaire, evil and the devil are symbolic representations of the human ability to act and to choose, which is at the same time continuous and irremediable, and human action can only guide us closer and closer to hell. Despite its secular underpinning, modernity in Baudelaire's eyes is a spiritual journey and undertaking, because it gives us the ability 'to explore the forbidden realm of *evil*' and allows the artist to transform banal reality through the imaginary 'where ephemerality and eternity are one' (Călinescu 1987: 54). While Baudelaire separates the poems in his famous work into two sections, Spleen and Ideal, the poems do not necessarily separate these two concepts, but instead blend them into one another: they become essentially the same, as one could not exist without the other: 'je ne conçois guère (mon cerveau serait- il un miroir ensorcelé?) un type de Beauté où il ny ait pas du *Malheur*' (1949: 22) ('I can scarcely conceive (is my brain become a witch's mirror?) a type of Beauty which has nothing to do with Sorrow') (2006: 43–44). For Baudelaire, this Sorrow is an uncanny strangeness that allows one to acknowledge something as beautiful:

> *Le beau est toujours bizarre.* Je ne veux pas dire qu'il soit volontairement, froidement bizarre, car dans ce cas il serait un monstre sorti des rails de la vie. e dis qu'il contient toujours un peu de bizarrerie, de bizarrerie naïve, non voulue, inconsciente, et que c'est cette bizarrerie qui le fait être particulièrement le Beau. C'est son immatriculation, sa caractéristique (1935: 216).

> Beauty always has an element of strangeness. I do not mean a deliberate cold form of strangeness, for in that case it would be a monstrous thing that had jumped the rails of life. But I do mean that it always contains a certain degree of strangeness, of simple, unintended, unconscious strangeness, and that this form of strangeness is what gives it the right to be called beauty. It is its hallmark, its special characteristic (1981: 119).

Here, Baudelaire points to a paradoxical sense of beauty: it can only exist when a form of strangeness shades it, becomes one with it. What is interesting is that Baudelaire peculiarly claims this relationship is not a 'monstrous' and disjointed experience, even though for Baudelaire, the monstrous is an uncanny result of joining together two opposites or the fusing of 'divergent perspectives' (Scott 2017: 71). As with his concept of evil, monstrosity seems to have a double connotation for Baudelaire: as an undesirable experience in regard to *ennui*, but also as a creative practice belonging to the liminal realm of art and imagination.[6] He directly connects the monstrous to beauty and sacredness in the poem "Hymn to Beauty" ("Hymne à la Beauté"),[7] even suggesting a correlation between monstrosity and God in "Mademoiselle Bistouri".[8] It is why many of the women in his poems are often regarded as monstrous, not necessarily as a criticism but almost as a sign of admiration and accomplishment (Stephens 1999: 146). Therefore, despite what Baudelaire claims in the previous passage, monstrosity, strangeness, beauty, and the sacred all seem to be interconnected for him.

This paradoxical relationship must be why Baudelaire struggled with these uncanny feelings throughout his life, forever pulled between the 'deux postulations simultanées' (1949: 62) ('two simultaneous allegiances'), between the

God and Satan that exist within everyone (2006: 73). He does not try to answer a mystery but sees this as a fact or detail, an entanglement due to the consequences of modernity and disenchantment. It is not that those are opposites in the sense that one needs the other to exist; rather, both are virtually the same thing. The positions of good and evil are presented allegorically through his depictions of urban life while exploring the newly paved boulevards of 19th-century Paris. It becomes a place where the lines between heaven and hell, dream and nightmare, begin to blur, where demons and angels soar to such an intensity that the poet and reader cannot tell them apart, making the distinction between these realms no longer substantial.

For both Leopardi and Baudelaire, the removal of humanity from the natural definitely revolves around the artificial. Leopardi eventually comes to the conclusion that all life is artificial, even nature, which gifted us illusions that give life meaning. The illusions of modernity are not able to hold up to the ancient ones that connected both human and nature. In Leopardi's poetry, the moon is often seen as a final representation of enchantment and sacredness, standing alone at night, projecting 'the shadow of its absence' (Calvino 24) that "allows for a certain interdeterminacy and openness to illusion" (Galassi xx). In this instance, Baudelaire's philosophy is slightly different. He sees nature in humanity as something disgusting and evil, and the artificial that separates us from it as something good and beautiful. The absence of stars in Baudelaire's poetry culminates in "Le Crépuscule du soir" ("Dusk") (Buck-Morss 1991: 193), as they fail to equal the artificial light brought on by the city's illumination, which gives power to the prostitution that 'blazes in the streets' (Baudelaire 2008: 193). The beauty of modern life must be found within artificial reality for Baudelaire, and that is why the majority of his work focuses on the modern city. Despite these differences, what Baudelaire and Leopardi acknowledge, in a greater degree than we saw with Shelley, is that the artificiality of humanity, and even of nature itself, furthers the destruction of the dialectical synthesis between natural and unnatural: reality and illusion. This monstrous artificiality, unnaturalness, or being out of place is far more entertaining and adventurous for Baudelaire than the modern monster that is *ennui*, once again expressing monstrosity's paradox: 'Quelles bizarreries ne trouve-t-on pas dans une grande ville, quand on sait se promener et regarder? La vie fourmille de monstres innocents' (1968: 204) ('The strange things one encounters in a city when no one knows how to move around it and look! Life is teeming with innocent monsters') (1968: 93).

As Walter Benjamin points out with the Baudelaire poems "Tu mettrais l'univers entier" ("You'd entertain the universe …") and "L'Avertisseur" ("The Cautioner"), Baudelaire 'has lost himself to the spell of the eyes which do not return his glance, and submits to their sway without illusions' (2007a: 190). The ambiguous eyes that resemble 'a mirror-like blankness' (ibid.) do not cause terror for Baudelaire as they did for Frankenstein when he first gazed into the watery eyes of the Creature. Instead, it is staring into the eyes that were 'illuminés ainsi que des boutiques' (Baudelaire 2008: 52) ('illuminated like boutiques') (ibid. 53) which plunged Baudelaire further into an enchanted state. For him, a secularized modern hell was the only possible place for the resacralization of the modern world. What mattered to Baudelaire was our engagement in our own heavens or hells that exist within both the depths of modernity and our psyche. In the poem "Le Voyage" ("Voyages"), beauty is found in both moral binaries, but only when diving into the new and unknown: '[v]ersenous ton poison pour qu'il nous réconforte!/Nous voulons, tant ce feu nous brûle le cerveau,/Plonger au fond du gouffre, Enfer ou Ciel, qu'importe?/Au fond de l'Inconnu pour trouver du nouveau!' ('[s]erve us your poison, sir, to treat us well!/ Minds burning, we know what we have to do,/ And plunge to depths of Heaven or of Hell,/ To fathom the Unknown, and find the *new!*') (ibid. 292–293). The 'new' relates not only to the contemporary, novel, and fleeting elements of modernity, but likewise to a form of creation of the self that exists within each individual.

The Modern Dantes: Wanderers of a Modern and Liminalizing Hell

Another notable connection between the two philosopher-poets conceivably stems from their relationship with the works of the celebrated Italian poet Dante Alighieri. What both Leopardi and Baudelaire took from Dante was an acknowledgement of the limits of reason, something that was far more substantial to them after the Enlightenment and French Revolution, alongside a blending of mythic and religious themes with present and historical reality (Barricelli 1986: 74). More importantly, both sought to describe a secularized allegorical interpretation of Dante's *La Divina Commedia* (*The Divine Comedy*) (1320/1998), or to be more specific, his *Inferno*. While the thought of bringing heaven to earth was being championed by the materialists and modern utopians, Baudelaire and Leopardi saw fit to look for the hell that came with it. This tradition, starting with Leopardi and Baudelaire, continued well into 20th-century modernism with the works of Samuel Beckett, T. S. Eliot, James Joyce, and Virginia Woolf, as many moderns saw Dante to be 'eminently modern in sensibility and in manner' (Hiddleston 1999: 78).[9] Leopardi and Baudelaire, as well as Frankenstein's Creature, share an affinity of being modern Dantes, and their alienation from travelling in an unknown world is all-encompassing. Throughout their journeys within secular hell as *flâneurs* or voyeurs, they are left ultimately alone, having neither a Virgil to guide them nor a concept of absolute and lasting Beauty in Beatrice as a goal to reach.[10] In "La Tromonto Della Luna" ("the Setting of the Moon"), Leopardi describes the wanderer within secular modernity:

Van l'ombre e le sembianze/Dei dilettosi inganni; e vengon meno/Le lontane speranze,/Ove s'appoggia la mortal natura./Abbandonata, oscura/ Resta la vita. In lei porgendo il guardo,/Cerca il confuso viatore invano/ Del cammin lungo che avanzar si sente/Meta o ragione; e vede/Che a se l'umana sede,/Esso a lei veramente è fatto estrano.

(The shadows/And the shapes of glad illusions/Flee, and distant hopes,/ That prop up our moral/nature up, give way./Life is forlorn, lightless./ Looking ahead, the wayward traveler/Searches unavailing/for goal or reason on the long/road he senses lies ahead,/and sees that man's home truly has become/alien to him, and he to it) (2014: 282–283).

Leopardi wrote this poem while caught in the threshold between his religious upbringing and the forming of his secular thoughts (ibid. 480), where his soon-to-be-annihilated Christian beliefs were juxtaposed with an idea of death as oblivion and nothingness (Rosengarten 2012: 150). Dante at least had a hell that served justice and provided order, but modern hell was a place of nothingness and boredom, to such a point that Leopardi tells the spectre of Dante in "A Angelo Mai" ("To Angelo Mai") (1820), "Beato te che il fato/A viver non dannò fra tanto orrore" ('You were lucky fate did not condemn you to live among these horrors') (2014: 18–19). Leopardi describes traditional Hell as a sanctuary from our world, from our modern notion of hell: 'Eran calde le tue ceneri sante,/Non domito nemico/Della fortuna, al cui sdegno e dolore/Fu più l'averno che la terra amico./L'averno: e qual non è parte migliore/Di questa nostra?' ('Your holy ashes still were warm,/undefeated enemy of fortune,/to those whose disdain and pain/ hell was friendlier than earth./ Yes, even hell: for what place isn't preferable to ours?') (ibid. 32–33). The world is forever condemned and 'somiglia a un vero inferno' (1983: 115) ('resembles hell itself') due to the implementation of reason over imagination (2013: 113).

Dante's influence on Baudelaire's work has been well documented, especially by the 20th-century moderns and equally by Walter Benjamin throughout his *Passagen-Werk* (1999: 233–234, 247, 251, 267, 271, 275, 289, 295, 305, 324, 363), even though the degree of Dante's direct influence on the French poet is debatable.[11] Barbey d'Aurevilly labeled Baudelaire as a 'deformed Dante' (Rainey 2005: 157), regarding him as 'a modern and atheist' version of the Italian poet, born as a result 'of a fallen age' (ibid. 157, n4), while later, T.S. Eliot emphasized Baudelaire's modern qualities by referring to him as the 'fragmentary Dante' (1932: 336) and as a Christian and a Classist "born out of his due time" (1936: 72). Although Baudelaire focused on sin, morality, and spiritual death, as did Dante, the structures of the worlds in which they existed differed prominently. Dante's spiritual universe was divided clearly and separately into *Hell, Purgatory*, and *Heaven*, whereas in Baudelaire's world the division between each realm is far more ambiguous. Morality has become uncannily unhinged and displaced in the modern world, becoming a place where good and evil have copulated, giving birth to a new liminal form of thought that exists between ancient moral boundaries. Modernity and secularism culminate in a hellish existential boredom for the stranger, resulting from the limitlessness of desire and the inability to cure it. Replacing a religious or mythological place where sins are punished, hell has become a psychological response to the ascending secularized world that forces individuals to place their dependence on abstract concepts such as happiness and joy onto material and physical pleasures and desires that ultimately leave one in a state of perpetual weariness. Modernity is characterized by its boredom, which itself is connected to a negation of lived experience and action, two fundamental attributes needed for the pursuit of linear progress.

Although not exactly identical, Baudelaire's *ennui* and Leopardi's *noia* roughly be can translated as a mixture of melancholia and boredom. Moreover, neither ailment can be alleviated by a forever-present and recurring sense of consciousness that comes from a desire to live a joyous life in a secular world based on pleasure. Each individual, according to Leopardi, is given the two-edged gift of self-love from nature. This is why every person seeks out good, which is nothing more than the search for pleasure; and since desire is superior to pleasure, pleasure can only satisfy desire in fleeting moments (Leopardi 2013: 333). Our desire for infinite happiness keeps desire in the realm of impossibility, because infinite desire cannot be satisfied by pleasure, thus 'tutti i piaceri debbono esser misti di dispiacere' (ibid. 1983: 135) ('all pleasures must be mingled with displeasure') (ibid. 2013: 130). We can see that, for Leopardi, the relationship between pleasure and desire—which is comparable to Jacques Lacan's (1977) psychoanalytic relationship between being, desire, and lack[12]—does not actually lead to happiness, because it lacks any positive qualities. Fundamentally, it is only 'privazione' (ibid. 1983: 818) ('privation') (ibid. 201: 1136). While Leopardi's concept of pleasure and desire is temporal, and therefore an indication of consciousness, it likewise implies a succession or chain of signifiers that both Lacan and Freud argue make up the unconscious (Rennie 2005: 199–200). Both Lacan and Lepoardi see desire and lack fundamentally bound together in an endless series of unfulfilled pleasure-seeking. For Lacan, desire 'is caught in the rails of metonymy, eternally extending towards the desire for something else' (1977: 431). The metonymic desire is never satisfied but always deferred, flowing from one to another (ibid. 379), making desire is a liminal process with no beginning or end. In the case of Leopardi, the modern citizen becomes spiritually empty and 'è tormentato da un desiderio infinito del piacere' (1983: 247) ('is tormented by an infinite desire for pleasure') (ibid. 2013: 229). Similar to Lacan's psychoanalytic description, Leopardi's philosophical understanding of pleasure, which for him is everything that we desire, never exists in the present moment, but is merely successive hints or an 'idea del futuro' (ibid. 1983: 306) ('idea of the future') (ibid. 2013: 290). Although desire for pleasure is innately human, for the modern individual alienated from nature, happiness is not possible after having acquired knowledge of 'le illusioni e il niente di... piaceri naturali' (ibid. 1983: 57) ('the emptiness of things and the illusoriness and nothingness ... of natural pleasures') (ibid. 2013:63). As a result, *noia* psychologically envelops the self once the individual acknowledges the futility of trying to satisfy infinite desire.

Noia is an existential pain brought on by reason and uniformity, even from a uniformity of pleasure, and essentially ingrained within homogeneity itself (ibid. 1085), making it "la passione la più contraria e lontana alla natura" (ibid. 1983: 732) ("the passion most contrary to and farthest from nature") (ibid. 2013: 952). Conversely, it is Leopardi's concept of *noia*, which continuously emerges throughout the *Zibaldone*, that led to his shift towards seeing nature as evil. *Noia* is what allows reason to destroy the illusions created by nature, and therefore is essential to what removes humans from Nature. Since human nature is finite, it is unable to satisfy our pleasure and desire, which are ultimately infinite, thus giving us eternal sorrow in exchange for fleeting happiness. As Leopardi maintains,

> La noia è manifestamente un male, e l'annoiarsi una infelicità. Or che cosa è la noia? Niun male n è dolore particolare, (anzi l'idea e la natura della noia esclude la presenza di qualsivoglia particolar male o dolore), ma la semplice vita pienamente sentita, provata, conosciuta, pienamente presente all'individuo, ed occupantelo. Dunque la vita è semplicemente un male: e il non vivere, o il viver meno, sì per estensione che per intensione è semplicemente un bene, o un minor male, ovvero preferibile per se ed assolutamente alla vita ec (1983: 1061).

> (Boredom is clearly an ill, and the experience of boredom brings unhappiness. Now what is boredom? No particular ill or suffering (in fact the idea and nature of boredom excludes the presence of any particular ill or suffering) but simply life itself fully felt, experienced, recognized, life fully present to the individual and taking him over. Life therefore is simply an ill: and not to live, or to live less; whether in duration or in intensity, is simply a good, or lesser ill, rather absolutely and in itself preferable to life, etc.) (ibid. 2013: 1719).

Noia is virus-like, a self-creating, self-feeding emotion based on nothingness that spreads and contaminates wherever it goes. Since *noia* is a never-ending feeling even worse than despair, Leopardi acknowledges a heroic quality in being able to inhibit its liminality on a daily basis (ibid. 2013: 186), thereby making it the most tragic yet inspiring emotion, since it insinuates that the human spirit, although fragile and uncertain due to modernity, is more important than the rest of the universe (Svendsen 2005: 58). While many personal experiences may have led to Leopardi's theory of pleasure and *noia*, such as his ailments and strict upbringing, the existential disillusionment and moral indifference surrounding modernity induced in him a creative outlook that would linger within the modern age.

Ennui too was a result of a spiritual malaise in the modern world; however, Baudelaire emphasized its development as a by-product of over-stimulation even more so than did Leopardi. Baudelaire saw *ennui*, which he also refers to as Spleen, as the greatest flaw of the modern age if not utilized properly. In "To the Reader," boredom is seen as humanity's greatest weakness: '[c]'est l'Ennui! L'oeil chargé d'un pleur involontaire,/Il rêve d'échafauds en fumant son houka./Tu le connais, lecteur, ce monstre délicat,/- Hypocrite lecteur, - mon semblable, - mon frère!' ('He is Ennui!—with tear-filled eye he dreams/ Of scaffolds, as he puffs his water-pipe./Reader, you know this dainty monster too;/-Hypocrite reader,-fellowman,-my twin!') (2008: 6-7). Benjamin Fondane argues that the theological malaise trapping Baudelaire is the 'boredom of the cosmos' (Fondane, 1947: 63), the boredom that represents all modern civilization, stimulating us to blindly proceed through the void. Although the abyss and *ennui* are existentially bound and should be a concern for all individuals, it is the stranger that forces itself to gaze into it and not turn away, something Baudelaire accuses his readers of being incapable of doing at the beginning of his most famous work. Baudelaire's introduction to *The Flowers of Evil* brings all of humanity into the same modern world in which boredom has made urban society assume a state of insomnia. Eluned Summers-Bremner argues in her intriguing book *Insomnia: A Cultural History* that modernity, 'like insomnia,' is 'akin to having a mental itch one cannot reach, a state of conscious enjoyment one can imagine but cannot get to. And insomnia, while frequently companioned by anxiety and conflict, is reliably an experience of boredom' (2008: 75). Not only does Summers-Bremner relate boredom to insomnia, she argues that modernity and insomnia are uncannily interrelated because they "show how unknown we can be to ourselves, and unknowable things often seem to come from outside" (ibid. 31–32). However, this liminal and almost unnatural state is where the stranger thrives and feels natural. Navigating the realm of boredom, in the unknown, is where the stranger begins to finally know itself.

Baudelaire's prose poem "Chacun sa chimere" ("to each his own Chimera") shows how everyone has a monster that imprisons and guides them without knowing, 'poussés par un invincible besoin de marcher' (1968: 46) ('impelled by an imperious need to advance') (1968: 112); however, 's'enfonça dans l'atmosphère de l'horizon' ('lost in the air of the horizon') (ibid.), the poet is weighed down by "Indifférence" (ibid.) ("Indifference"), and finding the mystery of each person's monster becomes a pointless endeavour for him. Baudelaire's capital "I" indifference results in his alienation from a world that solely believes in an aimless sort of progress, where the purpose of the movement is simply movement itself. The idea of alienation from indifference later becomes an important theme for modernists such as T.S. Eliot and Robert Frost, who were influenced by their *fin de siècle* predecessors (Gray 2005: 11), in which alienation is derived from the paradoxical notion of being detached from a world with entrenched meaning and yet still having a direct, albeit self-protective relation to that world (Jaeggi 2014: 150). Addressing Benjamin's *Passagen-Werk*, Susan Buck-Morss claims,

> ... natural history as prehistoric and modernity as Hell—the nineteenth-century origins of the most recent historical phenomena, when named as reincarnations of the most archaic, open themselves up to critical understanding. Both images contain the same conceptual elements—history and nature, myth and transitoriness—but in configurations so different that their meanings pull in opposite directions. If after a century the original arcades appear prehistoric, it is because of the extremely rapid changes which industrial technology has wrought upon the urban landscape. But the experience of time brought about by this rapid change has been precisely the opposite: hellish repetition (1991: 184).

Nonetheless, *ennui* is still a feeling that the modern artist or stranger must embrace to understand the world and him- or herself within it. In showing us the hellish truth of the boredom and repetition of modern capitalist life, *ennui* becomes almost a revolutionary aspect of modernity. Benjamin wanted to use the *Passagen-Werk* to show how the contemporaries of 19th-century Paris, which he felt mirrored his own time, experienced their age as exhausting, disillusioning, and boring, where in spite of the massive movement towards technology, secularism, and the reshaping of the city that usually defines the characteristics of progress, nothing new seemed to be emerging. In *The Communist Manifesto*, Karl Marx and Friedrich Engels state that the '[c]onstant revolutionizing of production' found in capitalism and modernity leads to the disenchantment of everyday life and corrosion of sacrality, in which 'all that is solid melts into air, all that is holy is profaned' (1848/2005: 7). Both modernity and capitalism effectively exploit our ability to live in repetition, yet simultaneously offer us illusory instances of new. With every product bought or every new boulevard created, the same repetitive joy is experienced anew. However, as the illusion begins to fade for some, or the repetition becomes one of emptiness, the receptiveness of modern life slowly leads the individual towards a state of existential boredom and malaise. Marx characterized the alienation of the worker from the '*product of his labour*' as an 'alien God,' where the more one puts into labour, the less it belongs to them (1844/2007: 70). Conjuring an image akin to Frankenstein's Creature, capital for Marx is the prevailing and alienating power over labour that assumes the form of an isolated and animated 'mechanical monster,' demonically possessed to 'work' through this alterity (1976: 302, 503).

In this light, we see that this vision of history is in many ways akin to Søren Kierkegaard's concept of *Gjentagelsen* (repetition), which means 'to take again'

(Lewis 2014: 79). Conceptually, recollection (*Erindringen*) and repetition are paradoxically the same movement, only heading in opposite directions: one moves backwards, the other forwards; one might be seen as inauthentic movement, the other authentic. If modernity becomes an existence of simply recollecting, the individual may fall into a mundane, 'meaningless noise' (Kierkegaard 1983: 149). Kierkegaard sees negativity in recurring alienation, but unlike Marx also recognizes it as something that can be positive and spiritual. Whereas recollection looks backwards, repetition is an action "to take back again"; therefore the action becomes something new, always moving forward. Repetition can assume the form of a spiritual or sacred struggle, as in being born again, where 'in the moment of despair a change takes place ... and freedom takes on a religious expression, by which repetition appears as atonement' (ibid. 320). Engaging with this paradox, repetition becomes an indication of spiritual intelligence and strength for Kierkegaard:

> The person who has not circumnavigated life before beginning life will never live; the person who circumnavigated it but became satiated had a poor constitution; the person who chose repetition—he lives ... Indeed, what would life be if there were no repetition? Who could want to be a tablet on which time writes something new every instant or to be a memorial volume of the past? ... If God Himself had not willed repetition, the world would not have come into existence ... Therefore, the world continues, and it continues because it is a repetition. Repetition— that is actuality and the earnestness of existence (ibid. 132–133).

Kierkegaard assigns both a liminal and religious element to repetition,[13] similarly to Baudelaire's use of the new, by considering it a type of restoration or cultivation of the self. In a psychoanalytic sense, '[t]rue repetition is a desire for a getting back of the Other, restoration of the God relationship. It is desire for the transcendent Other but, paradoxically, desire for restoration of a relationship that one cannot recollect from actuality' (McCarthy 2015: 91). True repetition is a movement forward, in which one is the same yet also becomes another.[14]

It is this perspective that makes such "pessimistic" and paradoxical thinkers as Baudelaire and Leopardi important to modern thought, secularization, and even the paradoxical notion of the resacralization. Their plight of living in liminal modernity could be summed up by a famous quote often attributed to Gramsci: '[t]he challenge of modernity is to live without illusions and without becoming disillusioned' (cited in Best 2011: xxiv). Although perhaps discouraging, while others were attempting to secularize the notion of heaven on earth, Baudelaire and Leopardi felt it necessary to acknowledge and examine the secularized hell that is so closely tied to heaven, by questioning not only the rational, technological, and capitalist aspects of modernity, but also the false historical, spiritual, and religious ones that came with it. Nonetheless, they exhibited an uncanny positivity, akin to Nietzsche's sense of affirmation or "tragic joy,"[15] in which tragedy is the experiencing of modern life. This paradoxical joy at the heart of their melancholic views was their challenge to appreciate liminal and secularized modernity for what it was. Through an acceptance of the paradoxical beauty found in ordinary and harsh modern experience, the poets looked to dissuade any illusory optimism of progress that refused to stare into the eyes of its own monstrosity or failed to embrace the modern condition of estrangement and alienation. Failing to do so would ironically result in an age of spiritual bankruptcy. Consequently, long before Camus' *Le Mythe de Sisyphe* (*Myth of Sisyphus*) (1942/1991), Baudelaire and Leopardi strove to envision a smile on the individual faced with the uncanny absurdity of the modern age, even if it was only an ironic one, merely for the reason that freedom must be free of illusions—if not completely, then at least of the unnurturing ones.

A Rupture in History and the Illusion of Progress

Modernity lives and breathes in a paradox of time. Born from a rupture in history and fostered on past ruins, it not only gazes towards the future, it is continuously haunted by its ahistorical spectres.[16] Whereas the future may be considered utopian, in that it contains a wealth of unknown possibilities, the disenchantment and demystification of modernity, paradoxically developed from a fear of the unknown,[17] can itself become a problematic roadblock built into progress itself. While most of their contemporaries continued to insist on a myth of constant societal growth, Leopardi and Baudelaire were beginning to see through the dream of modernity and the veil of progress cast over the eyes of society. And yet, although the two acknowledged a definite rupture in history with the advent of modernity, neither necessarily saw this disruption in history correlating to any real sort of progress.

Leopardi saw this distinct rupture between what he deemed ancient and modern civilization as an irreversible separation. According to him, we must not consider modernity 'come una semplice continuazione dell'antica, come un progresso della medesima' ('as a continuation of ancient civilization, as its progression'), but rather, 'queste due civiltà, avendo essenziali differenze tra loro, sono, e debbono essere considerate come due civiltà diverse, o vogliamo dire due diverse e distinte specie di civiltà, ambedue realmente complete in se stesse' (Leopardi 1983: 1094) ('[t]hese two civilizations, which are essentially different, are and must be considered as two separate civilizations, or rather two different and distinct species of civilization, each actually complete in itself') (ibid. 2013: 1820–1821). This contrast between the ancients and the moderns, spurred on by the Copernican and French revolutions, was a prevailing theme in Leopardi's work; and although it seems he tended to assign a superiority to the ancients and the classics, especially in his early, more nostalgic poems, the melancholic yet necessary demise of the classical age was always prominent in his writings and would further continue and expand throughout his life's work. Furthermore, Leopardi believed that an admiration of classical poetry should result in the love of one's contemporary age, since classical poets were themselves writing about their own present time and not partaking in some anachronistic practice (Rennie 2005: 135). One of the very first *canti* written by Leopardi, the Dantesque poem "L'appressamento della morte" ("The Approach of Death") (1816), echoed the tyranny and horrors of the *Inferno*, yet still reflected his own modern age rather than Dante's Italy of the 14th century (Rosengarten 2012: 142). As Leopardi laments in another poem dedicated to Dante, he sees historic ruins as spectres that should spur us on in the future: 'Mira queste ruine/E le carte e le tele e i marmi e I templi;/Pensa qual terra premi; e se destarti/Non può la luce di cotanti esempli,/Che stai? lévati e parti' ('Look at these ruins,/ these pages, canvases, these stones and temples./Think what earth you walk on. And if the light/of these examples fails to inspire you,/what are you waiting for? Arise and go') (2014: 26–27).

Leopardi's Italy seems to embody the turmoil and alienation of secularized modernity, completely caught in an illusion of progress and an undefined future.[18] In "Dialogo di un Venditore D'almanacchi e di un Passeggere" ("A Dialogue of an Almanac seller and Passer-by") (1832), the setting of Leopardi's narrative takes place in a modern European city and tells us of a fleeting conversation between an almanac seller on the street and a modern *flâneur*-like character. The passerby questions the seller's belief that the future should always be better than the past simply because the future has yet to come and thereby contains many possibilities. But as the passerby and Leopardi himself contend, this optimism towards the future is based on an illusion of the unknown, and that deeming the future better because of an assumption that the past is simply not good enough leads to a paradoxical position that if the past is never good enough, then how could the future ever be? The seller admits he is only willing to relive his life as a different person, which Leopardi shows as the greatest flaw of modern existence: reducing existence from repetition to pure novelty. By trying to evade the past, humanity has paradoxically continued on a cyclical path of recurring desire. For Leopardi, nothing is novel; everything is old; everything repeats.

Despite Leopardi's view that history is cyclical, he was never a supporter of restoring the past, especially in a civilization dominated by a Christian God. Leopardi endeavoured to search out modern and secular knowledge at all costs, believing that any nostalgic sentiment directed towards the past kept modernity rooted in its current existential predicament. This development of thought left Leopardi with an extremely paradoxical view of modernity, yet his disillusionment resulting from the 'sovrumani silenzi, e profondissima quïete' ('superhuman silences, and depthless calm') (2014: 106–107) found within modernity directed him to an anti-Platonic and relativist stance concerning life that eventually led him to proclaim God's death,[19] even before Nietzsche famously did.[20] In many of his poems, Leopardi placed himself in a liminal position within time, space, and society, unable to find complete solace in past wisdom, the present reality, or the 'promising' future ahead of him; 'Non io d'Olimpo o di Cocito i sordi/regi, o la terra indegna,/e non la notte moribondo appello;/non te, dell'atra morte ultimo raggio,/conscia futura età' ('I call not on the heedless kings of Olympus or Cocytus,/ nor on unworthy earth, nor the night before I die;/ and not you, conscious future generation,/ last hope of lightest death') (2014: 64–65). As Fabio A. Camilletti claims, 'Leopardi's style confirms this impression of immediacy, as if it aimed to capture a fading and indefinable sensation ... in which no chronological progression can be detected, nor any further analysis possible' (2017: 23).

What the ancients had over the moderns, according to Leopardi—and the essential difference that defines this historical rupture that is modernity—was their ability to nurture strong and life-giving illusions; while in the modern age, these illusions have become ultimately empty and baseless due to the absolute implementation of both reason and truth over nature. By stressing the idea of illusion, Leopardi rejects the mythologizing of human history and develops an animosity towards the notion of Christian perfection that has been secularized, and in turn resacralized, into modern society's concept of progress. As a result, Nature/God turns into something imperfect at the expense of the illusion of humanity's perfection (Z 235). In developing an attitude of secularization that is inadvertently similar to that of Charles Taylor, Leopardi argued that Christianity helped destroy these classical illusions through a championing of reason over nature, the same concept the Age of Enlightenment had ironically used to destroy the illusions that had been shaped by Christianity. As it was later for Nietzsche, Christianity is a primary cause of nihilism in the modern world. The problematic combination of Christianity's influence in seeking happiness from a world outside our own, plus scientific reason's emphasis on demystifying the natural world, has led humanity into a liminal state in which our world has become remarkably unhomely for us: 'Non è egli un paradosso' ('Is it not a paradox,') Leopardi argued, 'che la Religion Cristiana in gran parte sia stata la fonte dell'ateismo, o generalmente, della incredulità religiosa? Eppure io così la penso. L'uomo naturalmente non è incredulo, perchè non ragiona molto, e non cura gran fatto delle cagioni delle cose' (1983: 432) ('that the Christian Religion has in large part been the source of atheism or more generally of religious unbelief? Yet I think this is the case. Man is not naturally incredulous because he does not reason much and does not care a great deal about the causes of thing') (ibid. 2013: 502). This historical process leaves modern Europe in a continuous liminal position in which the re-enchantment brought on by the Enlightenment, which paradoxically coexists with its rationalizing and disenchanting element, puts society in a problematic situation where it constantly oscillates between enchantment and disenchantment: past, present, and future.

For Leopardi, the modern world, in comparison to the traditional, was akin to adults growing up from their childish past; however, he lamented our inability to fear the supernatural as we did previously as children:

Lascio stare il timore e lo spavento proprio di quell'età (per mancanza di esperienza e sapere, e per forza d'immaginazione ancor vergine e fresca): timor di pericoli di ogni sorta, timore di vanità e chimere ... timor delle larve, sogni, cadaveri, strepiti notturni ... L'idea degli spettri, quel timore spirituale, soprannaturale, sacro, e di un altro mondo, che ci agitava frequentemente in quell'età, aveva un non so che di sì formidabile e smanioso, che non può esser paragonato con verun altro sentimento dispiacevole dell'uomo. Nemmeno il timor dell'inferno in un moribondo, credo che possa essere così intimamente terribile. Perchè la ragione e l'esperienza rendono inaccessibili a qualunque sorta di sentimento, quell'ultima e profondissima parte e radice dell'animo e del cuor nostro, alla quale penetrano e arrivano, e la quale scuotono e invadono le sensazioni fanciullesche o primitive, e in ispecie il detto timore (1983: 305–306).

(To say nothing of the fear and terror typical of that age (due to a lack of experience or knowledge, and to the power of our imagination, still fresh and virgin): fear of dangers of every kind; fear of figments and chimeras ... fear of ghosts, dreams, dead bodies, noises in the night ... The idea of specters, that spiritual, supernatural, sacred, otherworldly fear, which frequently gripped us at the age, had something so dreadful and frenzied about it that it cannot be compared to any other pleasurable feeling felt by human beings. For childhood or primitive sensations, and this fear in particular, reach, assail, penetrate, and overwhelm the ultimate and deepest part and root of our mind and heart, which reason and experience render inaccessible to any kind of feeling) (2013: 289–290).

Although the modern world has predominantly extinguished its sense of supernatural fear, it has to deal with a new and subtle kind of terror. *Terrore* for Leopardi, took on an uncanny aspect in the modern world that 'determines an ambiguous feeling of surprise and shock' (Camilletti 2017: 126), since it 'e molto più avvilitiva dell'animo e sospensiva dell'uso della ragione' (Leopardi 1983: 822) ('is far more likely to cause the use of reason to be suspended') (ibid. 2013: 1160). This uncanny and monstrous terror was a form of fear that resulted from the post-Enlightenment. Reason thrusts us towards a terror brought on by an acceptance of a greater insignificance, a fear that goes even beyond the boundaries of the courageous individual or trailblazer. Leopardi contended that, while the courageous or wise man 'non teme mai ... sempre essere atterrito' (1983: 822) ('is never afraid ... he can always be terror-struck') (ibid. 2013: 1160). With fear, one can still be led by imagination and spirited action, whereas with terror, the individual becomes paralyzed. We see this distinction of fear and terror also in *Frankenstein*: Victor's fear of death propels him to create life, but the terror witnessed afterwards paralyzes him from action for large portions of the remainder the novel.

Leopardi similarly rejected the utopian enthusiasm of modernity's rational ideologies, arguing they are inauthentic forms of life. In the poem "La Ginestra O, Il Fiore Del Deserto" ("The Broom, or the Flower of the Wilderness") Leopardi disparaged the idea of progress, seeing it as regressive: 'Qui mira e qui ti specchia,/secol superbo e sciocco,/che il calle insino allora/dal risorto pensier segnato innanti/abbandonasti, e vòlti addietro i passi,/del ritornar ti vanti,/e procedere il chiami' ('Look here and see yourself reflected, proud and foolish century,/ who gave up the way forward/ indicated by resurgent thought,/ and having changed course,/ boast of turning back/ and call it progress') (2014: 290–291). In regard to spiritual evolution, Leopardi argued it stems from what we do not know, 'nel disimparare' (1983: 1104) ('in unlearning') (ibid. 2013: 1832). What the scientific method has shown us is that in actuality, we do not understand the laws of nature. The more we discover, the more we realize that we 'saper sempre meno' (ibid. 1983: 1104) ("know less and less") (ibid. 2013: 1823), and 'l'apice del sapere umano e della filosofia consiste a conoscere la di lei propria inutilità' (ibid. 1983: 211) ('the peak of human knowledge or philosophy is to recognize its own uselessness') (ibid. 2013: 195). Leopardi argued that the need to discover brought on by scientific process, the rational ideals of the Enlightenment, and the French Revolution, although reliable, had nonetheless weakened and challenged our profound notions of faith and meaning, leaving us with an insurmountable void to battle due to the deterministic and materialistic features of modernity, while still trying to satisfy the need for spiritual fulfillment. Leopardi did not completely refute the idea of progress, advocating for the notion of the social constructs designed by humans, such as civilization, that ultimately led to the constructions of cities. It is only when recognized as linear progress or historical optimism that progress, as an all-encompassing project, begins to fail.

Battling the Storm that is Modernity in the Streets of Paris

A similar anti-utopian shift is seen in the writings of Charles Baudelaire, for the optimism of revolution and creative spirit of progress found in "Aux Bourgeois" ("To the Bourgeois") (1846) slowly dissipated in his writings after the 1850s (Berman 1988: 138). In essays such as "De l'idée modern du progrès appliquée aux beaux-arts" ("On the Modern Idea of Progress as Applied to the Fine Arts") (1855) and throughout his later journal entries, Baudelaire moved towards the notion of the absurdity of infinite human progress: '[l]a croyance au progrès est une doctrine de paresseux' ('[t]he belief in Progress is a doctrine for idlers') for 'Il ne peut y avoir de progrès (vrai, c'est-à-dire moral) que dans l'individu et par l'individu lui-même' (1949: 60) ('[t]here cannot be any progress (true progress, that is to say, moral) except within the individual and by the individual himself') (2006: 71–72). Here, Baudelaire's concern resides with an internal or spiritual rather than external or socio-political perspective of advancement, rejecting any illusory ideas of progress based on modernity's teleological, scientific, materialist, and technological innovations that have become, for him, dazzling spectacles used to cover up the dark void existing within modernity's attractive façade. Baudelaire's writings begin to question humanity's messianic belief in unending progress and seriously consider whether this belief is humanity's greatest downfall:

> Je laisse de côté la question de savoir si, délicatisant l'humanité en proportion des jouissances nouvelles qu'il lui apporte, le progrès indéfini ne serait pas sa plus ingénieuse et sa plus cruelle torture ; si, procédant par une opiniâtre négation de lui-même, il ne serait pas un mode de suicide incessamment renouvelé, et si, enfermé dans le cercle de feu de la logique divine, il ne ressemblerait pas au scorpion qui se perce lui-même avec sa terrible queue, cet éternel desideratum qui fait son éternel désespoir? (1869: 220).

(I am leaving out of the account the question whether, in making humanity more sensitive in proportion as it adds to the sum of possible enjoyment, unending progress would not be humanity's most ingenious and cruel form of torture; whether by this process, which is a stubborn negation of itself, progress would be a constantly renewed form of suicide, and whether, imprisoned within the flaming circle of divine logic, progress this eternal *desideratum*, which is humanity's eternal despair, would not be like the scorpion that stings itself with its own tail) (1981: 122).

Instead of containing any substantial growth, the historical process outlined by Baudelaire is self-defeating and representative of the decline in human history, especially in regard to the moral and spiritual being. According to Jean-Paul Sartre, progress for Baudelaire was 'a continuous decline which was such that every moment was inferior to the one that preceded it' (1950: 168). For Sartre, Baudelaire's pessimistic experience of modernity and abhorrence of the idea of positive and effective progress was a circumstance of his age that 'snatched him away from the contemplation of the past and compelled him to turn his eyes towards the future. In this way he was made to live his age backwards; and in such a situation he felt as clumsy and embarrassed as a man who was being made to walk backwards' (ibid.). Sartre seems to depict Baudelaire in a similar vein as Benjamin's analytic account of the "angel of history" in Paul Klee's drawing "Angelus Novus" (New Angel) (1920),[21] as someone swept backwards against the wind of progress. Yet this description goes against the poet's emblematic liminal stance on life that juxtaposed binaries in order to fully experience the present day. Baudelaire was unable to gaze in one direction for too long and was far more Janus-faced than Sartre (1947/1950), who felt Baudelaire was simply a late-Romantic idle dreamer, wanted to admit. Progress and modernity were simply constant change for Baudelaire, and although change signifies something new, he understood that it also encompasses something that has decayed or been lost. In Baudelaire's famous poem "Le Cygne" (The Swan), faced with the urban restitution of Paris, the poet gazes into the face of progress, ripping away its utopian façade—'Paris change! mais rien dans ma mélancolie/N'a bougé! palais neufs, échafaudages, blocs,/Vieux faubourgs, tout pour moi devient allégorie/Et mes chers souvenirs sont plus lourds que des rocs' ('Paris may change, but in my melancholy mood/ Nothing has budged! New places, blocks, scaffoldings,/Old neighbourhoods, are allegorical for me,/And my dear memories are heavier than stone') (2008: 174–175)—only to conclude that 'À quiconque a perdu ce qui ne se retrouve/Jamais, jamais!' ('[o]f all those who have lost something they may not find/ Ever, ever again!') (ibid. 176–177). While Baudelaire is confronted with a physical and structural change of Paris, his thoughts flow towards the people, liminal figures that are captives but also historical exiles and outcasts. From Ovid to Andromache to an African 'negress' (ibid.) and the poem's allegorical swan, Baudelaire's historical journey of change is paradoxically caught in its static motion. According to Richard Terdiman, '[t]he process of memory carries an uncanny danger, which emerges in the paradigm of dispossession that organizes Baudelaire's poem. For the exiles of "Le Cygne," for the dispossessed, memory stages not recovery but *deficiency* ... memory figures the inauthenticity of presentness, the traumatic persistence of an irreversible experience of loss' (1993: 108). While all 'progress' signifies loss to Baudelaire, being a captive of memory and nostalgia is equally as damaging to the internal self, since both a total belief in progress and a clutching at the past imprisons the individual in a false sense of reality.

The poems in *Les Fleurs du Mal* (*The Flowers of Evil*) (1857/2008) depict much more than historical outsiders. They are littered with uncanny characters of Baudelaire's present time. For him, the strange characters that inhabitant the modern city—gamblers, prostitutes, alcoholics, drug addicts, his true heroes of modern life—become the uncanny allegories of modernity. Although the uncanny is best elucidated in literature, it was the metropolis that allowed it to surface in the public realm of everyday experience, looming through the void in urban space; a space ideal for the stranger who is alienated and estranged, who experiences homesickness due to the modern condition, which allows the uncanny to surface within the self and most notably in modern and avant-garde art (Vidler 1992: 5–13).[22] Baudelaire's allegorical use of his heroes of modern life was a violent means of destroying the modern myths that encased him, as '[t]he images disclosed behind this façade became emblems of his own inner life' (Buck-Morss 1991: 182). Baudelaire used allegory as a subtle weapon against his capitalist age, but also as a means of reading the world, of understanding the emotional and psychological aspects of the inner person by plunging oneself into the physical world. The reason Baudelaire's heroes of modern life are uncanny is because they should not exist in a utilitarian and bourgeois-utopian world built upon the idea of progress. The backdrop for many of his poems consists of the long and wide boulevards newly constructed in Paris during the time Baudelaire was writing. Commissioned by Napoleon III, Georges-Eugène Haussmann, also known as Baron Haussmann, set out to reconstruct and modernize Paris between 1853 and 1870, in an attempt to clear out slums, create 'breathing space,' and facilitate the traffic flow towards the centre of the city (Berman 1988: 150). In the process of leveling the old medieval city, Haussmann's renovation of Paris destroyed many arcades, the favourite home of the Baudelairean *flâneur*, which consisted of shopping malls made of glass and steel that had been created before the Second Empire while Baudelaire was growing up as a child. For Baudelaire, the arcades represented the dream of modernity, the possibilities and wonders it could provide. With the destruction of these arcades and his childhood fantasies, along with the failed revolution of 1848, Baudelaire quickly learned that modernity was a fleeting dream of destruction, failure, repetition, and boredom. The metropolis was a modern image of the chaotic flux of sensation into which the bourgeois rational dream world was beginning to dissolve (Ferguson 1996: 19, 31). However, thanks to the new modern reconstruction of Paris witnessed by Baudelaire, society could now see these marginalized figures more than ever, as the boulevards created more social contact between people of different classes.

Baudelaire's prose poem "Les yeux des pauvres" ("Eyes of the Poor") perfectly captures this confrontation. We are able to see how these new boulevards forced people to confront and deal with the image of the poor because they were no longer segregated in the underprivileged quarters of Paris, a monster that modernity could not cover up. "Eyes of the Poor" showcases Baudelaire's social conscience and critique of what Benjamin calls high capitalism. It is one of the poems that showcases Baudelaire 'as one of the great urban writers' (Berman 1988: 147). The narrator of the poem takes us back to a memory, which we discover is the cause of the hatred he feels towards the woman he once loved. The memory takes place in a café at the corner of the new boulevard. The narrator describes the scene in the café with dream-like quality, containing 'nappes éblouissantes des miroirs' ('dazzling mirror pools') and 'les nymphes et les déesses' (1968: 122) ('nymphs and goddesses') (1968: 52). A poor family walks up to the window, spellbound by the beauty they witness inside. At this moment, the narrator feels both guilt and shame and looks at his lover expecting her to feel the same thing. When she replies, 'Ces gens-là me sont insupportables avec leurs yeux ouverts comme des portes cochères ! Ne pourriez-vous pas prier le maître du café de les éloigner d'ici?' (1968: 123) ('I cannot bear those people with their eyes out on stalks! Tell the waiter to get rid of them') (1968: 53), the narrator realizes that his dream, 'deux âmes désormais n'en feraient plus qu'une" (1968: 121) ("two souls would be as one') (1968: 52), died along with that dream. The new boulevard not only creates an environment of 'splendeurs inachevées' (1968: 121) ('unfinished splendor') (1968: 52) in the modern city, but also has brought the poor family to the window of the café, and consequently face to face with the young bourgeois couple. As a result, the feeling of guilt and shame begin to crack through the recently paved boulevards of Paris (Berman 1988: 152). While the woman continues to repress these feelings, or rather is unable to see them with her own prejudiced eyes, the narrator is no longer able to ignore them, which leads to both his bitterness towards her and his questioning of himself. Whereas he originally saw her eyes as beautiful, in the end, they become a symbol of the inability to communicate, and represent "a shift from love to hate, from fantasy to reality, from closeness to alienation" (Rice 1999: 35). The breakdown in their relationship pushes the narrator to acknowledge that it is the woman he loves whose eyes are truly poor.

Although this poem does show the class division and inequalities that occur in the capitalist hub, it also shows Baudelaire's tendency to blur the lines between reality and dream. The tale is told through the memory of a couple inside the modern café, where the modern bourgeois reality is described by Baudelaire in dream-like fashion. The line between dream and reality becomes instantly blurred. When the narrator looks outside of his dream and into the harsh reality of the "eyes of the poor," he realizes that this 'utopian' experience is just a bourgeois modern dream, but also that this dream and the dream of eternal love are illusions and do not truly exist. On the other hand, the poor family on the other side of the glass window stands within the harsh reality of modernity yet looking into the modernist dream living within the café, believing in all its wonders. Baudelaire therefore creates a liminal world where both parties are caught within reality and dream simultaneously, encompassing the fragility of both. The narrator is first recalling a memory, in the same way one recalls a dream. However, in this dream he sees the failure of the modern dream and recognizes that we repress what makes us uncomfortable in our own skin. The narrator acknowledges his strangeness, locating the dark aspects that exist within both his dreams and reality. Although he has seen the death of the modern dream and, likewise, modern love, he nonetheless furthers his understanding of both his internal and external worlds as being interconnected, albeit fractured. While Baudelaire is often seen as a precursor for the decadence of the 19th-century *fin de siècle*, he, as with Leopardi, also foreshadowed the fragmented, opposing, and chaotic beginning of the next century that would plunge the world into its "greatest" war yet, and bring the modern stranger into a whole new realm of liminality and violence.

Notes: Chapter II

[1] As Daniel E. White points out, 'while there is neither evidence nor likelihood that Shelley read Leopardi while she was in Italy, in many respects Valperga was a production of the same cultural climate in which authors such as Leopardi ... voiced opposition to past and present histories of foreign domination in Italy' (1997: 8).

2 Cosmicism is the literary philosophy established by American author H P Lovecraft, which argues that in the face of no identifiable divine presence in the world, humanity has become fleeting and insignificant in regard to the cosmos. While the term is usually attributed to Lovercraft's work in the 20th century, I suggest that Shelley is its pioneer.

3 Schopenhauer wrote that Leopardi presented the 'mockery and wretchedness of this existence ... yet with such a multiplicity of forms and applications, with such a wealth of imagery, that he never wearies us, but, on the contrary, has a diverting and simulating effect' (1966: 588). Nietzsche was influenced by Leopardi and shared many ideas, such as an interest in the Copernican revolution and an admiration with ancient Greek civilization, along with ambivalent feelings towards reason and abhorrence for religion (Rosengarten 2012: 162–163). Nonetheless, Nietzsche criticized Leopardi as a 'suprahistorical thinker', who according to him only saw the nausea and decline in humanity (1997: 66). Nietzsche would regard this type of pessimism as 'weak pessimism' and his own as a 'pessimism of strength' (1999: 3–4). Although Benedetto Croce praised Leopardi as a great poet, he completely rejected Leopardi as a thinker and philosopher due to Leopardi's pessimism and outsiderness (1923/1935: 98–99).

4 According to Susan Blood (1997), post-Benjamin scholarship of Baudelaire has been broadly divided into two spheres: the historicist criticism that focuses on Baudelaire's work in context with the socio-political changes and thought that occurred in the mid-19th century, exemplified by the work of Richard Burton (1991) and Marshall Berman (1988); and the allegorical strain of Baudelairean scholarship associated with Hans Robert Jauß (1982), Paul de Man (1969/1971), and Blood herself, which takes, albeit in different directions, \a more aesthetic approach to the socio-historical question, since allegory 'involves a disturbance of historical categories' (Blood 1997: 14).

5 In response to a German critic who panned him in a similar vein, Leopardi laments: '[b]efore dying, I wish to protest against this invention of weakness and vulgarity, and beg my readers to try to controvert my remarks and my arguments, rather than accuse my ill-health' (cited in Origo 1999: 265 (*Epistolario*, VI, 24 May 1832)).

6 'La nature est laide, et je préfère les monstres de ma fantaisie à la trivialité positive' (1935: 263) ['Nature is ugly, and I prefer the monsters of my imagination to the triteness of actuality'] (1964: 180).

7 'Que tu viennes du ciel ou de l'enfer, qu'importe, Ô Beauté! monstre énorme, effrayant, ingénu!' ['What difference, then, from heaven or from hell, O Beauty, monstrous in simplicity?'] (2008: 44–45).

8 'Ô Créateur ! peut-il exister des monstres aux yeux de Celui-là seul qui sait pourquoi ils existent, comment ils se sont faits et comment ils auraient pu ne pas se faire?' (1968: 204) ['O Creator, can there be monsters in the eyes of Him who alone knows why they exist, how they *came into being*, how they might *not have come into being*?'] (ibid. 93).

9 Moreover, Erich Auerbach claims in his famous book *Dante: Poet of the Secular World* (1929/1961) that this extremely religious poet paved the way for imagination of the secular world through Mimesis.

10 In "Le Peintre de la vie modern" ["The Painter of Modern Life"] (1863), Baudelaire explains that modern beauty is something that is unstable and always in flux. Beauty itself is made up of dual components—'un élément éternel, invariable … et d'un élément relatif, circonstanciel' (1869: 54) ['an eternal, invariable element … and a relative, circumstantial element,'] (2010: 3)—and although it does contain an element that is constant and universal, it is only through the second element that humans are able to recognize beauty, for the first eternal and infinite constituent of beauty would be 'indigestible, inappreciable' (1869: 54)) ['beyond our powers of digestion or appreciation'] without the second (2010: 3). Furthermore, Leopardi's poem "*A Sylvia*" ["To Sylvia"] and Baudelaire's "À une passante" ["To a women passerby"], arguably the poets' most famous poems, are about the inevitability of unobtainable or unrequited love.

11 See "Baudelaire's Knowledge and Use of Dante" by James S. Patty (1956).

12 In "The Ego in Freud's Theory," Lacan argues that '[d]esire is a relation to being to lack. The lack is the lack of being properly speaking. It isn't the lack of this or that, but lack of being whereby the being exists' (1988: 223).

13 '… it is: transcendent, a religious movement by virtue of the absurd—when the borderline of the wonderous is reached, eternity is the true repetition' (Kierkegaard 1983: 305).

14 Kierkegaard's repetition shares some affinity with Nietzsche's concept of the eternal recurrence/return: 'Your whole life, like a sandglass, will always be reversed and will ever run out again,—a long minute of time will elapse until all those conditions out of which you were evolved return in the wheel of the cosmic process. And then you will find every pain and every pleasure, every friend and every enemy, every hope and every error, every blade of grass and every ray of sunshine once more, and the whole fabric of things which make up your life. This ring in which you are but a grain will glitter afresh forever. And in every one of these cycles of human life there will be one hour where, for the first time one man, and then many, will perceive the mighty thought of the eternal recurrence of all things:—and for mankind this is always the hour of Noon' (1911a: 250). Although both concepts share a paradoxical movement forward out of nihilism, one of the main differences between the two concepts, as Anna Strelis Soderquist points out, is that while Nietzsche's idea is more of a thought experiment or 'an exercise of the imagination, Kierkegaard's repetition must be an exercise in practice' (2016: 39).

15 'The saying of Yea to life, including even its most strange and most terrible problems, the will to life rejoicing over its own inexhaustibleness in the *sacrifice* of its highest types—this is what I called Dionysian, this is what I divined as the bridge leading to the psychology of the *tragic* poet. Not in

order to escape from terror and pity, not to purify one's self of a dangerous passion by discharging it with vehemence ... but to be far beyond terror and pity and to be the eternal lust of Becoming itself—that lust which also involves the *lust of destruction*' (Nietzsche 1911b: 120).

16 Frankenstein's Creature can be seen as epitomizing this notion of a modern ahistorical spectre.

17 Adorno and Horkheimer argue, 'Man imagines himself free from fear when there is no longer anything unknown. That determines the course of demythologization, of enlightenment, which compounds the animate with the inanimate just as myth compounds the inanimate with the animate. Enlightenment is mythic fear turned radical. The pure immanence of positivism, its ultimate product, is no more than a so to speak universal taboo. Nothing at all may remain outside, because the mere idea of outsiderness is the very source of fear' (1982: 16).

18 Interestingly, Mary Shelley saw the liminality of Italy—a result of its being a fragmented set of nation states—as its greatest hope, since it had not yet formed a 'nation' and therefore still contained in itself a possibility of creating something new. As Tilottama Rajan explains, Shelley saw that 'the sickness of contemporary Italy was also its potential' (1997: 30–31).

19 '... è chiaro che la distruzione delle idee innate distrugge il principio della bontà, bellezza, perfezione assoluta, e de' loro contrarii. Vale a dire di una perfezione ec. la quale abbia un fondamento, una ragione, una forma anteriore alla esistenza dei soggetti che la contengono, e quindi eterna, immutabile, necessaria, primordiale ed esistente prima dei detti soggetti, e indipendente da loro. Or dov'esiste questa ragione, questa forma? e in che consiste? e come la possiamo noi conoscere o sapere, se ogn'idea ci deriva dalle sensazioni relative ai soli oggetti esistenti? Supporre il bello e il buono assoluto, è tornare alle idee di Platone, e risuscitare le idee innate dopo averle distrutte, giacch è tolte queste, non v'è altra possibile ragione per cui le cose debbano assolutamente e astrattamente e necessariamente essere così o così, buone queste e cattive quelle, indipendentemente da ogni volontà, da ogni accidente, da ogni cosa di fatto, che in realtà è la sola ragione del tutto, e quindi sempre e solamente relativa, e quindi tutto non è buono, bello, vero, cattivo, brutto, falso, se non relativamente; e quindi la convenienza delle cose fra loro è relative...In somma il principio delle cose, e di Dio stesso, è il nulla ... Certo è che distrutte le forme Platoniche preesistenti alle cose, è distrutto Iddio' (Leopardi 1983: 483–484).
['... it is clear that the destruction of innate ideas destroys the principle of absolute goodness, beauty, perfection, and of their contraries. That is to say, the principle of a perfection, etc, that has a foundation, a logic, a form prior to the existence of the objects which contain it, and hence is eternal, immutable, necessary, primordial and existing before the said objects, and independent of them. But where does this logic, this form exist? And what does it consist of? And how can we recognize or know it, if we derive every idea

from sensations relating only to existing objects? To assume absolute good and absolute beauty is to return to ideas of Plato, and to revive innate ideas after having destroyed them, since once they are removed, there is no other possible *reason* why things should absolutely and abstractly and necessarily be thus or thus, with these good and those bad, independently of every will, of every accident, of *every concrete* circumstance, which in reality is the sole reason for everything, and is therefore always and only relative. Hence everything is not good, beautiful, true, bad, ugly, false except relatively, and hence the propriety of things with respect to one another is relative … … In short the principle of things, and indeed of God is nothingness … What is certain is that once the Platonic forms preexisting things are destroyed, God, too, is destroyed' (Leopardi 2013: 368–369).

[20] Although Nietzsche was an admirer of Leopardi, calling him one of the four 'masters of prose' (2010: 146), he could not have known of the reference to God's destruction, since *Zibaldone* was not published until after Nietzsche's death. However, Nietzsche's ridiculed madman, who utters Nietzsche's famous quote (1999b: 59; 2010: 181), ended up being an apt voice to paraphrase Leopardi.

[21] Benjamin writes of Klee's painting:
A Klee painting named Angelus Novus shows an angel looking as though he is about to move away from something he is fixedly contemplating. His eyes are staring, his mouth is open, his wings are spread. This is how one pictures the angel of history. His face is turned toward the past. Where we perceive a chain of events, he sees one single catastrophe which keeps piling wreckage upon wreckage and hurls it in front of his feet. The angel would like to stay, awaken the dead, and make whole what has been smashed. But a storm is blowing from Paradise; it has got caught in his wings with such violence that the angel can no longer close them. The storm irresistibly propels him into the future to which his back is turned, while the pile of debris before him grows skyward. This storm is what we call progress (2007b: 257–258).

[22] In *The Architectural Uncanny*, Anthony Vidler claims that space is inheritably, inherently uncanny since [s]pace, in the contemporary discourse, as in lived experience, has taken on an almost palpable existence. Its contours, boundaries, and geographies are called upon to stand in for all the contested realms of identity … space is assumed to hide, in its darkest recesses and forgotten margins, all the objects of fear and phobia that have returned with such insistence to haunt the imaginations of those who have tried to stake out spaces to protect their health and happiness … In every case 'light space' is invaded by the figure of 'dark space', on the level of the body in the form of epidemic and uncontrollable disease, and on the level of the city in the person of the homeless (1992: 167–168).

III

Violence, The Great War, and The Modern Stranger

Do not think that I have come to bring peace to the earth; I have not come to bring peace, but a sword.
—Matthew 10:44

La salute non analizza se stessa e neppur si guar- da nello specchio. Solo noi malati sappiamo qualche cosa di noi stessi.
(*Health doesn't analyze itself, nor does it look at itself in the mirror. Only we sick people know something about ourselves.*)
—Italo Svevo (*Zeno's Conscience*)

Let us remain soldiers even after the war ... for this is not war against an eternal enemy, as the newspapers and our honorable politicians say, nor of one race against another; it is a European civil war, a war against the inner invisible enemy of the European spirit.
—Franz Marc (quoted in Modris Eksteins' *Rites of Spring*)

"*When the world was in darkness and wretchedness, it could believe in perfection and yearn for it. But when the world became bright with reason and riches, it began to sense the narrowness of the needle's eye, and that rankled for a world no longer willing to believe or yearn.*"
—Walter M. Miller Jr., *A Canticle for Leibowitz*

Three men, resembling military soldiers and officers, are torturing a man, raping his wife, and holding the couple's child captive in a small attic. The executioners look calm and unemotional, as though they are mad scientists of pain and torture performing a sensible experiment. A dog is seen howling for help but is ultimately unheard as a phonograph plays, hiding the screams of the helpless victims. The noise of technological modernity, of the city, drowns out

---

How to cite this book chapter:
Beghetto, R. G. 2022. *Monstrous Liminality; Or, The Uncanny Strangers Of Secularized Modernity*. Pp. 75–102. London: Ubiquity Press. DOI: https: //doi.org/10.5334/bcp.d. License: CC-BY-NC

the violence taking place. This violent and grotesque scene is an illustration of Max Beckmann's post-WWI Expressionist painting *The Night* (1919). The work, which was influenced not only by the terrors of WWI but also by the outbreak of the November Revolution of 1918 in Germany, exemplifies a life ruled by violence, chaos, and murder. There is no purpose to the suffering shown in this painting, only senseless and meaningless violence executed out of perpetual boredom, if nothing else. Hiding in the painting's background appear another man and woman: the next victims or curious voyeurs? The answer is uncertain, but nonetheless, the painting implicates the viewer's scopophilic attraction to the violence in the horrific scene. Even the face on the child being carried away seems to have conflicted emotions. Clinging to one of the murders, the child's eyes seem to express a dejected state, but the child's smirk suggests a hint of pleasure. In the background is a window which seems to be the victims' only way of escape. However, one of the perpetrators is about to close the blinds, signifying that modern society has little time left before it is able to detect, or even more frightening, finally consent to the horror that has entered it. The moonlight shining in the night sky resembles a detached eye looking in on this ghastly scene; and despite the fact that the blinds are closing, it has already seen enough; the viewer has not just witnessed but rather was a part of the scene, and therefore lives in its memory. The painting is not a genuine account of a specific attack, but instead represents all of humanity caught in a vicious maelstrom of monstrosity and violence.

After the First World War, the modern stranger begins to figure more prominently in the literary and visual art world, but more importantly, starts to move from its individualistic and outsider beginnings and more into the collective sphere. Prior to WWI, modern strangers only manifested themselves in a handful of works by novelists, poets, and philosophers, and therefore were still peripheral and uncanny characters in secularized modernity. After the war, the philosophical and intellectual landscape of modernity changed, ushering in innovative or transformed avant-garde and literary movements such as Expressionism or the "Lost Generation" of the 1920s. These literary and art movements epitomized the soldier returning from trenches that embodied this new chaotic and ambiguous mindset, alongside the monster of modernity. These themes would once again manifest after WWII with the existentialism of Camus, Celine, de Beauvoir and others, as well as further into late modernity, when the concept of the modern stranger would be more properly defined in works of philosophy and critical theory by thinkers such as Bauman (1991) and Kristeva (1991). The relationship between war and the modern stranger put greater emphasis on violence as an essential characteristic of liminality, and can be seen as an examination of why in contemporary film and literature the modern stranger is usually represented as the violent anti-hero. World War I created an upheaval like no other, along with its postwar peace settlement, resulting in a global revolution (Sondhaus 2011), not just geographically and politically but also psychologically and artistically. This chapter will predominantly focus on the time period in and around WWI, including the modernism of the early 20th century, through avant-garde art movements such as Expressionism and Futurism, although I primarily focus on the significant painter Max Beckmann and filmmaker Fritz Lang. Moreover, the literature of Erich Maria Remarque, Robert Musil, and Italo Svevo will be addressed to examine the indirect influence of the modern stranger on these themes of violence, irony, utopia, and the paradoxical connection between them. Svevo and Musil's main characters Zeno and Ulrich have a historical literary connection as both men have often been characterized as "men without qualities."

Elizabeth Ziolkowski's "Svevo's Uomo Senza Qualità: Musil and Modernism in Italy" compares and contrasts the two celebrated characters: Ulrich and Zeno are both attractive, ironic, intelligent men, who are 'open to a range of perspectives, never committing ... to just one' (2010: 89), even morally ambiguous ones (ibid. 94). While the men do contain qualities, however indistinct, they are contrasted with the 'men with qualities' who falsely believe they possess control over own their lives, a trait that ultimately leads to their hubris and failure. As Ziolkowski proclaims, '[b]oth narratives suggest that the only genuine choice in the modern world is to be a man without qualities, a reflection of the crisis experienced during modernity in general and also of the crisis during the dissolution of Austria-Hungary, where identity was especially in flux' (ibid. 95). Notwithstanding the comparisons, Ziolkowski argues that the continuous and strong link between Zeno and Ulrich has a lot to do with the strong Austro-Italian literary relations of the time, especially since the term inetti (inept, passive, weak) that typically emphasizes Svevo's characters is not necessarily the best word to describe Ulrich (ibid. 84). Nonetheless, I will build on the connections between the two, through a more comprehensive examination of irony, violence, and liminality. Naomi Lebowitz also distinguishes the two by arguing that 'the presence of historical contemplation in Musil's novel is stirred to a high allegorical pitch,' while 'Zeno, still bound by sociability and his psychology, lives in historical comfort, despite all that rages around him' (1978: 204). Therefore, while both are modern strangers caught in the same historical and liminal time period, the two operate in different inside/outside thresholds, though they are bound by the same chaos.

Although this chapter focuses primarily on pre-WWII work, Walter M. Miller Jr.'s science fiction novel A Canticle for Leibowitz will also be discussed alongside the notion of divine violence, repetition, and messianic time, outlined by the works of Ernst Bloch, Walter Benjamin, and Giorgio Agamben. By doing so, I will shed light on the development and difficulties of the modern stranger within secularized modernity once the monstrousness of violence and war enters into the collective conscience of society, and whether it is possible to define violence as messianic—or is the modern era simply caught in a cycle of destruction?

The Great War, Irony, & Dark Utopias

Although it was the Romantics who first revolutionized irony, taking it from a literary device into a new form of consciousness of seeing the contradictions of everyday life, 20th-century romantic irony went further by focusing on the ambiguity of modern life by taking a more versatile, critical, and existential form, shaping a perspective that would dominate most of early- to mid-20th-century art and literature (Berg 2014: 53–56). The modern use of irony began to change after WWI as many of the 19th-century metanarratives began to crumble under the weight of modern warfare. The rise of irony in the 1920s, according to Paul Fussell (1975) and Susanne Christine Puissant (2009), is directly associated with the outbreak of WWI, which ushered in an ironic world that completely altered both literature and the modern consciousness. Modris Eksteins' remarkable book *Rites of Spring: The Great War and the Birth of the Modern Age* studies the cultural history of World War I and its aftermath. Eksteins also denotes WWI as the threshold of the changing ideological landscape, but his study of the war is inserted between an examination of the disordered society waiting to shatter and the postwar era looking to reassemble itself. Eksteins' book is extremely useful in constructing a correlation between the modern stranger, liminality, and WWI, as he defines the solider battling in the liminal chaos of No Man's Land as the representation of the new modernist era that is built on a paradoxical and ironic utopia grounded in hopelessness and faith. Eksteins declares the soldier 'not just a harbinger but the very agent of the modern aesthetic, the progenitor of destruction but also the embodiment of the future' (1989: 213).

By the 20th century, the monster of modernity had mutated into a disease, an uncanny sickness epitomized by violence that had spread throughout the world. While the Creature in *Frankenstein* personified monstrosity in its totality, especially for its creator (who falsely believed that the monster was something external from him), monstrosity became consciously acknowledged as part of humanity, yet something that was still foreign and invading. Rendering it a human sickness implied that it could be cured, a perspective that further allowed for the monster to be something external and alien even though it belonged to the human self and, therefore, was still able to be removed. However, the "solution" was as problematic as it was simple, and in the face of remedies conducted through modern science and psychoanalysis that looked to cure society, an ironic reading of post-WWI life challenged the rational binaries of sickness/health. Almost a century earlier, Kierkegaard (1841/1989) rightfully saw irony, as he did with despair, residing on a liminal plane between sickness and health, positivity and negativity, faith and incredulity, and the divine and secular.[1] This existential battle would become the stranger's most enduring war within the secularized modernity of the 20th century, where a cure for this sickness could only emerge from a 'mastery over irony' through a process of 'diving into the sea of irony, not in order to stay there, of course, but in order to come out healthy, happy and buoyant' (Kierkegaard 1841/1989: 326–327). Faced with the outbreak and aftermath of the First World War, many saw that looking into both societal sickness and the self's monstrosity was the best way to overcome its power over the individual, in an ironic and liminal space between the impulse of the utopian spirit and succumbing to nihilism, boredom, and dread. Shelley, Leopardi, and Baudelaire's monstrous modernity had finally exploded onto mass society.

Though the ironist may laugh at the absurdity of what the world holds sacred, irony does not necessarily negate through laughter, but is rather '[t]he said and unsaid working together to create something new' (Hutcheon 1994/2003: 61). In Hutcheon's seminal book, *Irony's Edge*, she defines irony in liminal, oscillating terms, where 'meaning is *simultaneously* doubled (or multiple)' (ibid. 58), and not a rejection of the literal. Since irony is the existence of opposing meanings at once, the ironist is never truly removed from the sacred while uttering the profane, but balances on the edge of the sacred/secular binary. Irony, especially modern irony, exists in liminality, occupying 'the space between face and mask' (Hermans 2007: 79), and even has the utopian ability to open up 'new space, literally between opposing meanings, where new things can happen' (Hutcheon 1992: 31). D. C. Muecke similarly claims that there is a transcendent element to modern irony, creating a liminal space between the spiritual and moral spheres of heaven and hell. Containing both a complete sense of freedom and an element of destruction, modern irony blurs the lines of 'above' and 'below,' thereby creating a void or 'bottomless pit' in the realm of ethics and morality (Muecke 1969: 229–230). Yet located in the darkness of this black hole, a new concept of utopia develops after the First World War, indebted to the works of German philosopher Ernst Bloch and his paradoxical vision of utopia.

Published in the immediate aftermath of WWI, Ernst Bloch's *The Spirit of Utopia* moved away from the blueprint form of utopia that had become analogous to totalitarian thought, in favour of a more radical and iconoclastic usage based upon a strong, critical form of irony. Influenced by two major events of the early 20th century, WWI and the Russian Revolution, Bloch's notion of utopian hope is born 'in the darkness itself' (1918/2000: 201). Utopia, according to Bloch, is inherent in the unhappiness, despair, and frustration found in the present. This internal darkness manifests itself in what is missing in each individual; within this internal darkness is where the "spirit of utopia" offers us hope that fuels or inspires our movement towards a better future. Bloch argues that it is through the "something missing" within our present world, the lack or blind spot, that subsequently shows us a better future by imagining or attempting to fill what is absent in our present. Therefore, the lived experience of the present is utopian in itself, given that it exposes what is lacking in our present world by showing us an opposite or alternate vision of the future outside of one curated by linear progress. Here, Bloch distances himself from Hegel, and even

Marx, in favour of the subjectivity found in the philosophy of both Kant and Kierkegaard. He supports Kant's pursuit of the secret of ourselves, a process of ongoing deepening or self-encounter, for it is in this self-encounter where the utopian spirit is created through an absence (ibid. 3, 187). Nonetheless, Bloch does not completely dismiss Hegel, but rather believes in a synthesis of both Kant and Hegel's philosophy, or as he expresses in the phrase 'Kant burning through Hegel' (ibid. 187), a point where the spirit of utopia contained within each individual channels itself into the external world or 'the world of the soul' (ibid. 3).

In *Prey Into Hunter: The Politics of Religious Experience*, Maurice Bloch further expands the liminal structure by magnifying the theme of violence that van Gennep and Turner only allude to in their liminal theories. Bloch claims that for van Gennep and Turner, violence is found only in the initial transcendent stage of passage from the everyday world into the liminal second stage, where he claims the 'native vitality' of the person is 'symbolically vanquished' (1992: 37); however, for Bloch, violence becomes a double passage that reoccurs in the last stage of the religious ritual as well, where the individual reintegrates him- or herself into the mundane world without cancelling the transcendental, making violence for Bloch 'a result of the attempt to create the transcendental in religion and politics' (ibid. 7). Finally, this dialectical oscillation consisting of utopia and violence culminates in the question of mystic violence and divine violence. The problem is first raised by Walter Benjamin in "Critique of Violence," in which he defines and structures the various discretions concerning violence and law. The difference between mythic and divine violence for Benjamin is that 'mythic violence is lawmaking, divine violence is law-destroying; if the former sets boundaries, the latter boundlessly destroys them; if mythic violence brings at once guilt and retribution, divine power only expiates; if the former threatens, the latter strikes; if the former is bloody, the latter is lethal without spilling blood' (1921/1986: 297). With mythical violence, Benjamin claims it is impossible to separate violence from law, in that 'violence ... is either lawmaking or law-preserving' (ibid. 287). Contrasting mythical violence is what Benjamin regards as divine violence, which exists outside the legal sphere and is a violence of "pure means," or means without ends. To differentiate the two, Benjamin uses the examples of the political strike as mythic law and the general strike as divine law. The political strike looks to change law in the existing social structure, therefore it is still lawmaking; whereas the general strike is revolutionary and looks to destroy state power and existing social order, thereby making it more anarchistic in nature (ibid. 291–292). Benjamin's resacralized notion of divine violence resembles that of God's, because it both protects the sacredness of human life and exists beyond the realm of human law. Benjamin's equivocal concept of divine law is nonetheless problematic, as the ambiguity in what Benjamin constitutes as divine law is subject to various interpretations, including ones that can lead to horrible consequences.

Benjamin's notion of divine violence is closely tied to his idea of messianic time, which contrasts with the 'homogeneous, empty time' of human history (2007: 261). While the secular time of progress is empty and repetitious, messianic time, the 'time of the now' (ibid. 263), is a monadic and momentary time that shatters the repetition of history and connects past, present, and future. This moment seems to be where both messianic time and divine violence intersect with one another to become whole, according to Judith Butler (2012: 218). Butler reaffirms Benjamin's argument in her assessment of "Critique of Violence," by asserting that

> [t]his sacred or divine sense of life is also allied with the anarchistic, with that which is beyond or outside of principle ... the anarchism or destruction that Benjamin refers to here is to be understood neither as another kind of political state nor as an alternative to positive law. Rather, it constantly recurs as the condition of positive law and as its necessary limit. It does not portend an epoch yet to come, but underlies legal violence of all kinds, constituting the potential for destruction that underwrites every act by which the subject is bound by law (ibid. 85–86).

Benjamin's concepts of the messianic and divine violence have likewise been very influential in the work of Italian philosopher Giorgio Agamben. For Agamben, messianic time is not necessarily removed from secular time but

> is that part of secular time which undergoes an entirely transformative contraction ... This is not the line of chronological time (which was representable but unthinkable), nor the instant of its end (which was just as unthinkable); nor is it a segment cut from chronological time; rather, it is operational time pressing within the chronological time, working and transforming it from within; it is the time we need to make time end: the time that is left us [*il tempo che ci resta*] (2005: 64, 67–68).

In regard to divine violence, Agamben expands on Benjamin's theory by interjecting his own concept of sovereign violence and the figure of the *homo sacer*. Although not exactly the same, a liminal correlation exists between the two because

> sovereign violence, like divine violence, cannot be wholly reduced to either one of the two forms of violence whose dialectic the essay undertook to define. This does not mean that sovereign violence can be confused with divine violence. The definition of divine violence becomes easier, in fact, precisely when it is put in relation with the state of exception. Sovereign violence opens a zone of indistinction between law and nature, outside and inside, violence and law. And yet the sovereign is

precisely the one who maintains the possibility of deciding on the two to the very degree that he renders them indistinguishable from each other (1998: 64).

Agamben's sovereign, who is both inside and outside the law, acts as the liminal link between the divine violence and the political, for 'the sovereign is the point of indistinction between violence and law, the threshold on which violence passes over into law and law passes over into violence' (ibid. 32). The protagonist of Agamben's study is the abstruse Roman figure *homo sacer* (sacred man), who was a criminal that was both excluded from and included in law, as he could be killed by anyone yet not sacrificed because he was considered sacred. Here the sacred oscillates between the pure and impure, which creates a liminal and ambiguous atmosphere where the impure is made from the pure, and vice versa (ibid. 77). Since the sacred man is outside both divine and profane law, it allows for the possibility of the *homo sacer* to become the threshold where sovereign violence and law are able to interconnect. Agamben concludes that with the indistinctness of the sacred, this stranger has entered the collective society in that 'we are all virtually *homines sacri*' (ibid. 115). Despite his post-9/11 critics (Butler 2004; Connolly 2005; Kalyvas 2007; Žižek 2002), who were concerned with the apolitical, totalistic and universalism of his claim, Agamben—by stating 'virtually'—is emphasizing the potential for the *homo sacer* to exist within everyone, as a hovering spectre of the modern political and secular age. Agamben's stranger is a reflection of modernity's liminality, as someone that is 'from the remote past who brings into focus a disturbing element in our political present—and points towards a possible future' (de la Durantaye 2009: 211). Yet both the opportunity and problem lie in the fact that the possibility that exists in statelessness is not actually defined, and as a result can manifest itself in violent extremes or even in an impasse.

From this perspective, Benjamin's ambiguity in completely outlining the idea of divine violence has also led to a problematic discussion of what represents violence that may be defined as sacred. Derrida's (1990/1992) criticism of Benjamin's essay revolves around the uncertainty and ambiguity that surrounds the secularized concept of divine violence, which could ultimately lead to the temptation to regard the Nazi final solution as divine violence. On the other hand, Slovenian theorist Slavoj Žižek ultimately disagrees with Derrida's assessment, arguing that Nazism simply represented mythical violence, as he infamously claims 'the problem with Hitler was that *he was not violent enough*, that his violence was not 'essential' enough. Nazism was not radical enough, it did not dare to disturb the basic structure of the modern capitalist social space (which is why it had to focus on destroying an invented external enemy, Jews)' (2009: 151). Although Žižek may be right in a traditional understanding of Hitler and Nazism as fascist and nationalist forces, the compelling recent work of Timothy Snyder has challenged this conventional assessment by arguing that Hitler's plan was to completely destroy the existing social structure through The Final

Solution, by creating a liminal world based on chaos and violence. According to Snyder, Hitler was a 'biological anarchist' (2015: 52) who sought to destroy ideas such as the state, nationalism, capitalism, communism, and monotheism by eliminating what he believed to be the artificial culture or "non-race" of the Jewish people, deeming them a universal enemy that created the new artificial world that surrounded him. At the very least, Snyder's new assessment of the final solution and WWII creates a new discourse on the subject that still makes Derrida's deconstructive criticism of Benjamin's essay a valid one and encourages certain understandings of the destructive forces of the present.

The Stranger in No Man's Land

Max Beckmann once said that the purpose of painting, especially after the war, was to show humanity their horrible fate (Elger 2007: 209)—a fate perhaps unknown to the general populace, but to the WWI solider, it was a doom that was ever-present in everyday modern life. *The Night* moves beyond time by encompassing Europe's past, present, and future of violence: the past through the imagery of the WWI solider, who still shows the wounds from battle; the present through the violence being depicted; and the future through the hint of pleasure we are subconsciously experiencing through the child's ironic smile. Beckmann went to war with patriotic enthusiasm, as did many young European men who quickly enlisted to serve their countries; however, once he experienced the violence and horror of modern warfare, he suffered a nervous breakdown and was invalided out of the military (Beckett 1997: 26). Like many artists of his day, Beckmann ingenuously believed that the war would be both a coming-of-age ritual process and a positive inspiration for his artistic work. In some sense, Beckmann was half right. The war failed him in his ritual process of passage to manhood, a failure that would see him fleetingly place that sacredness into the god-like character and 'social and political utopianism' of the artist (Clair 2004: 112). The sentiment would not last, however, as he would eventually mock himself as a messianic figure in *Selbstbildnis als Clown* (*Self-portrait of a Clown*) (1921),[2] as the war ultimately left him spiritually trapped in the liminal planes of the WWI battlefield. Nonetheless, the experience of modern trench warfare, although not the courageous and heroic experience the young German artist expected, significantly influenced his work through the haunting nightmares that remained. Suffering from traumatic "shell shock" (post-traumatic stress disorder), Beckmann's new attraction to violence seemed to be a search for an identity, a way of 'exorcising something within himself' (Beckett 1997: 21–22). The 'strange, and fatalistic feeling of safety' that surrounded him on that first day (Beckmann 1997: 163) dissipated bit by bit as the excitement of warfare gave way to the monotony of violence. The First World War was originally thought of as a meliorist war of progress, but ironically became the culmination of modernity's technological utopian values failing (Fussell 1975:

8), a blatant example of the return to barbarism that Leopardi had warned of. Although Expressionism retained its focus on the individual, the war nonetheless turned it from a private, egocentric art movement to one that encompassed a social and revolutionary atmosphere (Elger 2007: 205). Beckmann's works, like many postwar Expressionist art pieces, now examined humanity as a group of strangers, helplessly caught in a changing world of technological violence and absurdity (ibid. 211). The WWI solider entered a war that began traditionally on horseback, though quickly transformed into a modern horror of trenches, tanks, planes, Zeppelins, and gasmasks, while its aftermath marked the end of many European Empires. As with the French Revolution, WWI was an irredeemable break in history, which exposed the monster lurking along the borders of optimism, rationalism, and scientific discovery.

Notwithstanding the pivotal change in modern warfare, the conflict may not have ushered in a new age, but rather was the illuminating event of the chaotic modern world that led up to it. Philipp Blom argues that the time period between 1900 and 1914 was far less optimistic, enthusiastic, and naïve about the monster of modernity than many like to believe. It was an age characterized by velocity and the vertigo that came with the exhilarating, frightening nature of the modern age (Blom 2008: 2). Although the turn of the century was met with technological wonder and amazement, the years leading up to WWI were also defined by a multitude of theories clashing against the bedrock of positivism, leading to feelings of uncertainty, while rationality was challenged by Sigmund Freud's theories of the unconscious as well as the modernist and avant-garde art movements (ibid. 403–406). In response, young men like Beckmann were trying to solidify their identities and reestablish gender binaries, battling the rising suffragette movement with the traditional idea of masculine courage (ibid. 398–400). Soldiers looked to complete their rite of passage to manhood through warfare and patriotism and conclude their sacred journey by coming out of the war as masculine heroes. But the war seemed to reemphasize the ambiguous, liminal, and violent nature of the modern world for these young men.

The soldiers who were "lucky" to survive and return to civilian life became extremely alienated and detached from their fellow citizens, unable to reassimilate into regular society. In essence, postwar soldiers became a unified though unorganized front, as there seemed to be more of an affinity, through isolation and existential anguish, among each other than to their nation states. In spirit, the soldiers remained in No Man's Land long after the war. The liminal battlefield, located between the two trenches of rival nations or empires, ended up embodying a group that would forever be referred to as "the lost generation." British officer and author Charles Edmund Carrington argued that the soldiers returning from war shared a 'secret bond' that 'could never be communicated' (cited in Leed 1979: 12–13). The unsettling image of No Man's Land and "the unknown world beyond it" (ibid. 14–15) became something that was eternal for Carrington and most soldiers. Caught between two binary trenches, the violent space of No Man's Land is where the soldiers became modern strangers. If war was a rite of passage for these young men, it was one where they remained liminal, unable to fulfill the third and final reaggregation phase of the passage to manhood. Despite being driven into that void by their respective countries, the nationalism that was enforced in the trenches became suspended in No Man's Land. At that moment, they become strangers to the reasons of the conflict, leaving them only with the struggle for survival and constantly toeing the line between life and death. By 1916, the fraternization between fronts, exemplified by the Christmas truce of 1914, had dissipated. Soldiers were no longer under the illusory perception of being heroes. Instead, they lost their identities and individuality and became nameless, unknown, completely alienated from their commanding officers. British artist and solider Paul Nash perfectly captures this uncanny space in his painting *The Void* (1918) as he depicts the hellish desolation of war, where the lines between trench and No Man's land are virtually erased by all the carnage. For the soldier caught in No Man's Land, the war had lost its original cause; the lines of heroism became blurred or essentially destroyed, a sentiment that quickly seeped into the trenches, which no longer held any distinction from No Man's Land as the war progressed.

While Britain fought to preserve balance, order, and social values, the war for Germany was touted as a spiritual conflict, a chance to change the world and liberate it from a reality that had been fashioned up to that point, a reason why many German artists fully backed the war when it originally began (Eksteins 1989: 118–119). If the war originated as a spiritual conflict for many, it continued as such once it was finished, taking on a new identity as it progressed. Historian Modris Eksteins examines how Remarque's novel *Im Westen nichts Neues* (*All Quiet on the Western Front*) (1929/1984) created both a spiritual affiliation between soldiers and a reactionary attempt to destroy that connection. *All Quiet*, which follows German solider Paul Bäumer and his fellow combatants' passage from students to killing machines, is a novel more about the postwar disillusionment of the individuals in the trenches, even though it focuses on the experiences and events of the war that ultimately ruined them.[3] By 1916, many soldiers believed the war would be endless (Fussell 1975: 71), and although the conflict did end two years later, in many regards, those soldiers were quite accurate. As Eksteins argues of Remarque's novel, '[o]nly the fraternity of death remains, the comradeship of the fated' (1989: 281). Upon its release, the book was an accomplishment and enjoyed great success. It unified the spirit of the soldiers through the mutual horrors they suffered, regardless of what side they fought on; war veteran and poet Herbert Read acknowledged the novel as 'the Bible of the common soldier' (ibid. 286). With *All Quiet*, Remarque was able to describe the war and the soldier's experience of it better than any historian or politician, since the new horrors of trench life—the actual experienced war— were completely foreign to the outside observer.

The novel exemplifies this theme at the point when Paul returns home on leave and feels estranged from his family, unable to get rid of this *'Befangenheit'* ('sense of strangeness') that overcomes him and the 'Schritt' ('distance') and 'Schleier' ('veil') that exist between him and the rest of society (Remarque 1984: 138; 1958: 160). While on leave, he ultimately is excluded from a war discussion, and his experiences are dismissed by his old headmaster as merely individual or subjective (1984:142; 1958: 167). He is accused of being unable to see the bigger picture. Here, Paul is removed from a war he faces at every waking moment, furthering his alienation from society, which sadly leads to his acknowledgment that the only home he has left is on the front with his fellow soldiers, both friend and enemy. Only a few hundred miles away, the world of 'normal' society becomes completely alien and strange for Paul, while the war had slowly become strangely familiar. As a result, the novel's destruction of national boundaries, and subsequently blame and fault, became extremely problematic for many nationalists, politicians, and traditionalists, who tried to reinforce these divisions and binaries and reaffirm the war guilt of their former enemies, which ultimately led to numerous critical attacks by various journalists and politicians (Eksteins 1989: 293–299). Carl Jung argues that the war did not end with the battles of 1914–1918, but continued on to embody the other, the uncanny, and the unconscious of human psyche still lingering in a liminal battle (1946/2014: 2–3). The spiritually hollow war would continue to endure in the soldiers; however, once they returned to ordinary society, there was no liminal void in which to exercise these demons, leaving them in a difficult position of understanding the fragility of life but also, at the same time, the complete meaninglessness of it.

Trenches, Violence, and The City

Remarque's *All Quiet* and Beckmann's *The Night* reflect on the continuing violence in soldiers' everyday lives; however, Beckmann allocates or transmits the violence of postwar consciousness specifically inside the modern urban space. *The Night* carefully indicates how the violence of the war has entered the city's streets, as well as the homes and private lives of Europeans, though the painting could even be interpreted as arguing that it was the chaotic and artificial city that had entered the war. Commenting on his first day at the front, Beckmann uncannily connects its spectacle to city space: '[u]nforgettable and strange. In all those holes and sharp trenches. Those ghostly passageways and artificial forests and houses … strangle unreal cities, like lunar mountains' (1997: 163). While No Man's Land represents the spiritual battle and the liminal void embodied by each individual solider, the trenches uncannily represent the chaotic urban space of the modern city. The association of trenches with city streets has been well documented, from the British armies that allocated English street names to their channels (Fussell 1975: 42–43; Gilbert 2000: x; Pike

2007: 286) to the trenches' structure and atmosphere reflecting each country's culture (Fussell 1975: 44–45). Although these touches may have been added to give the trenches a sense of home, the ambiance of modern warfare was closer to urban life than the soldiers originally thought. Like the congested city, the trenches were made of twisting corridors and labyrinth-like streets and tunnels in which a "man without a map"[4] can easily become lost. Just as Baudelaire brought the uncanny from the Parisian underworld out into the consciousness of its citizens, 'the war signaled an unavoidable shift from conceiving the underground as a distinct space, either hidden in a world of metaphors or a separate physical realm, to accepting it as a dominant feature of everyday life' (Pike 2007: 301). While the majority of people were well removed from the war, WWI lessened the distinction between warzone and normal society. Although nowhere near the extent of WWII, violence entered the cities like never before, as demonstrated with the German Zeppelin raids over London.

Not only did the trenches have an uncanny relation to the modern city, constructing a 'parody' of them (Fussell 1975: 43), but they also reflected the noticeable fast-paced and ferocious atmosphere of the late 19th- and early 20th-century metropolis. While the Crimean War gave Europe a glimpse of a modern, meaningless conflict, the technological age had already cemented itself by the time of WWI, and the notion that warfare could remain traditional, pure, and even spiritual was now impossible. Years before WWI began, the Futurists had already amalgamated human and machine in their revolutionary and utopian ideal. Their 'artificial optimism' (Poggi 2009) celebrated technology through symbols of cars, machines, and cities, containing a resacralized spirituality in which the machine was able to transcend the desires and limitations of the human body and mind (ibid. 241). The horrific aftermath of the war did little to discourage most Futurists, even reinforcing their attitudes, despite the war having altered perception on a grand scale in regard to the relationship between human and machine. Despite having its critics from its inception, Futurism had a profound influence on the pre-WWI avant-garde art movements across Europe. It was after the war that the first phase of Futurism began to decline, largely due to the Futurists' utopian vision of violence (Bondanella & Bondanella 2001: 242), the synergism of human and machine, and the movement's newfound affiliation with Italian fascism. English painter Wyndham Lewis critiqued Futurism's romanticisation of machines as simply melodramatic or misguided (Rabaté 2007: 36; Ray 2001: 338). His depiction of war in *A Battery Shelled* (1919) presents soldiers as dehumanized killing machines, depicting the 'cult of machine' in far grimmer circumstances, while removing the glamour of violence that found Futurism in favour of representing warfare 'as an ordinary affair' (Mao 2013: 251). The sentiment of Futurism's "Extended Man," which depicted humans as virtually enslaved by advancing technology, would continue to be critiqued in postwar films such as Fritz Lang's *Metropolis* (1927/2002) and Charlie Chaplin's *Modern Times* (1936/2010). Shelley's cyborg nightmare and corresponding anxiety over humanity's obtaining too much knowledge became a self-fulfilling prophecy after the turn of the century in the modern city, culminating horrifically with WWI, two sentiments that Robert Musil's unfinished novel *Der Mann ohne Eigenschaften* (*The Man Without Qualities*) further explores.

The novel's protagonist, a modern stranger and ex-soldier named Ulrich, is an alienated intellectual caught in a time of rising uncertainty, largely due to a world of increasingly divided ideologies and illusions. Musil, who started the novel in 1921, sets the story's beginning in 1913 Vienna and opens with the line '[ü]ber dem Atlantik befand sich ein barometrisches Minimum' (1943/1967: 9) ('[a] barometric low hung over the Atlantic') (1995: 3), foreshadowing the war hanging over what Musil portrayed as an increasingly divided Europe ignorant of the violence fast approaching. The novel's beginning also shows how this technological violence had already emerged in the city streets before the war. The chaotic hustle and bustle of the modern city closely resembles the structure of both a machine and chaotic modern warfare:

> Autos schossen aus schmalen, tiefen Straßen in die Seichtigkeit heller Plätze. Fußgängerdunkelheit bildete wolkige Schnüre. Wo kräftigere Striche der Geschwindigkeit quer durch ihre lockere Eile fuhren, verdickten sie sich, rieselten nachher rascher und hatten nach wenigen Schwingungen wieder ihren gleichmäßigen Puls. Hunderte Töne waren zu einem drahtigen Geräusch ineinander verwunden, aus dem einzelne Spitzen vorstanden, längs dessen schneidige Kanten liefen und sich wieder einebneten, von dem klare Töne absplitterten und verflogen (1943/1967: 9).

> (Automobiles shot out of deep, narrow streets into the shallows of bright squares. Dark clusters of pedestrians formed cloudlike strings. Where more powerful lines of speed cut across their casual haste they clotted up, then trickled on faster and, after a few oscillations, resumed their steady rhythm. Hundreds of noises wove themselves into a wiry texture of sound with barbs protruding here and there, smart edges running along it and subsiding again, with clear notes splintering off and dissipating) (1995: 3).

This tumultuous scene ends with a fatal car crash, thereby foretelling the violence of the impending war, but more importantly the spectacle it creates and the question of guilt and responsibility it leaves with the reader:

> Diese beiden hielten nun plötzlich ihren Schritt an, weil sie vor sich einen Auflauf bemerkten. Schon einen Augenblick vorher war etwas aus der Reihe gesprungen, eine quer schlagende Bewegung; etwas hatte sich gedreht, war seitwärts gerutscht, ein schwerer, jäh gebremster Lastwagen war es, wie sich jetzt zeigte, wo er, mit einem Rad auf der Bordschwelle, gestrandet dastand. Wie die Bienen um das Flugloch hatten sich im Nu Menschen um einen kleinen Fleck angesetzt, den sie in

ihrer Mitte freiließen. Von seinem Wagen herabgekommen, stand der Lenker darin, grau wie Packpapier, und erklärte mit groben Gebärden den Unglücksfall. Die Blicke der Hinzukommenden richteten sich auf ihn und sanken dann vorsichtig in die Tiefe des Lochs, wo man einen Mann, der wie tot dalag, an die Schwelle des Gehsteigs gebettet hatte. Er war. durch seine eigene Unachtsamkeit zu Schaden gekommen, wie allgemein zugegeben wurde. Abwechselnd knieten Leute bei ihm nieder, um etwas mit ihm anzufangen; man öffnete seinen Rock und schloß ihn wieder, man versuchte ihn aufzurichten oder im Gegenteil, ihn wieder hinzulegen; eigentlich wollte niemand etwas anderes damit, als die Zeit ausfüllen, bis mit der Rettungsgesellschaft sachkundige und befugte Hilfe käme (1943/1967: 10–11).

(The pair now came to a sudden stop when they saw a rapidly gathering crowd in front of them. Just a moment earlier something there had broken ranks; falling sideways with a crash, something had spun around and come to a skidding halt—a heavy truck, as it turned out, which had braked so sharply that it was now stranded with one wheel on the curb. Like bees clustering around the entrance to their hive people had instantly surrounded a small spot on the pavement, which they left open in their midst. In it stood the truck driver, gray as packing paper, clumsily waving his arms as he tried to explain the accident. The glances of the newcomers turned to him, then warily dropped to the bottom of the hole where the man lay there as if dead had been bedded against the curb. It was by his own carelessness that he had come to grief, as everyone agreed. People took turns kneeling beside him, vaguely wanting to help; unbuttoning his jacket, then closing it again; trying to prop him up, then laying him down again. They were really only marking time while waiting for the ambulance to bring someone who would know what to do and have the right to do it) (1995: 4–5).

The role of responsibility keeps being passed on, only to finally rest on the deceased victim, because in actuality no one knows whom to blame. Later, Musil broadens the violent spectacle of modern culture and the problem of guilt with the story of Christian Moosbrugger, a condemned man on trial for the murder and rape of a prostitute. Ulrich, like many other people in Vienna, becomes completely fascinated with Moosbrugger, a seemingly gentle and friendly man who commits a grisly, shocking murder. The character Clarisse takes her fascination with the murderer past a mere interest to something far more obsessive and unhealthy, where 'Anziehung und Abstoßung mischten sich darin zu einem sonderbaren Bann' (1943/1967: 144) ('[a]ttraction and repulsion blended into a peculiar spell') (1995: 152). Because of Moosbrugger's liminal disposition in society due to his rebellious act against law and order, Clarisse places a heroic, even revolutionary quality upon him. Therefore,

Moosbrugger represents not just Ulrich's *doppelgänger*, but also modern society's uncanny and irrational underbelly and liminal disposition; like Frankenstein's Creature, Moosbrugger becomes the novel's uncanny other or stranger. Suffering from hallucinations, Moosbrugger is unable to distinguish illusion from reality, inside and outside, and therefore cannot establish a fixed identity, 'war das wie helles Wasser zu beiden Seiten einer durchsichtigen Glaswand' (1943/1967: 239) ('like clear water on both sides of a transparent sheet of glass') (1995: 258). As Stefan Jonsson states, 'Moosbrugger signals the end of character, an extreme example of a person who is no longer one, the opposite of order, stability, unity, coherence, and reliability. He is an incarnation of all conceivable terrifying qualities that a community would like to imagine that it has under control' (1996: 51). Through his presence, the notions of criminal and victim blur to similar effects, as in *Frankenstein*.

As in the opening scene of the novel, in which the accident's onlookers seek to project blame upon either the victim or chance, Moosbrugger, who lacks any moral understanding, is now seen as the victim by many, a victim of the modern experience. He becomes a problematic scapegoat as society projects its monstrosity onto the murderer, though paradoxically reflecting a sense of victimhood back towards the same society. Ulrich sees the correlation between society and the ambiguous darkness within Moosbrugger as a collective entity: 'Das war deutlich Irrsinn, und ebenso deutlich bloß ein verzerrter Zusammenhang unsrer eignen Elemente des Seins. Zerstückt und durchdunkelt war es; aber Ulrich fiel irgendwie ein: wenn die Menschheit als Ganzes träumen könnte, müßte Moosbrugger entstehn' (1943/1967: 76) ('[t]his was clearly madness, and just as clearly it was no more than a distortion of our own elements of being. Cracked and obscure it was; it somehow occurred to Ulrich that if mankind can dream as a whole, that dream would be Moosbrugger') (1995: 76–77). Not only does Musil address society's enchantment with violence, he also leaves us to contemplate whether Moosbrugger is a victim of the modern experience, simply a symbol of it, or both.

This question remains unanswered, for when Moosbrugger is sentenced to death, Ulrich and the rest of society are able to push him and what he represents back into the subconscious. Nonetheless, Moosbrugger, whose story is interspersed throughout the novel, plays a vital part in *Qualities*, where the sickness of a society is not an end but rather a path to healing a civilization (Payne 1988: 114). With the Moosbrugger question, Musil presents modern society with the problematic impasse between free will and responsibility, which essentially leaves us trapped in the moral space of Frankenstein—caught between causation and chance. Philip Payne claims in his study of Musil that through Moosbrugger, the author addresses the question of whether freedom is an illusion or not. Payne argues that Musil does in fact acknowledge the verity of free will as something containing "both fact and mystery" (1988: 131). However, Moosbrugger is also a product of his environment, an allegory of 'society's collective dream,' which 'suffers from the same unresolved tensions between fragmentation and unity' (Piser 2010: 10). It is because of this uncanny representation of society that the media and citizens of Vienna overstate the monstrousness of Moosbrugger in order to portray him 'as the ultimate other' (ibid.) rather than seeing him as the uncanny other. Musil uses the Moosbrugger affair as a symbol of the fascination with violence and chaos that turn-of-the-century Vienna, and as an extension Europe, was engulfed in.

WWI did little to weaken society's unconscious desire for or interest in violence. Depictions in art and cinema, especially in Germany, became much more violent in postwar Europe, not just with Expressionist painters like Beckmann and his contemporary Otto Dix, but also with new film directors. Along with his famous silent dystopian film *Metropolis*, Lang's thriller *M* (1931/2004) stands out as one of the filmmaker's greatest achievements. Written by his wife Thea von Harbou, *M* is a film about a serial killer who preys on little children and whose terror stretches across the streets of Berlin, its homes, the police department, and even the criminal underworld. Lang, who was greatly influenced by the Expressionist paintings of the modern city, channels the same sensations of fear, violence, and city space on to the screen.[5] For most of the film, the pathological killer is visible only as a shadow, a haunting spectre bringing fear to the city streets, able to strike at any moment. Lang's technique of not showing the killer dislocates the shadow from the rest of humanity, though when his physical form is finally revealed, he is no longer the monstrous entity from the beginning of the film, but simply a sick, pathetic, scared human being. In actuality, this becomes a far more monstrous scene, as Lang removes the illusion of the supernatural other and reveals that the evil plaguing the city is simply a normal person. Moreover, it points to the metropolis as a liminal space between human and inhuman, between connectivity and the ability to be dehumanized within the chaotic crowd. Musil and Lang's killers share a liminal strangeness. Both characters experience a fracturing of their identification with both society and himself. Moosbrugger's inability to differentiate between external and internal reality (Jonsson 1996: 52) is similar to society's inability to identify him as either victim or monster, sane or insane. This same ambiguity shows up at the end of *M*, shortly after Lang transforms his killer from a spectre into a human. Unlike Moosbrugger, whose crime only came to light for society after he had been arrested, Lang's serial killer Beckert is not a 'monster' locked away, whose situation can be intellectually pondered or fetishized; rather, Beckert is a prevailing problem in the streets of Berlin, where the uncanny fear and violence he represents cannot be repressed in a cage. Lang reveals the killer's name quite early in the film, yet the name Hans Beckert still lacks any concrete identity or any tangible relationship with the shadow that haunts Berlin. Through most of the film, Beckert's identity, for both him and society, is tied to the haunting spectre and not the tangible person.

The physical Beckert is even dislocated from the shadow itself, to a point where the shadow haunts the killer: 'It's there all the time, driving me out to wander the streets, following me, silently, but I can feel it there. It's me, pursuing myself. I want to escape, to escape from myself! But it's impossible' (Lang 1931: 01:42:55–01:43:25). Lang depicts the serial killer not necessarily as an evil other, perpetrating violence on the good citizens of the city, but rather as an illness, a disease of modernity that exists within society. Like Moosbrugger, Beckert portrays himself as both victim and perpetrator. His defense is that he is as much a victim of the spectre as of the rest of society: 'I can't help myself! I have no control over this evil thing that's inside of me, the fire, the voices, the torment! ... Who knows what it's like to be me?' (ibid. 01:42:25–01:44:33). Maria Tartar has stated that by the film's end, Beckert transforms from a 'cold-blooded murderer to abject victim' (1995: 161). Alternatively, Stephen Brockmann argues in *A Critical History of German Film* that Lang makes it difficult to completely sympathize with Beckert, or with either the criminal underworld or the police, who exercise their own rational sense of judgment, leaving 'its viewers profoundly unsettled with no easy answers' (2010: 126). Brockmann presents a strong argument in that Lang makes it quite equivocal, since it is never revealed, as to whether any 'capital punishment, imprisonment, or institutionalization in a psychiatric ward' is the best sentence as a means of attaining justice, especially since none of the choices are able to erase any of the crimes committed (ibid.). Moreover, like Moosbrugger, Beckert is the uncanny representation of his society, and therefore unable to be truly judged by a society that is both fascinated by and responsible for him. The ending of *M* is terrifying and unnerving because it leaves both the individual and society once again in a liminal state, with no one to turn to, no real sense of order or judgment to cling to. 'Who knows what it's like to be me?' becomes the mantra that can epitomize all of modernity.

Sickness and Irony: Zeno's Ironic Utopia

With its illusions cast off, the world after 1918 faced a grim reality. Yet out of this chaos, new forms of utopia still managed to foster hope in the modern era by paradoxically diving into its terror rather than ignoring it. Chaos-turned-utopia, or at least the hope of it, continues secularized modernity's act of resacralization, between what is said and unsaid. The restoration of irony leads a utopian viewpoint that essentially rises from the ashes of violence, and also one based on the internal darkness of the modern stranger. The returning soldiers of the Expressionist movement began a paradoxical messianic drive that was biopolitical but strictly formed through an internal void. However, this resacralizing messianic spirit was not just a characteristic of the Expressionist art movement. Lisa Marie Anderson uses the term *Expressionist Messianism* to build upon the study of expressionism and the messianic (Sokel 1959; Vietta

& Kemper 1997) by arguing that the messianic spirit is not simply found in a branch of Expressionism, but is actually a representation of Expressionism in its entirety, and more importantly, also a configuration of the modern age but a representation of all of Expressionism.[6] For her, the "reconstruction of Jewish and Christian Messianic is a part of all modernism" and that 'Expressionism as a whole demonstrates one configuration of messianism in the modern era' (Anderson 2011: 10–11). I agree with Anderson's comprehensive definition of the messianic which I have attempted to outline in this work, in that messianism 'is not always characterized by an outward turn to the socio-political, but sometimes involves the process strictly internal to he artist or human being' and that it signifies, 'a particular constellation within the Modernist reworkings of the sacred' (ibid. 11). As with the modern stranger, post-WWI messianism in particular operates in an internal/external paradox of self and other, between the spiritual becoming of the individual and the world at large.

The postwar Expressionists quickly located themselves and their mission in the city, for the 'sickness, crime and sin' (ibid. 168) that the city shared with the war allowed for a space that embodied the struggles they had experienced on the front. The anti-bourgeois and metropolitan fascination seemed to once again give the modern stranger the early urban spark that was originally unearthed in *The Flowers of Evil*. Returning from the war, Beckmann channelled the creative spirit he had expected to gain from the war back into the modern city streets—streets that symbolically spawned modernity's violence. In the spirit of Baudelaire, Beckmann argued that the rightful place of the artist is in the city and its crowds:

> But right now, perhaps more than before the war, I need to be with people. In the city. That is just where we belong these days. We must be a part of all the misery that's coming. We have to surrender our heart and our nerves, we must abandon ourselves to the horrible cries of pain of a deluded people. Right now we have to get as close to the people as possible. It's the only course of action that might give some purpose to our superfluous and selfish existence—that we give people a picture of their fate. And we can only do that if we love humanity.
>
> Actually it's stupid to love humanity, nothing but a heap of egoism (and we are a part of it too). But I love it anyway. I love its meanness, its banality, its dullness, its cheap contentment, and its oh-so-very-rare heroism. But in spite of this, every single person is a unique event, as if he had just fallen from Orion (1997: 184).

In this passage, Beckmann admits to the inanity of hope in a world of nothingness, but he nonetheless still opts for choosing to see its beauty and sacredness through an ironic perspective. The contradictory axioms of WWI, such as "the Great War" and "The War to End All Wars," allowed for effortless ironic criticism from many postwar writers and artists who had fought in the trenches.

The anti-modern element of modernity could no longer be suppressed, allowing for an intensification of modernity's "waste," namely ambivalence and chaos (Bauman 1991). As Fussell states, '[t]he irony which memory associates with the events, little as well as great, of the First World War has become an inseparable element of the general vision of war in our time' (1975: 33). Irony was one of the few possible ways for soldiers to cope with or protect themselves from the meaninglessness of modern warfare, and also an outlet to critique the violence engrained in liminal modernity.

In Italo Svevo's third and final novel *La coscienza di Zeno* (1923/2015) (*Zeno's Conscience*) (2000), the author constructs an ironic position encompassing themes of identity, sickness, science, and progress through the eyes of an elderly stranger reminiscing about his past life and experiences. Svevo, a 'master ironist' (Moloney 1972: 311), produces a protagonist in Zeno Cosini who represents a modern twist on, or ironic use of, Stoic philosophy. Reflection and meditation are seen through a lens of the psychoanalytic practice of free association, resulting in an ironic conclusion that is both a positive and negative assessment of modern science. There is an insurmountable division for Svevo, between his partiality towards 'depth psychology' and the psychoanalytic principle of curing disorders (ibid. 312). Through his own introspection, Zeno's irony comes to its most devastating yet utopian conclusion in the closing of the book, when he imagines a superbomb exploding at the centre of the earth. Besides foreshadowing events that would take place during the world's second "great" war, Zeno views the destruction of the world as the only possible way to remove the sickness from humanity:

> Forse traverso una catastrofe inaudita prodotta dagli ordigni ritornerem alla salute. Quando i gas velenosi non basteranno più, un uomo fatto come tutti gli altri, nel segreto di una stanza di questo mondo, inventerà un esplosivo incomparabile, in confronto al quale gli esplosivi attualmente esistent saranno considerati quali innocui giocattoli. Ed un altro uomo fatto anche lui come tutti gli altri, ma degli altri un po' più ammalato, ruberà tale esplosivo e s'arrampicherà al centro della terra per porlo nel punto ove il suo effetto potrà essere il massimo. Ci sarà un'esplosione enorme che nessuno udrà e la terra ritornata alla forma di nebulosa errerà nei cieli priva di parassiti e di malattie (Svevo 1923/2015: 480–481).

> (Perhaps, through an unheard-of catastrophe produced by devices, we will return to health. When poison gases no longer suffice, an ordinary man, in the secrecy of a room in this world, will invent an incomparable explosive, compared to which the explosives currently in existence will be considered harmless toys. And another man, also ordinary, but a bit sicker than others, will steal this explosive and will climb up to the center of the earth, to set it on the spot where it can have maximum

effect. There will be an enormous explosion that no one will hear, and the earth, once again a nebula, will wander through the heavens, freed of parasites and sickness) (2000: 436–437).

Zeno is not advocating a senseless destruction of the world, but in its inevitability sees the only way to free humanity from its inherent sickness, an apocalyptic remedy for a fractured, unsettled world. Living on the brink of WWI, Zeno affirms the material victory of not necessarily the weak, but of the 'the man with ambiguous qualities,' or as James Joyce's brother Stanislaus argues, a weakness that has nothing to do with ineptness but instead with a detached skepticism that allows for 'the obtuseness of critics' (cited in Lebowitz 1978: 208). After gaining self-consciousness of his "weaknesses," Zeno begins to understand where truth and strength truly lie for him. Brian Moloney argues that Zeno's irony exists within his own self-deception, for like many moderns, 'Zeno has to pay a price for his hope: that price is self-deception … It may well be that we have no freedom, that our behaviour patterns are predetermined, but it may well be too that our illusions are our protective devices' (1972: 318). Throughout the novel, Zeno is able to build and simultaneously cast off his own illusions with his use of irony, which allows him to make sense of the absurd world surrounding him.

Throughout his confessions, we see that Zeno's ironic disposition towards himself is a result of his placing a sort of perfection on certain people around him, which leads him to both inaction and a lack of responsibility. His '[s]elf-deprecating Irony is designed to exculpate him, by making him appear to be the buffoon or blunderer who has in no way been responsible for what has happened, the perpetual victim either of circumstances or his own good intentions' (ibid. 312). However, as he grows older, Zeno is able to realize that all the people in his life that he thought to be stronger or better than him were actually just as weak or strange. Once he is able to see the sickness in that image, he starts to feel more comfortable within his own self. Zeno now begins to realize that the perfect image of health he has sought his whole life has been merely an illusion based on utilitarian and rationalist ideas about progress. In contrast to a world built upon specialization, Zeno's inability to be interested in one idea or profession alienates him from family and society. As with Musil's Ulrich, his 'openness to all perspectives creates the potential for moral ambiguity' (SE Ziolkowski 2010: 94), which leads to a metaphor of humanity where sickness exists at every position:

> ad un capo della quale sta la malattia di Basedow che implica il generosissimo, folle consumo della forza vitale ad un ritmo precipitoso, il battito di un cuore sfrenato, e all'altro stanno gli organismi immiseriti per avarizia organica, destinati a perire di una malattia che sembrerebbe di esaurimento ed è invece di poltronaggine. Il giusto medio fra le due

malattie si trova al centro e viene designato impropriamente come la salute che non che una sosta. E fra il centro ed un'estremità – quella di Basedow – stanno tutti coloro ch'esasperano e consumano la vita in grandi desiderii. ambizioni, godimenti e anche lavoro, dall'altra quelli che non gettano sul piatto della vita che delle briciole e risparmiano preparando quegli abietti longevi che appariscono quale un peso per la società. Pare che questo peso sia anch'esso necessario. La società procede perché i Basedowiani la sospingono, e non precipita perché gli altri la trattengono. Io sono convinto che volendo costruire una società, si poteva farlo più semplicemente, ma è fatta così, col gozzo ad uno dei suoi capi e l'edema all'altro, e non c'è rimedio. In mezzo stanno coloro che hanno incipiente o gozzo o edema e su tutta la linea, in tutta l'umanità, la salute assoluta manca (Svevo 1923/2015: 358).

(At one end is Basedow's disease, which implies the generous, mad consumption of vital force at a precipitous pace, the pounding of an uncurbed heart. At the other end are the organisms depressed through organic avarice, destined to die of a disease that would appear to be exhaustion but which is, on the contrary, sloth. The golden mean between the two diseases is found in the center and is improperly defined as health, which is only a way station. And between the center and one extreme—the Basedow one—are all those who exacerbate and consume life in great desires, ambitions, pleasures, and also work; along the other half of the line, those who, on the scales of life, throw only crumbs and save, becoming those long-lived wretches who seem to burden on society. It seems this burden, too, is necessary. Society proceeds because the Basedowians push it, and it doesn't crash because the others hold it back. I am convinced that anyone wishing to construct a society could do so more simply, but this is the way it's been made, with goiter at one end and edema at the other, and there's no help for it. In the middle are those who have either incipient goiter or incipient edema, and along the entire line, in all mankind, absolute heath is missing) (2000: 316).

As critics have argued (Saccone 1973: 66; Minghelli 2002: 196), *Zeno's Conscience* is a novel about the sickness and disease found in modernity. In the previous quote, Zeno's dream sees humanity being pulled between two extreme diseases. On one side there is what Zeno regards as the Basedowians, who push society towards a future of technology and science, while its religious and conservative counterpart pulls it back in order to keep things from collapsing. Not only does sickness reside in both extremes, but also in a life of the stranger living betwixt and between them, making sickness exist 'along the entire line,' and therefore removing the notion of perfect health for all of humanity. Therefore, strangerness is still a type of sickness for Zeno, but is also something unique that allows him to distinguish and understand the absurdities and illness of modern society, rather than being unaware of them. If initially Zeno was a stranger because he rejected the values and ideas that were conjured in the modern world, which made him subjectively sick, he nonetheless continues to remain a stranger by not only accepting this sickness, but also taking pleasure in it.

Zeno refuses to define life as strictly progressive, and instead describes it as something in constant motion. In order to appreciate it, one must be in constant motion oneself: 'Già credo che in qualunque punto dell'universo ci si stabilisca si finisce coll'inquinarsi. Bisogna moversi. La vita ha dei veleni, ma poi anche degli altri veleni che servono di contravveleni. Solo correndo si può sottrarsi ai primi e giovarsi degli altri' (Svevo 1923/2015: 359) ('I already believe that at any point of the universe where you are settled, you end up being infected. You have to keep moving. Life has poisons, but also some other poisons that serve as antidotes. Only by running can you elude the former and take advantage of the latter') (2000: 317). Zeno's deluded and self-conscious world ends up being a microcosm of the world that surrounds him, and comes to recognize that humanity can only conquer the world by conquering itself. He comes to this conclusion once he is able to conquer, or at least understand, his own fears and sicknesses as well as those that reflect the characteristics of a world he once deemed strong. The novel's final chapter sees Zeno connect the inner and outer worlds through the outbreak of World War I, as the absurdity of humanity now crashes against the absurdity of his own world. The only antidote for this poisonous world, outside of its pure annihilation, is paradoxically found within, as other poisons, such as self-consciousness, allow the individual to explore the beauty and originality of life. As with Beckmann turning violence, demons, and nightmares into captivating works of art that question the modern world's thirst for violence, the poisons and diseases of modernity ironically become moments of resacralization for Zeno, and a possible means of allowing oneself to transcend those same poisons. In the early 20th century, irony acts as a replacement for spirituality and sacredness in secularized modernity, based on the analogous character of divine God-like language and irony (Berg 2014: 54; Booth 1983: 737). As with the clouds in Baudelaire's "The Stranger" that show us what is absent or lacking in the present world, this ironic spirit allows us to imagine a better future by trying to fill in what is absent and wrong in modern society. As with Zeno's Basedowian utopia, Blochian utopia begins in the darkness and must manifest internally, within the individual, beginning as something spiritual and subjective before it is able to spread across the collective.

However, creating a utopian vision based on the ephemeral, fragmented aspects of the modern stranger and an ironic use of despair can be problematic. Even though Bloch's view is not a cynical one, if despair is necessary in realizing hope and a spirit or vision of utopia, then a utopian world will always be paradoxical, since it must continuously be flawed. How can we achieve the best possible world when we are reliant on not just a flawed world that lacks something, but also one that needs to reach total darkness and desolation in order for us to see it? A continuous process of the utopian spirit must consist of a state of despair, and as a result, motion can paradoxically become stagnation. An ironic utopian vision based on the gaze of the modern stranger—transitory, ironic, even malicious—may have saved the utopian spirit for the modern age, but nonetheless can lead to questions that recognize it as ultimately self-defeating. What does this alternative, modern notion of utopia say about the violent ways one will use to engage with it in order to realize one's imaginings? This problematic tension may have been why Baudelaire, Leopardi, Beckmann, and Svevo (through Zeno) distanced themselves from ever coming to terms with utopian progress. In the poem the "L'Albatros" ("Albatross"), Baudelaire captures the essence of what he felt utopian ideals amount to. Whereas the albatross flies powerfully and gracefully in the sky, on land, in the space of lived experience, it transforms into an awkward, clumsy animal easily susceptible to human violence.

Divine Violence & Messianic Time in Miller's *Leibowitz*

The relationships between the violence and utopia became so strong that after witnessing the atrocities of WWII, Karl Popper (1950) ultimately declared the two inseparable. However, if modern society cannot remove violence from its existence, is it truly wrong to attempt a resacralization of it? In consideration of Maurice Bloch's notion of rebounding violence, the outsider not only consumes the world left behind but also expends the liminal violence of the rite of passage. Bloch's theory of violence creates a journey that is more cyclical than linear. It is at this stage of rebounding violence that Bloch argues the religious turns into the political, and the individual must recognize the collective and the other (1992: 6). It is 'symbolism of rebounding violence, which at bottom is concerned with the universal social, political, intellectual and emotional problem of human fluidity' (ibid. 98).

Although Bloch's study focuses on the religious ritual outside of modern Western culture, his theory can be applied to secularized modernity and the process of resacralization, especially as he claims that this idea of rebounding violence is 'quasi-universal' (ibid. 1), since it attempts to solve the intrinsic impasse of the human condition, which is 'how human beings can be the constituent elements of permanent institutional structures' (ibid. 19). For Maurice Bloch, the idea of rebounding violence allows the human to become political. These ruminations on a form of violence that remains with the individual allow them a transformed vivacity, because the second stage of violence becomes something external. This notion of the other differentiates the first violent stage from that of the second in a rite of passage, in that the second stage includes an 'alien' or 'external' validity. The rebounding violence manifests after the ritual is completed either as 'symbolic construction of a permanent order,' outwardly as a military conquest, or, finally, culturally inwards towards people of a lower class (ibid. 81). According to Bloch, the individual therefore retains a spiritual and violent facet of the past, and in turn creates new ones during the violent liminal phase. Therefore, the question arises: how do we extrapolate this "intrinsic" violence to everyday life? These biopolitical and spiritual elements of violence become the core of messianic time and of the problematic dilemma of divine versus mythic violence. The messianic drive of modernity may well be why Paul de Man characterized modernity as being obsessed with 'radical renewal' and 'new beginnings' (1971: 150, 152). This obsession could potentially lead to a predicament that holds humanity in a perpetual state of negative liminality, a series of cyclical violence filled with destruction and rebirth, and apocalyptic repetition. In contrast, Agamben, paraphrasing Gianni Carchia, argues that messianic time cannot be apocalyptic since the 'messianic is not the end of time, but *the time of the end* ... the time that remains between time and its end' (Agamben 2005: 62; Carchia 2000: 144). Here, Agamben incorrectly argues that '[t]he apocalyptic is situated on the last day,' because the apocalyptic can likewise be viewed the same way that Agamben views messianic time, as "the time that remains between time and its end" (ibid.).

In *A Canticle for Leibowitz*, Miller blurs the lines between messianic and apocalyptic time, while divine violence can be seen as either remaining in its ambiguous state or not existing at all. Situated in an environment of a post-apocalyptic world, *Canticle* focuses on the Abbey of Saint Leibowitz, which duplicates and archives the scientific and cultural knowledge of the pre-apocalyptic 20th century, hoping that humanity can once again learn and progress through experience and knowledge. What makes Miller's apocalyptic/post-apocalyptic work so distinctive is that the novel is separated into three new yet familiar epochs, each spanning 600 years: *Fiat Homo* (Medieval/Dark Ages), *Fiat Lux* (Renaissance/Enlightenment), *Fiat Voluntas Tua* (Industrial Age/Modernity). The book ends with a new apocalypse that represents either the messianic coming through an act of divine violence or the continuous apocalyptic cycle of destruction and rebirth with no end in sight. Similar to that of Benjamin and Agamben, Miller's messianic time exists in conjunction with the empty, homogeneous time that waits to manifest itself. This is shown through the character of the nomadic Jewish wanderer, whom Miller alludes to as living through all three epochs, only under different names. Although it is never stated that it is the same man throughout the whole novel, all three men look familiar and seemingly know information from past epochs that would otherwise be impossible to know. Moreover, in the second epoch, this wandering nomad regards himself as immortal and is seemingly waiting for the messiah.[7] Living in secular time, the wanderer waits for the messianic moment to uncannily manifest as either disastrous or illuminating, to either continue the cycle or break it. As Ralph C. Wood explains, *Canticle* 'is not apocalyptic merely because it concerns the final culmination of things in an atomic holocaust. Rather it is an *apocalypsis* in the literal sense: an "unveiling," a revelation of the deeply destructive urges at work in late modern life,' which is able to 'unveil and bring to light what is otherwise hidden—not only the causes of our culture's deep self-destructiveness but also its cure' (2001: 27, 29).

The novel's open ending leaves us with two possibilities of hope: the first comes from the monastery leaving the planet before the end of the world with all the knowledge it has accumulated in the last thousand years or so. This action offers a glimmer of hope as humanity looks to re-establish itself far away from earth, in an attempt to break the apocalyptic cycle. However, humanity's escape from this planet in search of another does not allow humanity to escape from itself. With the monastery bringing with it all the knowledge that arguably led to its destruction, what makes this attempt to escape the cycle any different than previous ones? As the Abbot Zerchi asks God/himself: 'Listen, are we helpless? Are we doomed to do it again and again and again? Have we no choice but to play the Phoenix in an unending sequence of rise and fall? Assyria, Babylon, Egypt, Greece, Carthage, Rome, the Empires of Charlemagne and the Turk ... *Are we doomed to it, Lord, chained to the pendulum of our own mad clockwork, helpless to halt its swing?*' (Miller 2007: 266–267). This possibility of escape does not exclude the disillusionment that may come with the failure of realizing the messianic moment. After WWI, the Expressionists' understanding of violence as a sense of renewal, faith, and hope quickly faded to disillusionment, which essentially ended their messianic vision and the movement itself (Anderson 2011: 176–177). Somewhat similarly, Futurism's love of the artificial came to its ironic apex when the pre-war ideology of man over machine changed into a divination of machine under fascism. Hollow, artificial Catholic messianic symbols were secularized into Futurist art under fascism, and as a result, destroyed its original ideology, while its revolutionary movement of speed slowed under its political alignments (Poggi 2009: 244–245). The notion of waiting for a messianic moment in time, or forcing it through a confusing notion of divine violence, has recently led Žižek to give us a sobering message: 'This, perhaps, is the most depressing lesson of horror and suffering: there is nothing to be learned from it. The only way out of the vicious circle of this depression is to change the terrain towards concrete social and economic analysis' (2016: 42). Redemptive violence is a myth based on artificially constructed binaries of good and evil, and instead increases violence through the amplification and exchange of irrational fears.

The novel's second messianic possibility exists in the character of Rachel. Rachel is the conjoined dead twin of the poor tomato farmer Mrs. Grales, who constantly seeks Rachel's baptism--something Abbott Zerchi is hesitant to perform. During the climactic new apocalypse, Mrs. Grales' death becomes the birth of Rachel, who exhibits a new childlike personality upon reanimation. Ironically, the radiation that will eventually eliminate humanity is what brings Rachel to life, giving her a transcendent, divine, and eternal quality. Rachel becomes a particularly symbolic representation of the modern stranger or even *homo sacer*, for she is beyond human, both pure and impure, neither dead nor living: 'Who, then, was Rachel? And What?' (Miller 2007: 334). Rachel, animated from the nuclear fallout, is born of the darkness and violence of our world, but becomes a true messianic figure when she rejects Zerchi's baptism. She requires neither the old world's religion nor its scientific discovery. Even when she gives the Eucharist to Abbott Zerchi, it is for his salvation rather than hers; as a result, she breaks away from the previous cyclical world. 'As a creature neither conceived in sin nor having had any occasion for sin' (Wood 2001: 40), Rachel represents 'a promise of resurrection' (Miller 2007: 336), a messianic figure that is a 'dispenser rather than a receiver of grace' (Wood 2001: 40). Miller seems to be reversing Bloch's spirit of utopia in that society's collective violence and darkness are manifested within the individual rather than the other way around. *Canticle*'s ending still leaves us with an uncanny monster created from scientific destruction and violence, although one born of the 'Immaculate Conception' (Miller 2007: 279) and is removed from the original sin of the society that created her, allowing us a new form of hope. Rachel therefore becomes the new uncanny creature without having to deal with the patriarchal, imposing, and detrimental figure of a Frankenstein, and at least at some level she is free to cultivate herself on the liminal world that is made up of the ruins of the past but is also on renewed ground.

The book must end there for the utopian character to exist. Just like Musil's *Man Without Qualities*, which has critics divided on whether a finished novel would have produced a utopian vision of a different outcome to history or simply ended in the historical failure of WWI (Grill 2012: 162), *Canticle* ends in liminality, with an ambiguous, sideshadowing possibility rather than having an either/or utopian or anti-utopian vision. By sitting between the said and unsaid, Miller gives humanity the free will to ultimately choose for itself. Through the monster/spectre Rachel who ends the novel standing over the ashes of a failed world, Miller ultimately leaves us with the ironic hope of transcending the past through the "monstrous," though still acknowledging that humans may well choose a cyclical repetition of violence and monstrosity. De Man is correct in diagnosing modernity's obsession with new beginnings, even violent ones; yet in a liminal and fragmented world of conflicting perspectives and moral ambiguities, it seems that the two are inseparable. Reminiscent of Baudelaire's albatross, Musil's Ulrich aptly argues, 'Roheit und Liebe nicht weiter von einander entfernt seien als der eine Flügel eines großen bunten stummen Vogels vom ändern' (1967: 29) ('brutality and love are no farther apart than one wing of a big, colorful, silent bird is from the other') (1995: 25).

As we have seen, the stranger is often associated with dread, violence, and a fear of the unknown, frequently represented by a shadowy figure lurking in alleyways, the dark corners of city streets, and our unconscious imagination. Yet the modern stranger more often than not offers us an ironic, paradoxical perspective that challenges the violence of modernity through a counter or 'rehearsal of violence' that 'opens up a space for the critique and resignification of accepted cultural practices' (Sanyal 2006: 30). The modern stranger's use of irony as a counterviolence to violence itself allows us to expose modernity's violent tendencies through self-reflectivity, both internal and societal, creating a liminal space of violence and nonviolence, of action and inaction.

Notes: Chapter III

[1] 'Irony is healthiness insofar as it rescues the soul from the snares of relativity; it is a sickness insofar as it cannot bear the absolute except in the form of nothing, but this sickness is an endemic disease that only a few individuals catch and from which fewer Recover' (Kierkegaard 1841/1989: 77–78).

[2] The description of the painting in the book *The Great Parade* argues that '[h]ere the prophet is revealed as buffoon, the guide as martyr. Beckmann's image of himself as clown is presented in a pose borrowed from gothic renderings of the mocking of Christ ... for reality is impervious to utopianism; the artist is condemned to be the ephemeral dissipater in his own inexorable ennui' (Clair 2004: 112).

[3] The postwar consciousness of the novel was missed by many critics, which ultimately led Remarque to write a sequel *Der Weg zurück* (*The Road Back*) (1931) that clearly addressed the sentiment of "the lost generation" (Eksteins 1989: 283).

[4] I am evoking James Donald's notion of feeling the city that he explores in *Imagining the Modern City*. For him, the city does not consist of the objective/subjective binaries. He rather sees it far more 'abstractly conceptual and intensely personal,' something that links all cities together: '[i]t is *the* city, not *a* city' (1999: x). This, along with Donald's interesting view of city exploration, is similar to the morally ambiguous WWI solider caught in No Man's Land, where the experience of city dwelling is like the film *Moetsukita chizu* [*The Man Without a Map*] (1968). Based on Abe's novel of the same name [*The Ruined Map*] (1967/2011), the film follows a detective who cannot solve a case because he does not know what the case actually is anymore.

[5] The serial killer's first victim has the last name of Beckmann.

[6] In terms of Expressionism, Anderson follows the claim by expressionists such as Walter Rheiner (1919) and Iwan Goll (1921) that the movement is more of a worldview [weltanschauung] (Anderson 2011: 12) or a 'designation of an attitude (Gesinnung) rather than an artistic configuration' (ibid. 13).

[7] The character refers to himself as Lazarus, whom Jesus raised from the dead, and is also alluded to as the mythical figure of the wandering Jew, a Jewish man in medieval Christian folklore who is cursed by Jesus with immortality when he is unwilling to help Jesus carry the cross.

IV

Boredom – An Infinite Epilogue to the Modern Stranger

Boredom is an experience of modernity, of modern temporality.
　　　—Elizabeth Goodstein, *Experience Without Qualities:*
　　　　Boredom and Modernity

At first boredom drove me to despair, but then, as it increased instead of diminishing, habit little by little made it less frightening to me and more susceptible to patience. My patience with boredom finally became really heroic.
　　　—Giacomo Leopardi, *Zibaldone*

Boredom is the threshold to great deeds. —Now it would be important to know: What is the dialectical antithesis to boredom?
　　　—Walter Benjamin, *Passagen-Werk*

A utopia cannot, by definition, include boredom, but the 'utopia' we are living in is boring.
　　　—Lars Fr. H. Svendsen, *A Philosophy of Boredom*

Action films—predominantly 'characterized by propensity for spectacular action, a narrative structure involving fights, chases, and explosions, and in addition to the deployment of state-of-the-art special effects, an emphasis in performance on physical feats and stunts' (Neale 2000: 48)—have become a cornerstone of not just Hollywood but films across the world (Artz 2015: 196), usually dominating lists of the highest grossing films of the year. Action as a film genre is a relatively new phenomenon, evolving around the 1980s, when its entertainment factor was fixated typically on glorifying violence (Kendrick 2009: 83). Up until then, action was simply an umbrella term conveying 'a sense of movement, of velocity, of thrills' (ibid. 82), a fundamental element that is

---

How to cite this book chapter:
Beghetto, R. G. 2022. *Monstrous Liminality; Or, The Uncanny Strangers Of Secularized Modernity*. Pp. 103–122. London: Ubiquity Press. DOI: https: //doi.org/10.5334/bcp.e. License: CC-BY-NC

found in most, if not all, films (ibid. 83). Action, therefore, is a result of "something happening'" in a story; the more that something happens, the more the narrative is established, and the less boring we tend to find the film, novel, or show. Consequently, the more we tend to view movies as entertainment rather than art, as embarking on "a thrill ride," the more action we require from them. Yet in regard to the films of Michelangelo Antonioni, words such as "action," "adventure," and "violence" become radically different and take on new meaning. Ironically, these new meanings are intertwined with one of action's antitheses: boredom.

What is boredom? Answering this question is both important and challenging, since the word carries a lot of weight today; yet the description of boredom as a mood remains extremely vague. Its usage is heavily dependent on subjective feelings and opinions, notwithstanding its shifting definitions throughout time. Boredom's equivocal nature has been examined and debated by philosophers in some aspect or other for centuries. From Isocrates to Plutarch; from Pascal to Schopenhauer, Leopardi, Baudelaire, and Nietzsche; from Kierkegaard to Russell, to Heidegger, Sartre, Camus, and Eric Fromm, the topic has been endlessly debated yet never pinned down by any sort of clear designation. Despite the subject's apparent exhaustion, it has not diminished in contemporary discussions (Schneider 2016; Svendsen 2005; Toohey 2011), although one might ask if boredom is still a significant problem in our society. Is it even possible to be bored anymore, since socio-technological advancements have given us the opportunity to escape (or at least the illusion of escaping) boredom whenever possible? Asking such questions about boredom might be considered gratuitous compared to more troubling societal questions that we currently face; yet as I have established, especially in regard to the modern stranger, uncanny and liminal struggles that haunt us from the shadows may point to larger problems that exist in society. This chapter examines this "exhausted" concept that was touched upon while discussing Baudelaire and Leopardi in Chapter 2. There, I discussed how boredom (*ennui* and *noia*) for the two philosopher-poets is an intrinsic and melancholic characteristic of modernity itself. The world for them was an incessant theatre of dreams and illusions that played out as repetitious boredom bordering on tragedy. As argued by Baudelaire and Leopardi, boredom was not an ailment that could easily be cured or forgotten, but rather something that was entrenched in, even intrinsic to, the human spirit. It was a forever-present, recurring sense of consciousness that comes from both a desire to live and, as Luce Irigaray maintains, an impulse for death (1977/1985: 115). The connection between boredom and secularized modernity is apparent through the fact that it has been largely discussed in philosophy and literature since the advent of modernity; nonetheless, it would be imprudent to think it a mood that is restricted only to the modern age.

Instead of breaking boredom into categories or binaries, I am arguing that the modern age actually creates a more ambiguous and fragmented understanding of boredom—as an uncanny, liminal state of in-betweenness and displacement which, at the same time, shares the burden of being part of the encompassing and significant aspects that define secularized modernity. From postwar *ennui* to contemporary boredom, I shall confront this enigma by examining the films of Antonioni and the writings of contemporary American author Tao Lin. Antonioni's masterful existential "trilogy" of *L'Avventura* (1960), *La Notte* (1961), and *L'Eclisse* (1962), along with the appendage *Il Deserto Rosso* (*The Red Desert*) (1964), are connected not only through actress Monica Vitti but likewise through the examination of an alienated society located in a postwar Italy/Europe, where the lingering horrors of WWII were mixed with the "economic miracle," resulting in an apathetic hangover that underscored the contemplative triviality of secularized modernity and the difficulties of interconnecting with one another in said world.

Lin tackles the same themes of alienation and boredom. Although his novel *Taipei* (2013) partly takes place in the Taiwanese capital, Lin's stories are predominantly located in contemporary America and focus on a generation ingrained in a world where communication is dominated by social media and technology. Both artists assess similar themes that simultaneously express the various types of boredom and show how these tend to blend into one another, defining the modern experience of the stranger. Boring is never a positive attribute one would assign to a film or novel, yet both Antonioni and Lin force the reader and viewer into a state of boredom, to fully experience the sensation, and as a result, connect the audience and characters in innovate ways. Notwithstanding that both exclude any spiritual or transcendental aspects from their work, it is through this void or exclusion that they paradoxically move towards the threshold of sacredness. By adding the work of Sara Ahmed, I shall also discuss how mood and boredom in the 21st century are still tied to a tradition or spirit of the modern stranger, yet look to reimagine the figure for an ever-changing modernity.

The Difficult Task of Defining Boredom

One of the challenges of analyzing boredom stems from the fact that boredom, and any mood in general, is ambiguous and 'usually described as ambient, vague, diffuse, hazy, and intangible' feelings we tend to fall into, rather than obtain (Ahmed 2014: 13). In *A Philosophy of Boredom*, Lars Svendsen asserts that 'moods, generally speaking, are seldom intentional subjects as far as we are concerned—they are precisely something one finds oneself in, not something one consciously looks at'; this description is particularly true of boredom, which is a 'mood that is typified by a lack of quality that makes it more elusive than most other moods,' to the point where one might not even know one is actually bored or have any direct reason for feeling boredom (2005: 14). Ambiguity has not stopped individuals from trying to understand the different types of boredom they may encounter in life. One of the most famous, and often-cited, 20th-century theories of mood and boredom comes from Martin Heidegger's lecture-course *The Fundamental Concepts of Metaphysics*. Heidegger sees mood (*Stimmung*) as something defined by our attunement towards the world and 'not something merely at hand. They themselves are precisely a fundamental manner and fundamental way of being, indeed of being-there' (1995: 67). Heidegger also characterizes boredom's liminal nature by describing it as '*a silent fog in the abysses of Dasein*' (ibid. 77), although he does compartmentalize its ambiguous essence into three different forms, each becoming more "profound" or deeper. The first form of boredom Heidegger discusses occurs when an individual is bored *by something*, as in waiting for something, which is a type of boredom that depends on the spatiotemporal situation, and not the individual's place in the world. The second form arises when one is bored *with something*, and although this form is less intense than the first and may not be acknowledged by the individual at the time, it is more lasting and troubling because it is essentially about being bored with the ways of alleviating boredom. Lastly, and most importantly, is what Heidegger refers to as 'profound boredom,' a feeling of emptiness where all things are enveloped in indifference and seem to lose meaning. This form of boredom is immeasurable and endless and not confined to certain situations. Profound boredom is 'being held in limbo' and, unlike the other two, is the fundamental attunement of the modern age (ibid. 164). Boredom as indifference may seem to fall under what Heidegger categorizes as a lack of attunement; however, since 'we are never without an attunement,' a lack of attunement is still an attunement but one that is uncanny, since it 'remains concealed or hidden from us' but is nonetheless present (ibid. 68).

As Heidegger argues, boredom becomes a "telling refusal," in which a lack of possibilities enables an understanding that this non-attunement points to our very existence and also our own possibilities. Heidegger's concept of a "lack of attunement" is reasonably very ambiguous, since its basis is of a liminal understanding. Sara Ahmed defines Heidegger's lack, or non-attunement, as an experience of 'how we can be in a world with others where we are not in a responsive relation, where we do not tend to 'pick up' on how they feel' (2014: 18). Ahmed appropriately likens this vague attunement of 'not being in harmony' to that of the stranger in that '[s]trangers … appear at the edges of a room, dimly perceived, or not quite perceived, lurking in the shadows' (ibid.). The link between the two is prominent enough that one may even argue that without some sort of modern understanding of boredom as emptiness, the concept of the modern stranger, and modernity itself, could not even exist.

This does not mean that there was no understanding of an existential boredom until secularized modernity. Christianity, for example, understood *acedia*, a form of spiritual melancholy or apathy of the soul, as a significant problem of the Middle Ages. The sentiment reappears in modernity: Kierkegaard famously asserts that 'boredom is the root of all evil' (1987: 285), while Baudelaire refers to *acedia* as "the malady of Monks" (2006: 42). In mapping out a complicated history of boredom, Patricia Meyer Spacks, however, maintains that a delicate distinction exists between boredom and *ennui/acedia*. To begin with, Spacks states that the English word 'bore' did not exist until the late 17th century, while boredom was not widely used until the beginnings of 19th-century modernity (1996: 8). Spacks describes a continuing shift of boredom due to secularization and a collapse of the Christian worldview (ibid. 11), resulting in a 'change from a moralistic to a sociological view of boredom' (ibid. 21). Following Seán Desmond Healy's (1984) division of boredom into "simple" and "hyper," Spacks examines how boredom breaks away from the French *ennui* that had been used until then: 'Boredom,' according to Spacks, 'was not (is not) the same as ennui, more closely related to acedia. Ennui implies a judgment of the universe; boredom, a response to the immediate' (Spacks, 1996: 12). Spacks goes on to argue that '[e]nnui belongs to those with a sense of sublime potential, those who feel themselves superior to their environment ... If only because it seems more dignified, many people would rather suffer ennui than boredom, despite its presumably greater misery' (ibid.). Spacks' analysis is a crucial addition to the long history of work on boredom, yet her linguistic interpretation tends to eliminate the ambiguous nature of the word's meaning. Although useful, there is a problem when trying to compartmentalize boredom into various categories, because boredom operates in the realm of liminality. Seeing that words such as *ennui* and *noia* in their native languages (French and Italian, respectively) retain boredom's ambiguity and multifaceted definitions, it is difficult to preserve the 19th-century uses of the words boredom and *ennui* as the defining differences between them, since the meanings of these words alter depending on context. Explicitly separating boredom from *ennui* is also problematic, since it was also in the 19th century that Baudelaire reinvented the word *ennui* by connecting boredom with melancholy, thereby changing it into something far more existential than its meaning during the Middle Ages. Furthermore, since the word boredom is virtually the only word we presently use in the English language for the mood itself, could it not be argued that the word boredom has now gained the same liminality and ambiguity that *ennui* and *noia* retained in their native languages?

Nonetheless, these divisions—or lack thereof—in boredom are still continuously debated. In *Boredom: A Lively History*, Peter Toohey, working from Spacks and Healy, separates boredom into the binaries of simple and existential; however, the separation is actually a ruse, as he essentially argues that existential boredom is a myth of modern society, in that it is not really boredom at all but part of depression. Like Spacks, Toohey argues that for 19th- and 20th-century writers, existential boredom is "described as a kind of 'emptiness' resulting from the sufferer's seeing him- or herself as isolated from others," where "such individuals are living in a secularized world where religion no longer offers solace. They inhabit a fragmented and divided world where regional and even personal loyalties have been lost" (2011: 196). In contrast, Toohey claims that our current society is one in "which tradition and community have disappeared" (ibid.). Toohey deceptively solves the problem of ambiguity in boredom by shifting existential boredom into another ambiguous term—depression, though he fails to acknowledge any connection between the two.[1] Neither does Toohey examine any correlation between hopelessness, permanent liminality, and boredom (Szakolczai 2000; Thomassen 2016), and how these relate to secularized modernity. For instance, in *Liminality and the Modern: Living Through the In-Between*, Bjørn Thomassen claims that '[t]he incitation of constant and instant liminal experience that so characterizes cultural life in our contemporary period easily turns into nullifying boredom, senselessness and normative nihilism' (2016: 2). A more interesting re-examination of boredom comes from Sianne Ngai with her concept of 'stuplimity,' which she describes as 'a concatenation of boredom and astonishment—a bringing together of what "dulls" and what "irritates" or agitates; sharp, sudden excitation and prolonged desensitization, exhaustion, or fatigue' (2009: 271). According to Ngai, the paradoxical fusion of boredom and sublime 'holds opposing affects together' (ibid.), and although she does set up a binary, she nonetheless keeps boredom in a more ambiguous and liminal light. Keeping with the more recent examination of boredom, Ngai positions the shift in boredom as part of the secularization process of the modern age, in that it removes the sacred transcendence of the sublime in favour of repetition or 'a series of fatigues or minor exhaustions, rather than a single, major blow to the imagination' (ibid. 272).

The major separation between boredom and existential boredom seems to exist for many scholars—Ngai, Spacks, Toohey, as well as Elizabeth Goodstein—because it is a historically specific experience. Boredom is not exclusively a modern characteristic, but with the advent of secularized modernity it gains a shifting importance as it moves from a metaphysical problem to a psychological one, and from the individual to the masses. As Goodstein writes, it 'is not that boredom as such is the key to theorizing modernity, but rather the problems of theorizing boredom are the problems of theorizing modern experience more generally' (2005: 407). I do agree with these arguments; but due to boredom's liminal essence, and since the sacred can equally exist in the profane world, I do not necessarily believe that these occurrences result in a clear dislocation between boredom and *ennui*, or a total removal of the sacred, as Toohey and Ngai suggest. As Mladen Dolar argues of boredom's liminal companion, the uncanny, the sacred or spiritual aspects are not necessarily removed but instead distilled into profane existence, remaining hidden in society's shadows but not complexly absent. Either as a part of the spiritual or as a psychological understanding, sacredness has become a spectre with secularized modernity, or what Tillich (1965/1987) describes as "sacred emptiness" or the "sacred void." In a world where God is absent (nonexistent) and religious traditions and symbols have lost meaning, the resulting void or empty space defines our contemporary existence entrenched in *ennui*/boredom. Yet paradoxically, it is the same space where the sacred resacralizes into new ideas.

The (In)Action Films of Michelangelo Antonioni

In discussing Russian filmmaker Andrei Tarkovsky, philosopher Thorsten Botz-Bornstein describes the director's use of action in his films as 'no action,' or rather '[t]he kind of action that cannot be seen' (2007: 6). This uncanny form of action that Tarkovsky implemented was highly influenced by the works of Antonioni. Beginning with his 1960 breakthrough film *L'Avventura*, Antonioni deconstructed the concepts of both action and plot, marking a stylistic shift that better captured the psychological elements of modern *ennui* than his previous films had. This lack of plot and slow pacing in his films may estrange many viewers, but it is precisely why his films succeed in capturing the film's subject matter of alienation and boredom in a much more captivating and satisfying way. The dissolving of action into inaction is what constructs the action of the film.

As Seymour Chatman argues, anxiety in Antonioni's films 'occurs in visual details of plot, behavior, and composition so veiled and subtle that Antonioni risks making the audience impatient and bored' (1985: 66); however, by bringing the audience into the same physiological and emotional state as the characters, the more boring the film becomes, the more interesting it turns out to be. For example, *L'Avventura* is about the disappearance of a young woman named Anna during a Mediterranean boat trip with her lover Sandro, best friend Claudia, and a group of friends. While searching for the vanished woman, Sandro and Claudia become attracted to one another, yet at the same time, this "plot" has little to do with what the film is about; it is neither a murder-mystery nor really a romantic love story. This groundbreaking film lacks any real plot or focus, but instead is driven by the film's characters, their inner turmoil and relationships (or lack thereof). The "adventure" that the characters embark on is internal, 'an emotional adventure ... a physiological and moral adventure which makes them act different to the established conventions and criteria of a now outmoded world' (Antonioni in Chatman & Duncan 2004: 71). Action in Antonioni's films establishes revolutionary ideas through invisible and uncanny conduct; action is recognized through the characters' emotions in a modern age where people have become 'spiritually adrift' (Chatman & Duncan 2004: 71) and fearful of the 'moral unknown' (1963: Antonioni 33).

By distancing the film's meaning from narrative plot, and thereby dissolving the narrative itself, 'Antonioni's camera often lingers on *temps morts* or dead time, where the central element in the camera's focus is the light or the tone of objects,' and 'invites viewers to collaborate in the film's creation of meaning, which remains, however, far from arbitrary' (Carlorosi 2015: 61, 63). Doing so made Antonioni a master of deconstructing the MacGuffin, distinct from that of Alfred Hitchcock, who used objects as false plot motivators in order to establish the plot; Antonioni used the plot itself as a MacGuffin, thus undermining the narrative rather than using narrative to establish plot. In this regard, while greatly influenced by Hitchcock, Antonioni can also be seen as "anti-Hitchcock." Instead of using the MacGuffin to create suspense, Antonioni's use of it gradually removes any suspense from the film (Chatman & Duncan 2004: 75), leaving the audience to ponder an unsolved crime or wonder whether there was any crime to begin with. As *L'Avventura* progresses, Anna is slowly forgotten, and her disappearance becomes less important to both the characters and audience. This technique allows Antonioni to show the inner turmoil of human relationships as well as that of the self and other, not through dialogue or narration, but rather through the cinematic image and "inaction" between characters.

The inaction or slow movement of both plot and Antonioni's camera, what David Bordwell describes as 'dedramatization' (2005: 152), replicates the boredom and alienation of Antonioni's characters. Antonioni uses dedramatization to great effect, as the more 'boring' the film becomes, the more interesting the development of both his film and characters. Unlike contemporary Federico Fellini's *La Dolce Vita* (1960), which used the exhaustion of the spectacle to reach similar themes, Antonioni explores *ennui* through tediousness, as the more time passes with nothing happening, the more we feel connected to the characters' state of anxiety and alienation. It is no wonder Antonioni's work is shrouded in ambiguity. His characters lack traditional character development, but are used instead as cinematic devices latched onto their surrounding landscapes, allowing for symbolic expressions and explorations of the philosophical dilemmas and questions that humans endure within the confines of modernity. In *The Material Ghost: Films and Their Medium*, Gilberto Perez argues that '[p]lace rather than action, situation rather than event, is Antonioni's chief concern' (1998: 370). Even this form of symbolic alienation is hard to pin down in Antonioni's films, since it is done predominantly through landscapes that offer differing, often contradictory, interpretations. For example, the volcanic Island of Lisca Bianca—the setting for both Anna's disappearance near the beginning of the film and the image of Mount Etna that makes up the foreground of the film's final shot—bookends *L'Avventura* with landscapes that simultaneously reflect beauty, terror, infertile violence, and a sensuousness that exists within the human condition; though like the volcanoes themselves, these elements remain dormant or silent within us.

As stated, one of Spacks' defining distinctions between boredom and *ennui* is that boredom does not place any individuals above or superior to their environment. The deserted, lonely settings and landscapes in Antonioni's films mirror the characters' psyches, blurring the characters into the landscapes that surround them. Antonioni achieves this by using distant shots, giving us a dislocated, alienated 'stance of critical detachment' (Perez 1998: 90), thereby linking 'the idle periods of everyday banality' and the dehumanizing of both the characters and landscapes (Deleuze 1989: 5). Gilberto Perez brilliantly aligns Antonioni's camera with the perspective of the stranger:

> The paths of strangers in Antonioni, the paths of the stranger that is his camera, are an unsettling relativistic geometry mapping the space and time of modern life, a web of lines of orientation and disorientation that come together at unexpected meeting points and drift apart in directions unforeseen (1998: 382).

Describing the scene in Antonioni's *L'Eclisse* in which Monica Vitti's character Vittoria stares out of her window only for her gaze to come upon a stranger watching her from his window, Perez describes how all the strangers' gazes (Vittoria, the stranger watching her, the camera, and the audience) create 'the effect ... of our suddenly seeing ourselves as the world distantly sees us' (ibid. 379). This is taken to its limits at the end of the film, when all the humans completely disappear from the film's final shots, although the removal of characters does not necessarily diminish their presence. In *L'Avventura*, Anna's disappearance is foreshadowed while she is in the film, through her attitude. The little time she is on screen, Antonioni makes it evident that Anna is both emotionally and spiritually absent. We instantly see that Anna wishes to be alone and is bored with herself, her friends, and her relationship with Sandro. Anna even announces her '*noia*' with the whole trip and leaves to swim on her own (Antonioni 1960: 00:14:20). When everyone joins her, Anna lies about a shark swimming around, ending the fun. Although she states to Claudia that she does not know why she made up such a story, Anna's malaise suggests that she wishes for some kind of excitement, or possibly even death, to extinguish her anguish. The main thing that separates Anna from her friends is not necessarily her *ennui* but the fact she acknowledges and to some extent embraces it. Yet once Anna disappears, she becomes the film's spectre that haunts the rest of the cast, especially Sandro and Claudia.

In *Cinema 2: The Time-Image*, Deleuze argues that 'in *The Adventure* [*L'Avventura*], the vanished woman causes an indeterminable gaze to weigh on the couple—which gives them the continual feeling of being spied on, and which explains the lack of co-ordination of their objective movements, when they flee whilst pretending to look for her' (1985/1989: 8). However, Anna haunts the others through her *ennui* and existential boredom, which infects both Sandro and Claudia, who appeared cheerful prior to her disappearance before slowly becoming alienated and bored with modern life and its relationships.

Paradoxically, by fading his characters into their environments, Antonioni dislocates the viewer from the same environment or space. Even if boredom is a 'response to the immediate,' as Spacks (1996: 12) claims, in film and literature artists still tend to place their characters above the environment

(Lundin 2014: 240, n31). A paradoxical combination of Antonioni's dislocation and absorption leads us back to a connection with *ennui*, where the individual is part of both the immediate and the infinite, placing humanity in an interior/exterior state of a liminal environment. This is especially evident in *Red Desert*, a film whose landscapes are dominated by grand images of industrialization and technology, a symbolic image of human achievement and modernity conquering nature. The factories represent the world that has absorbed the characters, but it is also a world that signifies humanity's ability to produce their own environments: 'I think the complex horizon filled with factories is much more beautiful, even esthetically, than the uniform green line of the pine forest. Because behind the factories, you sense the presence of human beings. They're alive' (Antonioni 1964: 00:03:38–00:03:57). Antonioni now points to a world where the sublime has been technologized and produced by humanity instead of by God/Nature. Antonioni's changing landscapes juxtapose humanity's natural and artificial characters, symbolizing both what we cannot escape and what we can modify within ourselves.

Antonioni's films may dwell on the theme of a sacred void within a modern technologizing world,[2] but he does not place blame on technological progress. Antonioni's themes of boredom and alienation are reflections of our ambiguous and liminal world, in which a nostalgic view of tradition and the past collides with optimism for the future, leaving us with the inability for action and communication. In a statement released during Cannes in 1960, Antonioni argued that

> we make use of an aging morality, of outworn myths, of ancient conventions. And we do this in full consciousness of what we are doing. Why do we respect such a morality? The conclusion which my characters reach is not that of moral anarchy. They arrive, at best, at a sort of reciprocal pity. That too, you will tell me, is old. But what else is there left to us? (Antonioni 1963: 144).

For Antonioni, the temporal-liminal enigma of secularized modernity has resulted in the inability for people to properly communicate with one another, and has become a catalyst for alienation and boredom. The result is an indication of the frailty of modern love, one of secularized modernity's last standing habitats of secularized sacredness. The fleeting moments of connection in *L'Avventura* and *L'Eclisse* may ostensibly point to a difficulty or even inability to achieve modern love and communication for extended periods of time, leaving us with a sense of 'solipsism' (Brunette 1998: 47), where the 'failures of human connection emphasize the death impulse found in boredom' (Paliwoda 2010: 166). Although the genuine connection between the two modern strangers Giuliana and Corrado in *Red Desert* does in fact dispute this idea of solipsism as an explicit theme of Antonioni's films, and despite the fact both characters finally meet someone who may truly understand their strangerhood, this relationship does not lead to any form of sustainable happiness or love, since it is difficult for even a substantial connection in liminal space to solidify into promising or utopic resolutions.

Digital Boredom

Bertrand Russell commented in *The Conquest of Happiness* that '[w]e are less bored than our ancestors were, but we are more afraid of boredom. We have come to know, or rather to believe, that boredom is not part of the natural lot of man, but can be avoided by a sufficiently vigorous pursuit of excitement' (1930/2015: 37). Since Russell's statement, this fear of boredom has been exacerbated rather than alleviated, even leaving us with a fear of becoming bored by what we use to alleviate boredom, which may result in a transition from simple boredom into a profound, more existential boredom. This is the space in which the writings of Tao Lin are situated, with stories that carry the torch of the modern stranger living in *ennui*, in much the same vein as Antonioni did with his films. Despite using a different medium, Lin's work seems to continue and develop these lingering themes of boredom, unhappiness, and the hardships of communication. Lin links his contemporary generation to the early modernist existentialists of the 19th and 20th centuries. While the latter suffered from the boredom caused by an onslaught of the modernist spectacle, Lin's generation suffers from the *ennui* and meaninglessness that manifests itself in the bombardment and totalizing discourse of information. His themes rest on millennial boredom and laziness told through 'plotless,' detached narratives that can unquestionably result in a hypnotic and frustrating reading experience. In focusing on the boredom of daily activities, Lin's "Kmart realism" shadows Jean Paul Sartre's famous novel *Nausea* (1938/2007),[3] what many consider the cornerstone novel of existential sickness and boredom. Although Sartre's first novel is possibly a significant inspiration for Lin's work, Lin advances Sartre's novel by focusing on modern strangers rather than outsiders. Whereas Sartre's protagonist Antoine Roquentin is mainly a recluse in the mould of Fyodor Dostoevsky's Underground Man, someone who abhors the contact of others, Lin's characters are highly social beings, contemporary *flâneurs* who are engaged yet simultaneously feel removed from their physical and digital surroundings, which in many cases become hard to distinguish from one another. Due to its permanent liminal characteristics, cyberspace no longer has the ability to dislocate someone from the physical world, since being in a state of dislocation has become commonplace.

While Lin's early work, such as *Eeeee Eee Eeee* (2007), *Shoplifting from American Apparel* (2009), or his short story collection *Bed: Stories* (2007), showcase a promising talent in modern literature, his last novel *Taipei* (2013) establishes him as one of the great voices of contemporary America. *Taipei*, like most of Lin's writings, focuses on the current generation born into internet culture, social media, and smart phones, immersed in tools that, at least initially, cast away boredom at will. It also emphasizes the struggle for meaning in a modern age while containing the lingering discontent of generations past. Lin, however, shows how monotonous the alleviation of boredom can become, pointing to an uncanny unhappiness that we should no longer be feeling. As the main tool we use to hastily end boredom, and with our ability to access it at any place and time, the internet has led many of us to assume we have ended boredom, or at least reduced the amount of it we must endure (Mann 2017: 115). The characters he portrays constantly reaching for social media are never far away from the 'bored expression' (Lin 2013: 5, 8, 27, 29, 138, 157, 170) that dominates their emotions. Lin likens the world of social media to drug use, something that can alter reality and create excitement but can also lead us into a perpetual liminal state, back into boredom if overused; his characters live constantly in a drug- or social media–induced tedium.

The internet, or more specifically the language of social media, seamlessly blends into ordinary life as words such as 'unfriendable' (ibid. 15) jump between online and offline life. This interchange alters even what the novel's main protagonist Paul, who is strongly based on Lin himself, believes an intimate and physical relationship should be: something that is simply just around or "on" in the background, something always there and used but not necessarily something to fully engage with. Paul continuously associates his life and other humans with computers, compares the city lights to GIF files, and obsesses over a girl's Facebook page but never shows the same obsession with the physical girl herself. In Paul's internet life, conversations are to be stored and returned to later, or possibly never; all the while, he spends his day doing prescription drugs and 'refreshing Twitter, Tumblr, Facebook, Gmail in a continuous cycle—with an ongoing, affectless, humorless realization' (ibid. 76), thereby making the two lives indistinguishable. The internet easily blends into Paul's life and does not need to be extensively referred to, since it is always there. As Paul himself states, 'technology seemed more likely to permanently eliminate life by uncontrollably fulfilling its only function: to indiscriminately convert matter, animate or inanimate, into computerized matter, for the sole purpose, it seemed, of increased functioning, until the universe was one computer.' (ibid. 166–167). By being omnipresent but also 'an abstraction undetectable in concrete reality' (ibid. 167), technology, dominated by the internet, is able to subversively control one's perception or attitude towards life, without allowing for any sacred space. While floating in the background, virtually unseen, the internet is not something you necessarily need to activate, like the jacking in and out as described in William Gibson's cyberpunk novels. There is no action; there is no immersing yourself in it and then getting out.

Similarly, boredom assumes a liminal stance for Paul and his social group, in that its continuous presence makes it seem it is not even there; when it completely surrounds the individual, boredom becomes hard to acknowledge:

> Paul became aware of himself staring, "transfixed," at the center of the screen, with increasing intensity and no thoughts. He focused on resisting whatever force was preventing him from moving his head or neck or eyeballs until finally—suddenly, it seemed—he calmly turned his head a little and asked if Erin was bored.
> "I don't know. Are you?"
> "I can't tell," said Paul. "Are you?"
> "Maybe a little. Do you want to go?"
> "Yeah," said Paul, and slowly stood (ibid. 214).

Boredom also seems to be a result of too much information and a lack of mystery. Everything is out in the open in the lives of Paul and his friends; from his love life to his drug use, nothing is secretive; but unlike Frankenstein, who was horrified by learning the truth, Paul's group is simply bored. Paul and Erin may have a relationship of full disclosure, but in the end, they fail to communicate meaningfully and also lack a mysteriousness to be excited about; there is never anything they could learn from each other in the future of their relationship. And although total disclosure allows them to understand more about themselves and their future, as Brian Willems says of the novel, '[t]he enumeration of possible futures closes down future possibilities' (2015: 232). Echoing Leopardi, since the possibility of a better future is always in the cards, the present becomes worthless; as a result, so does the future, therefore keeping Paul in a continuous process of permanent liminality and boredom. However, as with Antonioni, Lin does not seem to portray social media (technology) as the cause of his generation's ills but rather more of a catalyst in understanding the void left by modern existence.

This critique does not come from an outsider, from an older individual who cannot understand modern technology. As it does with all modern strangers, the critique comes from within, from someone born into its world. This is the reason why boredom and even a breakdown of communication may be attributed to social media use; Lin does not shy away from showing us that Paul and Erin's "digital" relationship also flourishes in communication and creativity as much as it seems damaged by it. The problem comes from the fact that young people like Paul and Erin are not allowed to be bored; the fear of boredom forces them to constantly seek entertainment, which eventually leaves them exhausted by the very concept of constantly trying to entertain themselves. While seeing his reflection in his computer screen, Paul links humanity and technology together within a liminal space, as a place of both utopian possibility and the secular void:

> He minimized Safari and saw his face, which seemed bored and depressed, his default expression. He maximized Safari and imagined millions of windows, positioned to appear like one window. He

closed his eyes and thought of the backs of his eyelids as computer screens; both could display anything imaginable, so had infinite depth, but as physical surfaces were nearly depthless (Lin 2013: 170).

It is a profound boredom that allows Paul to witness a lack that in turn serves as a thirst for desire. Paradoxically, it also serves as knowledge that desire is perpetually unquenchable, thereby leaving Paul in a state of inaction and boredom. According to Ahmed in *The Promise of Happiness*, since '[h]appiness is an expectation of what follows' and '[t]he very expectation of happiness gives us a specific image of the future,' it actually 'provides the emotional setting for disappointment' (2010: 29), especially if we continually wait for happiness or continuously feel that the future is lost for us.

The fear of the future, of modern boredom's immortality (Goodstein 2005: 6), pulls Paul into the past, possibly in an attempt to find remnants of the sacred. His family's Taiwanese culture and his racial background are a part of—yet also detached from—his identity, since he is very much a modern American product. Lin seamlessly brings the modern stranger into his protagonist through a liminal interpretation of Paul's social, racial, and geographical character. Paul lives in a world where the traditional myths have fractured and crumbled but, as in Antonioni's films, remain as spectres to haunt us in the background. He is being pulled between the present/future of his current life of friends, drugs, and social media that defines his contemporary New York existence, and the cultural and traditional values of his parents, represented by Taipei. While these values do not directly speak to him, they nonetheless continuously preoccupy him. Paul is caught in a liminal sphere of past/future and tradition/advancement, where falling back into tradition paradoxically allows him the illusion of new sensations. This is something that Antonioni's characters are unable to achieve because tradition for them is repetition of their daily lives. As for Paul, who lives a stereotypical New York lifestyle, in order to 'feel "out of character"' in a world that is itself out of character, or to experience "blandly otherworldly excitement" (Lin 2013: 41), which a modern stranger such as Paul needs, he must go visit his parents in Taipei, the only place where he is able to feel this uncanny displacement. Visibly belonging yet socially estranged, Paul begins to experience the uncanny when he visits Taiwan, as Taipei is able to "disrupt the out-of-control formation of some incomprehensible worldview" (ibid. 164). Although he never used to leave his parents' or uncle's apartment on previous visits, he begins to 'internalize' and view the foreign Taiwanese capital in subsequent trips as 'less like a city than its own world, which he could leisurely explore ... for years, or maybe indefinitely' (ibid.). In Taipei, his displacement is much more uncanny than it is continual, as life for him is in New York; this displacement allows him to experience some sort of sacred or utopian perspective, removed from social media and the internet yet linked through exploring the physical city itself. While back in New York and looking at the movies that he and his new wife Erin filmed there, 'Taipei seemed gothic and lunar ... with the spare activity and structural density of a fully colonized moon that had been abandoned and was being recolonized; its science-fictional qualities seemed less advanced than ancient, haunted, of a future dark age' (ibid. 240). Being in Taipei reveals uncanny truths, not only about his own life but also about his relationship with his casual friend-turned-wife.

Yet a modern stranger in liminality cannot simply fall back into tradition as a solution, especially with customs that no longer fit the fleetingness of the modern world. For example, Paul and Erin bring their New York life of computers, social media, and drug use to Taiwan, something he tended to exclude on previous visits. Even though these activities are not exclusive to New York, and certainly exist in modern Taiwan, Paul is no longer able to differentiate his spatiotemporal binaries, as his New York life and Taiwanese life become the same. The illusion has lasted only so long for Paul, until he comes to terms, as Adorno once claimed, with the notion that 'distant places are no longer—as they still were for Baudelaire's *ennui*—different places' (1991: 191). Additionally, Paul and Erin subscribe to the old tradition of marriage not necessarily out of a want or desire, but simply because it is still customary for a relationship to culminate there in our society. A marriage ceremony is supposed to complete the rite of passage from child/adolescence into maturity and adulthood, yet Erin and Paul's relationship is grounded too much on a liminal plane for it to succeed in such a way. Their relationship, which is originally "solid" or working in its liminality, does not change after marriage; yet it is the expectation that something should in fact change, but fails to do so, that proves to be the demise of their relationship. Lin argues that revisiting the past and tradition can allow one to experience emotions and feelings that seem uncanny and therefore exciting, but he adds that conforming to traditions and customs that no longer speak to our needs, without at least a reimagining of them, can no longer advance or save us from our liminal existence. Thus the modern stranger persists in a 'default expression' of *ennui*.

A Heroic Lack of Attunement

As we see with the work of Lin, Antonioni's expressions of modern malaise depict significant problems in contemporary and modern times. It is true that stories about bored, well-to-do white people, as in Antonioni's films, are not as attractive as once perceived, especially in a world where far more significant social injustices have become prevalent. But that argument would be misleading, especially if we ignore the ironic and spiritual spark that exists within those stories. William Pamerleau recognizes what Tillich regarded as 'sacred emptiness' in Antonioni's films, which refers to the absence of God or the spiritual, or rather the 'awareness of the loss of meaning' (Pamerleau 2011: 47). The sacred void epitomized by existential boredom identifies a moral or existential problem or void that essentially becomes spiritually substantial in the modern world (ibid. 5–6). Although stating a materialist argument, Henri Lefebvre's claim that 'space is never empty: it always embodies a meaning' (1991: 154) nonetheless applies to Tillich's ironic and paradoxical understanding of empty space, because even nothing must contain something. Metaphorically, we can compare Tillich's view of empty space with a quantum theory of empty space in that it is not really empty but bursting with energy (Habegger 2013: 92). The idea of sacred emptiness acknowledges a sacred spark or energy in emptiness, an energy in boredom.

Antonioni's films are also important for their portrayal of female protagonists and therefore "female" boredom, especially in *The Red Desert*, which highlights what Ahmed (2010) and Betty Friedan (1963/2010)[4] claim as the 1960s myth of the happy housewife. Even prior to the optimism and economic boom of the postwar years, women were not allowed to be happy, let alone bored; therefore their boredom would not be taken seriously, and was unfairly connected to 'selfishness as opposed to the benevolence that engages one in meaningful action' (Spacks 1996: x). For the most part, boredom or *ennui* was historically considered an unacceptable trait for a woman to possess, commonly disregarded as superficial or lacking any self-reflection or soulful weight (Pease 2012: 22–23). Whereas male *ennui* was regarded as soulful and 'ennoblingly individualized,' women faced a double standard, as boredom for them was symptomatic of a lack of self (ibid. 23). Yet in spite of this, it was the upper-class women of the 18th century, most notably in Britain, that transformed boredom into a literary endeavour, as 'boredom haunts the margins of much women's fiction' (Spacks 1996: 70). This, however, did nothing to transform the misconception of bored women throughout modernity. By the 19th and early 20th centuries, boredom became predominantly generalized as an upper-class woman's problem or experience, either romanticized or portrayed as a mental illness (Pease 2012: 25). Doctors and psychologists of the time blamed these discontents on women's inability to cope with modernity (ibid. 30), when the actual problem was simply that they were not allowed to partake in it. Even when the newly educated New Woman rose in society at the end of the 19th and early 20th centuries, modernist texts rarely showed women struggling for independence in the workplace, but instead portrayed them as bored characters stuck at the typist desk and lacking agency (ibid. 21).

This is a reason why women frequently have been overshadowed by men as modern strangers or outsiders in both literature and film, despite continuously being 'affect aliens' (Ahmed 2010: 49). In 1888, British writer Amy Levy argued, '[t]he female club-lounger, the *flâneuse* of St James Street, latch-key in pocket and eye-glasses on the nose, remains a creature of the imagination' (cited in Elkin 2016: 11), largely due to the fact that women were not allowed the freedom and independence to access public space in the same way as men (Wolff 1990: 34–35). Levy's statement is somewhat ironic because the *flâneuse*, although perhaps 'invisible' (Wolff 1985/1990; Gleber 1999), did exist. The rise of shopping malls allowed women to experience the art of *flânerie* in public spaces (Wilson 2003: 101), while George Sand (born Amantine Lucile Aurore Dupin), who dressed as a man in order to experience the freedom of modern urban space, the quintessential space of modernity, offers a more radical example of the *flâneuse*. Deborah Parsons claims that women were able to bring something different to the act of flânerie:

> A female observer corresponding to the social figure of the *flâneur* can be found in the late nineteenth and early twentieth centuries, when women were achieving greater liberation as walkers and observers in the public spaces of the city ... Whereas Benjamin's *flâneur* increasingly becomes a metaphor for observation, retreating from the city streets once the arcades are destroyed to a place of scopic authority yet static detachment, women were entering the city with fresh eyes, observing it from within. It is with this social influx of women as empirical observers into the city street that aesthetic, urban perception as a specifically masculine phenomenon and privilege is challenged (2000: 6).

While traditionally the concept of modern strangers or boredom with "weight" has been dominated by the male perspective, authors such as Virginia Woolf, and filmmakers such as Agnès Varda and Chantal Akerman, continued to challenge the boundaries of patriarchal society by focusing on the women strangers of modernity.

Antonioni's bored female characters carry with them the soulful and individualistic *ennui* that was wrongly associated only with men; and while a feminist critique of boredom exists in these films, Antonioni does not divide boredom into male or female, but instead uses these women characters to represent the everyday bored individual of secularized modernity. Regardless of whether Antonioni's films were intentionally feminist or not,[5] the heroines played by Monica Vitti helped change the dynamics of how women can be portrayed in films by shedding light on a growing, unspoken problem for women, as well as how that problem connects to everyone. This brings us to the question: "Can being bored or unhappy be revolutionary or heroic?" Predominantly, boredom is described as a negative mood or experience, usually referring to a lack of something: spiritual sacredness, meaning, or simply entertainment/enjoyment. All forms of boredom contain their own nuisances; however, all seem to be defined as a mood or disposition measured as negative. From the sinful, evil, or the devil devil's slothful device that characterized *acedia*, to the contemporary nihilism attached to its modern equivalent, boredom seems to lack any positive elements. The fact that boredom, or 'not being in the mood,' is so closely tied to evil or nihilistic predispositions compels us to render it as a negative and unfortunate, though necessary, 'side effect' of modern secular life, similar to the way Durkheim (1897/1975) aligns suicide with the "free inquiry" of Protestantism.

Nonetheless, boredom can still be seen as a catalyst for change, creativity, and progress. A 2011 psychological study showed that "[p]eople who feel bored experience that their current situation is meaningless and are motivated to reestablish a sense of meaningfulness" (van Tilburg & Igou 2011: 1690), and therefore attempt to escape from it. Ironically, escapism lies in a similar, liminal realm as boredom, and likewise shares a negative and passive undertone to it—escapism is often seen as an immature reaction to being unable to cope with reality. If boredom is a kind of over-dwelling on reality and escapism an outright rejection of it, a combination of the two can be seen as a movement in liminal space with the potential to create a realm of possibility, both permanent and temporary. In his study of escapism, Ty-Fu Tuan states that escapism allows us to do 'something extraordinary, namely 'see' what is not there. Seeing what is not there lies at the foundation of all human culture' (1998: 6). As with liminality, both boredom and escapism can therefore be positive elements in one's life, though either can become problematic if prolonged or perpetual, resulting in unhappiness.

Despite having reservations about producing 'a heroic model of the unhappy revolutionary' (2010: 169), Ahmed sees a politicized notion of unhappiness, which seems to be intrinsically related to the stranger:

> The history of the word *unhappy* might teach us about the unhappiness of the history of happiness. In its earliest uses, unhappy meant "causing misfortune or trouble." Only later, did it come to mean "miserable in lot or circumstances" or "wretched in mind." The word wretched also has a suggestive genealogy, coming from wretch, referring to a stranger, exile, or banished person. The wretch is not only the one driven out of his or her native country but is also defined as one who is "sunk in deep distress, sorrow, misfortune, or poverty," "a miserable, unhappy, or unfortunate person," "a poor or hapless being," and even "a vile, sorry, or despicable person." Can we rewrite the history of happiness from the point of view of the wretch? If we listen to those who are cast as wretched, perhaps their wretchedness would no longer belong to them. The sorrow of the stranger might give us a different angle on happiness not because it teaches us what it is like or must be like to be a stranger, but because it might estrange us from the very happiness of the familiar (ibid. 17).

The 'sorrow of the stranger,' living in a liminal or sacred void, allows us an alternative view or shadow of modernity, even while modernity was establishing itself. The same spectre that has haunted secularized modernity, and which haunts the ending of *Frankenstein* through ambiguity, has remained, although mutated, altered, or adapted to the uncertainty and liminality that is modernity. Ahmed gets closer to the idea of boredom and even inaction when discussing moods, specifically the concept of non-attunement in her essay "Not In the

Mood." In the face of a fictional public mood of happiness and nationhood, Ahmed claims '[n]ot to be made happy is to refuse the promise of this conversion' and to 'withdraw from the situation' or 'not being in the mood for happiness becomes a political action' (2014: 28). Once again, Ahmed brings in the concept of the stranger, the person who is out of place or alienated from her surrounding environment, an environment that has shifted due to the consequences of modernity, thereby radicalizing the stranger. Ahmed may have concentrated her analysis of the stranger to simply indicate migrants, queers, and women, those she regards as 'affect aliens,' a definition that goes beyond the modern stranger. However, Ahmed's work channels the same essence of the monstrous, uncanny, and liminality that has defined the concept of the modern stranger throughout secularized modernity.

There is a correlation between the relationship Ahmed sees among non-attunement, the stranger, and political action, and Adorno's arguments of boredom and political indifference. I am not entirely convinced of Adorno's argument that '[w]henever behaviour in spare time is truly autonomous, determined by free people for themselves, boredom rarely figures,' (1991: 192) since it is arguable whether truly autonomous time is even achievable, and that no matter how free people are, repetition is unavoidable, as is the boredom that will ultimately be a part of it; I do, however, agree that boredom and political apathy can be closely related. On the other hand, Ahmed in *Happiness* warns us against viewing unhappiness as a heroic stance because it can lead to indifference (2010: 169); but neither inaction nor boredom necessarily mean "doing nothing," just as not selecting a side does not automatically result in indifference. The liminal space between the attitudes of "you are with us" and "you are against us" can be considered a political action in itself. The inaction of kneeling for national anthems by black American athletes, for example, becomes a political action that, while stemming from violence and unfair treatment of black Americans, eventually works as protest by exposing the singing of the national anthem before sporting events as a boring symbol of the recurrent, illusory, and repetitive mythos of a happy and united nation. The ironic statement is not necessarily against the *idea* of a united and happy nation, but rather against what the current belief of a united and happy nation is. People may argue that nothing is held sacred anymore and tradition no longer matters, but protests such as these are not against the secularized sacredness of nationhood, but rather against a failing illusion of sacredness; in a way, sacredness can only be challenged by sacredness itself.

Boredom is an essential and ineradicable aspect of modern life, especially since contemporary ways of evading it, using tools such as the internet and social media, paradoxically also allow for its perpetualization. Existing in secularized modernity therefore depends on how we navigate and channel the liminal mood of boredom, both internally and externally, while likewise being cautious in circumnavigating the fascinating new digital technologies.

Notes: Chapter IV

1. In contrast, Reinhard Kuhn argues that the dissimilar types of 'are often confused with ennui because they can never be completely divorced from it. They do contain certain elements of ennui, they often coexist with ennui, and they sometimes even bring about ennui' (2017: 9). More recently, Michael Raposa reestablishes the relationship between the two by defining *ennui* as 'boredom colored by melancholy' (1999: 34).
2. Speaking of *Red Desert*, Cooper and Skrade claim that they 'cannot conceive of a more powerful, gripping, unrelenting illustration and experience of Tillich's analysis of the sources and reality of contemporary man's dilemma than Antonioni's [film],' in that the individual's 'place does not know him anymore' (1970: 8–9).
3. Lin's most obvious Sartrean allusion to boredom and absurdity may come in the short story "Love Is a Thing on Sale for More Money Than There Exists" from *Bed: Stories*, although it is much more playful:

    > People began to quit their jobs. They saw that their lives were small and threatened, and so they tried to cherish more, to calm down and appreciate things for once. But in the end, bored in their homes, they just became depressed and susceptible to head colds. They filled their apartments with pets, but then neglected to name them. They became nauseous and unbelieving. They did not believe that they themselves were nauseous, but that it was someone else who was nauseous—that it was all, somehow, a trick. A fun joke (Lin 2007: 10).

4. In the revolutionary book *The Feminine Mystique*, Friedan unearths 'the problem with no name,' an unspoken and widespread *ennui* that housewives endured during the postwar years that consisted of a 'strange stirring, a sense of dissatisfaction, a yearning that women suffered in the middle of the twentieth century in the United States' (2010: 57).
5. As Peter Brunette argues, Antonioni 'genuinely seems to have mixed feelings towards men as men, toward the male way of being in the world. (Or do we read the films this way because feminism has altered our interpretive frame? Certainly our reading of *L'Avventura*'s gender dynamics would have been different in 1960).' However, Brunette goes on to say that even '[w]hen men become the central characters ... the critique becomes subtler and more conflicted, but it does not disappear' (1998: 34).

V

The Sacredness of Digital Liminality

"And where does the newborn go from here? The net is vast and infinite."
—*Ghost in the Shell* (1995)

Men seldom moved their bodies; all unrest was concentrated in the soul.
—*"The Machine Stops"*, E.M. Forster

"'If God made anything better, he kept it for himself.'"
—*Neuromancer*, William Gibson

There is no such thing as either man or nature now, only a process that produces the one within the other and couples the machines together. Producing-machines, desiring-machines everywhere, schizophrenic machines, all of species life: the self and the non-self, outside and inside, no longer have any meaning whatsoever.
—*Anti-Oedipus*, Deleuze & Guattari

Werner Herzog's documentary *Lo and Behold, Reveries of the Connected World* begins with computer scientist and internet pioneer Leonard Kleinrock taking us through what Herzog describes as 'ground zero of one of the biggest revolutions we as humans are experiencing … the birthplace of the internet' (2016: 00:00:56–00:01:05). Opening the door to the small computer lab, Kleinrock looks into the camera and claims, '[w]e are now entering a sacred location … it's a holy place' (ibid. 00:01:34–00:01:38). This sacred space, preserved—or rather re-assembled—to its 1969 aesthetic, is a secular shrine venerating the advent of the sacred and liminal space of our contemporary world—the threshold between reality and virtuality, between the physical and digital worlds, that is the internet. Many scholars and academics have labeled, both positively and negatively, the internet or virtual space as liminal (Holt 2011; Madge and O'Conner 2005; Pimenova 2009; Yang 2006), in that it dissolves various borders

---

How to cite this book chapter:
Beghetto, R. G. 2022. *Monstrous Liminality; Or, The Uncanny Strangers Of Secularized Modernity*. Pp. 123–143. London: Ubiquity Press. DOI: https: //doi.org/10.5334/bcp.f. License: CC-BY-NC

but also signifies the main source of a shift of uncertainty in how we define the human. Cyberspace uncannily blurs the lines of what is alien and what is familiar in an entirely new way, especially in regard to the human consciousness. While the cyborg is the technological transformation of 'meat' to metal, or the breakdown of such binaries, cyberspace dissolves this material relationship altogether, establishing something more abstract and immaterial.

In a similar sense, the internet has even replaced God as our source of a spiritual mechanism. The self-proclaimed technopagan Mark Pesce believes that 'computers can be as sacred as we are, because they can embody our communication with each other and with the entities—the divine parts of ourselves—that we invoke in that space' (cited in Davis 2015: 176). William Indick similarly claims in *The Digital God: How Technology Will Reshape Spirituality*:

> [t]he internet has already been compared to God. Like the monotheistic God, it is abstract and distant; yet, simultaneously, it can be personalized and contextualized into the present. In its own way, the internet shares with God the same divine qualities of omniscience, omnipresence, and possibly even omnipotence. It is quite possible that the internet will give rise to a new form of spiritual perception … a Digital God (2015: 206).

This new 'Digital God' is paradoxical; unlike spiritual insight, which is internal, the new sacred space is an 'external sensation … a place where everyone is perpetually 'online.' For many people, being connected to the internet at every moment has become a psychological necessity, an existential lifeline' (ibid.). Seeing God within the internet is part of the ongoing process of secularization/resacralization that largely epitomizes modernity. In "The Internet as a Metaphor for God?" Charles Henderson states that '[i]f the Internet is coming to be seen as a metaphor for God, it is not because the new metaphor dropped magically from heaven, but by the same process through which most religious symbols have been born: naturally out of the everyday experience of real people' (2000: 80). Oliver Krueger uses Thomas Luckmann's individual and modernity-induced theme of 'invisible religion' to argue that the internet can act as a provider but also a mirror of religion, as 'the Internet reveals not only the developments of institutionalized religions like Christianity but also, in an extensive way, of the individual constellations of Thomas Luckmann's *invisible religion* or the so-called individual 'patchwork-religions' in Europe, North and South America, and Japan' (Krueger 2004: 184). The internet is not an entity of mythical perfection and flawlessness as God has been perceived by traditional monotheistic religions, but instead can be seen as an even more liminal representation of Frankenstein's Creature, a reflection that conceptualizes the fractured modern human existence. Cyberspace, therefore, seems to further challenge the idea of the unitary self by dissolving the binary of both self and other, alongside the self and self, in that unlike the cyborg that is still confined to the idea of the corporeal, cyberspace predominantly removes, or at least manipulates, the use of the physical body. Yet, although we seem to have a complex situation where individual and community are intertwined online, we have also seen an intensification of surveillance and loss of privacy as a consequence.

The internet has further infringed on our private space, more than any metropolis could ever imagine. Whereas one may lose one's privacy in a city simply during social interactions, the internet haunts us like a spectre by recording and remembering everything about us, making social and public life a continuous experiment and never-ending spectacle; and all this despite the internet's paradoxical anonymity, thus making it just as secretive and mysterious as it is revealing. As a result, the Internet Age seems to have placed us deeper in a realm of permanent liminality. Arpad Szakolczai describes this liminal 'condition when any of the phases in this sequence becomes frozen, as if a film stopped at a particular frame. This can happen both with individuals undergoing an 'initiation rite' and with groups who are participating in a collective ritual, 'a social drama"(2000: 212). Szakolczai uses the example of monks living in monasteries who continuously perform rites for a 'performance which will only be given in the next world' (ibid.). The most unlikely of the different forms of permanent liminality manifests when '[t]he stage of preparation can be played endlessly while the performance is postponed forever,' though Szakolczai also points to the opposite being true: '[o]ne can also imagine situations in which it is the performance that is being staged endlessly, and all the actors become pinned down or identified by their roles' (ibid. 214). Szakolczai seems to find this state 'less believable,' even though he acknowledges that in *Ulysses*, James Joyce uses the individual who is 'worn out by the duty of permanent performance' as 'archetype for the modern condition' (ibid.). Joyce's representation seems more in line with the modern stranger of the 19th and early 20th centuries, since his two main characters in the novel were outsiders to the rest of their social environment rather than part of the norm; however, the notion of a permanent performance being staged endlessly as an archetype seems to be more indicative of the current Internet Age.

This chapter focuses on the literary interpretations of cyberspace and the symbolic space of the internet, from incarnations of cyberpunk, beginning with Gibson's Sprawl trilogy and the Ghost in the Shell series, to more current and "realistic" depictions of social media and online life in literature such as *The Circle* (2013) by Dave Eggers. What we notice is that there is, at least initially, a continuation of similar themes of secularization/resacralizat ion. However, there seems to be more of a negative shift in how we ultimately view the internet the more entrenched it becomes in our reality. The concept of the Internet as a resacralized source of the divine and that of the modern stranger were resurrected and intertwined in the early 1980s through the fascinating literary and film movement of cyberpunk. Ridley Scott's *Blade Runner* (1982/2007), *Neuromancer* (1984), and *Ghost in the Shell* (1995/1998) are three of the most widely known cyberpunk works and can be considered as a sort of "holy trinity" of the science fiction subgenre. These three major works have several themes in common: all are influenced by noir crime fiction; all describe worlds in which the divisions between West and East are beginning to break down in one way or another; all deal with the uncanny relationship connecting humans, technology, and self; and finally, all in some way deal with the concept of the modern stranger. However, since this chapter's main topic is the internet and cyberspace, I will concentrate on William Gibson's Sprawl trilogy (*Neuromancer*, *Count Zero*, and *Mona Lisa Overdrive*), the first novels that exposed the notion of cyberspace into the public sphere (Hayles 1991: 36), and the famous Japanese series *Ghost in the Shell*.

The dystopian settings of these two universes exist in similar post-WWIII, balkanized worlds, where the United States has fractured into various sections or city states and where Japan has become the strongest and most stable economic nation in the world. More importantly, they are worlds in which these geopolitical locales are continuously subjugated by corporations and, crucially, pervasive technology, where both cybernetic implants and artificial intelligence culminate in the creation of cyberspace. With all the similarities these stories share, they ironically differ from one another by focusing on contrasting perspectives of a similar world. While *Ghost in the Shell* follows a group of individuals who try to uphold the law, the Sprawl novels concentrate on the underworld of crime and the personalities that navigate the space within it. The Sprawl trilogy's[1] emphasis is on one of the fractured sections of the Unites States known as the Boston-Atlanta Metropolitan Axis, a "sprawling" megacity that encompasses most of the Eastern American Seaboard. The Sprawl's influence on the novels is overshadowing. While only *Count Zero*'s setting is located there, as Tom Henthorne argues, it 'serves as an emblem' for Gibson's concept of the universal cityscape and his fictional world as a whole, since the 'entire world seems to be developing a sprawling monoculture that incorporates into itself elements from most of the industrialized world' (2011: 114). Several critics (McHale 1992; G. Miller, Jr. 2016; Rapatzikou 2004) reference Foucault's *heterotopia*[2] when describing both cyberpunk and the Sprawl, rightly directing us away from seeing Gibson's world as simply dystopian; in particular, Wendy Hui Kyong Chun makes convincing claims of seeing the Sprawl as a *heterotopia* since it 'simultaneously represents, contests, and inverts public spaces and places' (2006: 52). This is also emblematic of the main characters Gibson centres his stories on, as its criminals, mercenaries, hackers, and drug addicts have almost a physical, even transcendent, connection to the Sprawl's fragmentation, either through cyberspace or the subcultures found within the city's streets. The Sprawl becomes an overarching symbol of the fragmented self of the modern stranger, and not just of the world that constantly surrounds it.

The setting of *Ghost in the Shell*, on the other hand, is mainly the economically and nationally sound country of Japan, seen mostly through the perspective of the members of Section 9, an anti-terrorist and intelligence department led by the series protagonist, the cyborg Major Motoko Kusanagi. Section 9 was established in order to stop the criminal cyber-hackers that Gibson's novels tend to romanticize. However, the department's independence from government supervision likewise removes them from the nation state and establishes them within their own liminality. Although it can be argued that the two stories examine different sides of the same cyberpunk coin, it is through the internet that the two worlds cross one another. Cyberspace acts as a liminal space where one is able to gain control that one normally would not have held, but is also a space where that freedom can be regulated and controlled, allowing for both perspectives to intersect one another, thereby continuously blurring the lines between restriction and liberation.

Mike Featherstone and Roger Burrows define cyberspace as 'an information space in which data is configured in such a way as to give the operator the illusion of control, movement and access to information, in which he/she can be linked together with a large number of users via a puppet-like simulation which operates in a feedback loop to the operator' (1996: 2). In regard to cyberpunk, Featherstone and Burrows emphasize the relationship between human and technology:

> The term cyberpunk refers to the body of fiction built around the work of William Gibson and other writers, who have constructed visions of the future worlds of cyberspaces, with all their vast range of technological developments and power struggles. It sketches out the dark side of the technological-fix visions of the future, with a wide range of post-human forms which have both theoretical and practical implications; theoretically, in influencing those who are trying to reconstruct the social theory of the present and near future, and practically, in terms of those (largely young people) who are keen to devise experimental lifestyles and subcultures which aim to live out and bring about selected aspects of the cyberspace/cyberpunk constellation (ibid. 3).

This 'illusion of control' seems to become an even more significant theme in contemporary cyberpunk literature than in its earlier depictions. Although cyberpunk does concentrate on 'the dark side of the technological-fix,' it is as much about its utopian and resacralized aspects as it is of its technophobic ones. According to William Covino, cyberpunk exercises an uncanny association of the sacred and profane, as it contains 'an impulse that locates magico-religious behavior in the secular realm,' even though 'it also represents the implicitly sacrilegious attitude of the socio-cultural rebel' (1998: 41), though as I have argued, these two are not as mutually exclusive as once thought. Silvio Gaggi argues in "The Cyborg and the Net" that

[n]ovels like *Neuromancer* and films like *Ghost in the Shell* contain examples of such entities [having a will of their own different from their creators]—Wintermute and Neuromancer in *Neuromancer*, the "Puppet Master" in *Ghost in the Shell*. Such entities present themselves as hostile forces, though in the end, as is the case in these instances, they may reveal themselves to be quasi-religious higher beings, the next stage in an evolutionary process towards a higher form of consciousness" (2003: 135).

Similarly, Frank McConnell connects religious spiritualism with Gibson by arguing that the novel *Neuromancer* is a 'gnostic skewing of the *Divine Comedy*' (2009: 149), thereby continuing to secularize/resacralize the tradition of the modern stranger that was laid out by Baudelaire and Leopardi in the early 19th century. This liminal perspicacity of secular/sacred process with regard to technological media, interestingly enough, was carried out by 19th-century Evangelical Christians in Antebellum America. In the absorbing *Secularism in Antebellum America*, John Lardas Modern examines the resacralization process behind the evangelical passion of media technology and communication networks: '[t]he difference that new media technologies and semiotic strategies made in recasting the production, distribution, and reception of evangelical words was substantial in making secularism a metaphysical solvent' (2011: 9). As Modern describes, the secularizing religious movement believed in a 'system' of evangelical media that was crucial in regards viewing religion as a 'personal concern' (ibid. 65). By incorporating sacred Biblical text with not just ordinary life, but also secular reason and technological progress of mass media, the evangelical Christians of Antebellum America saw this paradoxical mixing of sacred and secular as 'true religion,' which 'revolved around voluntary attention and systematicity' (ibid. 11). Sacrality, therefore, was merged with a semiotic belief in technological progress, social connectivity, and media circulation. Evangelical secularism, as with cyberpunk depictions of cyberspace, saw the transitory power of technological media as an '[e]nd to bondage' and the beginning of individual freedom and belief (ibid. 112).

The central difference between cyberpunk and previous works regarding resacralization and the modern stranger, therefore, is not necessarily a breaking away from Judeo-Christian teachings, since cyberpunk is laden with its symbolism, but rather due to cyberpunk establishing itself within a world of postglobalization. Cyberpunk amalgamates Christian mythos with other religious and sacred images. This is why the internet plays such a powerful and important role in cyberpunk, as Ronald Cole-Turner writes in "Science, Technology, and the Mission of Theology in a New Century": 'for many, the Internet is not merely the key symbol of globalization; it is its driving force … we must recognize that the Internet links but does not homogenize or reduce cultures to a common global culture … it brings the diversity of the world to consciousness'

(2010: 147). Especially when it still encompasses an element of science fiction, cyberspace is a hybrid utopia of interconnecting knowledge and values, having the uncanny ability to blur borders and binaries while still being the perfect representation of both society and the individual in a liminal modern age. This immaterial, even spiritual value of globalization is differentiated from the more dystopian, physical or material aspects of globalization found within the technological cities and dehumanizing multinational corporations that control these cyberpunk worlds.

Cyberpunk depictions of technology and cyberspace are as much about autonomy as they are about control and addiction. As Chun points out, cyberpunk is more than fiction dealing with the technological fetishism of society. Equally, it is about self and other, as its 'global vision ... stems from its conflation of racial otherness with localness' (2006: 29). Chun states that cyberpunk classics like *Neuromancer* and *Ghost in the Shell* embody a sense of 'high-tech orientalism' which 'enables a form of passing—invariably portrayed as the denial of a body rather than the donning of another—that relies on the other as disembodied representation' (ibid. 177–178), leading to a process of self-alienation but also a source of sexual fetishizing. Both stories, according to Chun, orientalize the other—Japan in *Neuromancer* and Hong Kong in *Ghost in the Shell*—which thereby configures the internet as a space of escape from these locations. As Chun argues, 'cyberspace allows for piracy and autonomy' and 'allows the hacker to assume the privilege of the imperial subject' (ibid. 187–188). Chun's assessment, however—which does well in arguing for cyberspace as a space of control over the colonized other—overreaches with its orientalizing claims, especially in regard to *Ghost in the Shell*. Since director Mamoru Oshii chose Hong Kong as the main inspiration for his unnamed Asian metropolis because he felt it represented an optical depiction of information, making it a perfect visual companion to the invisible cyberspace, Chun argues that Oshii fetishizes Hong Kong as a city of data, seeing it as a disorienting metropolis with no past or future. However, Oshii was also heavily influenced by the cities of Europe, particularity Eastern Europe, especially for the second film of the series, *Ghost in the Shell 2: Innocence*, and his live-action film *Avalon*, which takes place in a comparable universe (Hanson 2005: 161). Therefore, Oshii's films, like other cyberpunk works, portray a sense of futuristic universalism and even normalness through their depictions of urbanism, while containing the idea of being a tourist or an alien within this normalness. Although these cyberpunk works address the concept of the other, they ultimately destroy these binaries to establish a more post-globalized and 'culturally ambiguous' (Dorman 2016: 43) philosophy of self/other than critics such as Chun acknowledge.

Relatedly, Andrew Ross famously critiqued cyberpunk as a genre that fanaticizes the male "white middle-class conception of inner city life" (1991: 146), and said that 'cyberpunk was a tale about the respective psychogeographies of country (suburb) and city' (ibid. 147). According to Ross, cyberpunk's 'main claim to postmodernity lay in its treatment of the less geographically distinct realm of space and time that was now available through information technologies, the cartographic coordinates of technosimulated space that have no fixed geographic referent in the physical landscape' (ibid.). Despite this critique, there is a direct link to the global cities that span the works of Gibson and Oshii, and their unique visions of the internet that cannot be ignored, in that both seem to tear down boundaries in favour of a universalism. Samuel R. Delany rightly sees Ross' critique as suggesting 'the wearing away of the rural/urban divide' as '[t]he microtechnology, that in cyberpunk, connects the streets to the multinational structures of information in cyberspace also connects the middle-class country to the middle-class city' (cited in Dery 1994: 198). While Chun and Ross's arguments examine the acts of racial, class, and gender displacement in cyberpunk, the major emphasis of the chapter is on the act of displacement in regard to resacralization and in relation to the modern stranger within cyberspace.

Hybrid Religions of Cyberpunk

The Sprawl trilogy and *Ghost in the Shell* series are witnesses to cyberpunk's liminal world of cyberspace, which, although it removes the physical properties of the city, nonetheless retains, and in fact supersedes, the city's uncanny and liminal characteristics of fractured and technological space. The genre's assessment of progress takes a similar approach to that of *Frankenstein*, in that social evolution—most notably technology—is far too complex to designate with any indication of linear progress. Although technology is ever-present and dominates these future worlds, they are also continuously haunted by it: 'In stories and films like *Neuromancer*, *Ghost in the Shell*, and *Blade Runner*, spectral entities unleashed by the modern machine haunt dark cities teeming with nocturnal life. The future they evoke is obscure and unknown, totally unlike well-illuminated destinies guaranteed by the predictable march of progress' (Greenspan 2014: 76). Yet in this case, the worlds in cyberpunk fiction are liminal in their totality. Traditional boundaries are broken down on every level in worlds where humans are machines, technologies are human, and corporations appear to be both: 'Power ... meant corporate power. The zaibatsus, the multinationals that shaped the course of human history, had transcended old barriers. Viewed as organisms, they had attained a kind of immortality' (Gibson 1984: 203). This is not to say that cyberpunk's defining theme is centred on a negative perspective of the technological progress of humanity, for at times it also argues that technology is its uncanny salvation. If corporations are liminal and therefore immortal, the humans in cyberpunk stories seem to be fairly influenced by them, and also look towards the liminal in order to gain immortality. That being said, these tales of futuristic underworlds of crime, deceit, and technology also consist of themes regarding the sacred and human connection.

It is these human qualities of resacralization, such as human connection, which tend to be at odds with the technocratic world that propels most of the outsiders into a cybernetic world, and not only a sense of the power and money that control or define their societies.

Cyberpunk may seem to be anti-religious, especially in regard to Christianity. However, this is a symptom of its anti-authoritarian character rather than any abhorrence of anything of a religious nature. To be certain, Christianity as an organized religion is portrayed negatively in Gibson's Sprawl novels whenever mentioned. However, its symbolism survives, which seems to be a common theme in a lot of cyberpunk, despite Samuel R. Smith's argument that cyberpunk never portrays Christianity in a positive light (1998: 245).[3] For instance, *Neuromancer* revitalizes both Christianity's apocalyptic focus (Di Tomasso 2014: 482) and its messianic mission, while also addressing the Christian dualism of body and mind presented through the AIs Wintermute and Neuromancer: 'Wintermute was hive mind, decision maker, effecting change in the world outside. Neuromancer was personality. Neuromancer was immortality' (Gibson 1984: 269). The division between the two AIs also indicates a semblance of the hybridity of Christ, in that Wintermute elicits a God-like entity, especially through its omnipresence, though it needs to merge with Neuromancer in order to establish a personality and unite with humanity through a resurrection of sorts.[4] Gibson warps these Biblical metaphors in a similar way that Shelley does in *Frankenstein*. Wintermute ironically references the Biblical God when sarcastically asking the novel's main protagonist Case if it should appear to him in the matrix like a 'burning bush' (Gibson 1984: 169), or when telling Case 'I am that which knoweth not the word' (ibid. 173), symbolizing a fractured God. If God's word, through scripture, is complete and final, Wintermute acknowledges that without Neuromancer, it is incomplete and really no different from humans: a fractured god that is unable to fully understand itself. Neuromancer, on the other hand, through individuality, is likened to Milton's Satan. When Wintermute is able to finally integrate with Neuromancer at the end of the novel, despite the latter's unwillingness, it claims a sense of unity, of completeness through otherness: "I'm the matrix, Case.' Case laughed. 'Where's that get you?' 'Nowhere. Everywhere. I'm the sum total of the works, the whole show.'" (ibid. 269). When Case asks, somewhat ironically, if this means it is God, the newly amalgamated digital deity responds, 'Things aren't different. Things are things.' (ibid. 270). Case expects something to change;[5] he expects something different, even though he is only able to appreciate Wintermute-Neuromancer in a familiar or traditional Western religious understanding. However, the Wintermute-Neuromancer entity understands that nothing has changed. It is simply continuing a secularizing-resacralizing process that motors throughout secularized modernity.

Even in a Japanese anime like *Ghost in the Shell 1 & 2*, Christian references are extremely prominent and an important aspect of series' philosophy, as director Mamoru Oshii was greatly influenced by the religion and often includes many references in his films (Ruh 2014: 43). This influence is most evident in the many Biblical passages the characters quote throughout both films. The most important occurs when the first film's complex villain, The Puppet Master, quotes Paul in *1 Corinthians* 13:12[6] to the series protagonist Major Motoko Kusanagi, insinuating that, although powerful, both the Major and The Puppet Master are incomplete, what each of them knows is partial. However, like a possible Wintermute–Neuromancer merging, once they unite, they will be whole and all-knowing. At the end of the film, the Major–Puppet Master creation references the *I Corinthians*' passage that precedes the previously mentioned line[7] to Major's partner BatÛ, completing the Biblical quote but more importantly, acknowledging that the fusion of the two in yberspace brought them to a higher spiritual level of consciousness. In *Innocence*, BatÛ's 'guardian angel' (Oshii 2004: 01:09:45) no longer needs a shell to host her ghost, similar to Jesus, who no longer needed his human body after rising from the dead.

However, Christianity's vital yet understated role in cyberpunk only tells us half the story. When examining the divine/human hybridity of Christology in cyberpunk, it is obviously more complicated than simple references to Christian thought and mythos. For one thing, in both *Ghost in the Shell* and *Neuromancer*, we see a reluctance of one of the entities that must merge with the other, essentially because one of the beings is the other to the other's self. The fusion of the two in both instances does not seem to be two halves of one thing uniting in perfection, but is far more symbiotic as two "others" uniting in hybridity. This is also reflected in the most prominent religion in the Sprawl novels, Vodou, most notably in *Count Zero*. In comparing Vodou to Christianity and Scientology, the matrix cowboy Beauvoir likens it to the streets because it refocuses life back towards the physical and material world instead of otherworldly phenomena. The sacred must live within the Earth and community:

> "Vodou isn't like that," Beauvoir said. "It isn't concerned with notions of salvation and transcendence. What it's about is getting things done. You follow me? In our system, there are many gods, spirits. Part of one big family, with all the virtues, all the vices. There's a ritual tradition of communal manifestation, understand? Vodou says, there's God, sure, Gran Met, but He's big, too big and too far away to worry Himself if your ass is poor, or you can't get laid. Come on, man, you know how this works, it's *street* religion, came out of a dirt-poor place a million years ago. Vodou's like the street" (Gibson 1986: 76–77).

Gibson's vision of the urban streets is similar to Baudelaire's poetry and Lang's *M*, depicting it as a complex, fragmented space consisting of different individual lanes that intersect with one another, a 'patchwork' (1984: 48, 103, 176) that determines its own liminal understanding. Beauvoir is effectively linking religion and the sacred to the streets in a similar perspective as Michel de

Certeau's view of the city. Referencing de Certeau, Scott Bukatman argues that '[c]yberpunk narratives construct trickster tactics within the 'machineries' of cybernetic culture' (1993: 212).

One viewpoint is created by the strategists, consisting of institutional bodies who have a synoptic view of the city as a unified whole. On the other hand, the city dweller is far more tactical and never completely controlled by the strategies of these organizations. On a literal level, the Vodou disciples and corporations create this division in the actual physical city. However, this conflict is also noticeable in how the followers of Vodou deal with the sacred and God. For Beauvoir, trying to find God or transcending into one a futile endeavour. To them, the matrix, or 'God,' represents 'the world' (Gibson 1986: 114). As we find out in *Count Zero*, the Wintermute-Neuromancer AI that united in *Neuromancer* has fragmented into many different Vodou deities and was not 'the whole show,' as it had stated it was; its unification simply led to even further distortion and fragmentation. But Gibson's use of multiplicity is what separates his work from the binary structures that de Certeau engages in, as the lines between tactics and strategies in regard to the sacred use of space are not clearly defined. It is the notion of hybridity that allowed Vodou to have a lasting impression on Gibson and why it is such a powerful and essential theme of his Sprawl novels. After reading an article on Haiti's Vodou beliefs, Gibson was greatly affected by learning that it was a hybrid faith made up of West African ancestral religions and Roman Catholicism, in which theologies intersect and saints and ancestral gods unite, resulting in a third religion, a religion of international diversity or 'spiritual collage' (Olsen 1995: 305). Vodou becomes the trilogy's most important religious symbol, not only because it is 'an outlaw religion, created by those whom the dominated society marginalized' (ibid.), a perfect representation for the cyber cowboys that dominate his stories; moreover, it supposedly is a liminal religion that transcends boundaries and borders, especially in a fictional world where nations, and therefore traditions, do not seem to exist anymore, surpassed by the matrix, thus going beyond any illusory borders that remain.

Ghost in the Shell similarly extracts the idea that a fragmented world is defined by its greatest technological accomplishment, the internet. In this futuristic world, society has become heavily balkanized. Even what had been the United States is no longer united, but fractured into various sections. Conversely, Japan's borders remain intact: an island unified yet seemingly isolated from the rest of the world. Still, in a world dominated by cyberspace, Japan's notion of strongly defined borders is also highly illusory. Within the future society of *Ghost in the Shell*, 'recognizable Japanese urban characteristics are difficult to distinguish among the intricate sprawl of multiple languages of ethnicities'" (Dorman 2016: 43). This use of multiculturalism goes beyond the notion of immigration and merging cultures that is common inside a global city space. The merging in cyberspace of Major Kusanagi, a Japanese cyborg, and The

Puppet Master, an American sentient computer, bypasses any designated national or cultural boundaries. No matter how much Japan deems itself secluded, the Puppet Master's infiltration of Japanese cyberspace, and subsequently of the Major, liquefies the once-considered-strong boundaries of the nation state that Japan believes are still intact. In fact, even the idea that the Puppet Master is American and the Major Japanese is equally dissolved. Likewise, in the second film, BatÛ becomes almost a quoting apparatus, frequently referencing various religious and cultural traditions, from the Bible to Buddhism, from Weber and Descartes to Saito Ryokuu, indicating that knowledge and culture have become universal, intersecting, globalized, predominantly due to the Internet Age. More so than during the advent of modernity, everyday life continuously becomes more liminal and culturally ambiguous, as both the cyborg and cyberspace go beyond notions of race, culture, and knowledge.

God is (In) Cyberspace

Despite the fact that Gibson's novels portray a world where nature is dead, leaving 'a bleak future where humans can be cloned, cryogenically frozen, or surgically manipulated to resemble computers' (Stiles 2011: 186), technology actually plays a far more multifaceted role in cyberpunk, offering just as many possibilities of freedom and notions of the sacred as it does of corporate control or secularization. Gibson's novels are not simply cautionary tales about a possible future where the escape from reality has taken over most people's lives; they also explore how one will navigate and find meaning in such a world. Gibson does this by continuously alluding to cyberspace as a religious space of salvation and transcendence of the spirit, removed from the human body (which the hackers consider "meat").[8] In *On Belief (Thinking In Action)*, Žižek states that 'in cyberspace, we return to the bodily immediacy, but to an uncanny, virtual immediacy,' thereby linking it to a type of 'spiritualized materialism' found in Gnosticism (2001: 54). The movement towards "a 'higher" BODILY reality, a proto-reality of shadowy ghosts and undead entities,' ultimately leaves us to digest the idea that through the removal of a corporeal body, we must realize that such a body must never have existed in the first place, and that 'our bodily self-experience was always–already that of an imaginary constituted entity' (ibid. 55). However, the characters in the Sprawl novels endlessly oscillate between both bodily entities. The physical body that is a cage of the self, and the cyber-body that lacks any corporeal restraints of the self, are constantly being exchanged whenever the hacker jacks in and out of the matrix.

For the cyber-hacker Case, the restriction from cyberspace and subsequent imprisonment in his physical body is likened to Adam and Eve's banishment from the Garden of Eden; in both cases they are punished for breaking the one rule: theft of knowledge.

He's made the classic mistake, the one he's sworn he'd never make. He stole from his employers ... Strapped to a bed in a Memphis hotel, his talent burning out micron by micron, he hallucinated for thirty hours. The damage was minute, subtle, and utterly effective. For Case, who'd lived for the bodiless exultation of cyberspace, it was the Fall. In the bars he'd frequented as a cowboy hotshot, the elite stance involved a certain relaxed contempt for the flesh. The body was meat. Case fell into the prison of his own flesh (Gibson 1984: 6).

In a world where knowledge is power, the multifaceted character Case equally represents Adam and Eve, but also Prometheus, or in modern terms, both Frankenstein and his Creature. Even more so than cybernetic implants, which are still just technological extensions of the physical body, cyberspace is an infinite realm of possibility, described as a 'colorless void' (ibid. 5) or 'endless beach' (ibid. 258), and acts as a palpable, recognizable afterlife that allows hackers like Case to transcend from 'meat' to immortal beings like the AIs that inhabit cyberspace. Seeing a vision of his dead girlfriend Linda Lee when he jacks at the end of the novel, Case alludes to cyberspace as a technological afterlife. Moreover, the idea of God as either living in or actually comprising cyberspace—a concept first expressed in *Neuromancer*—becomes more blatant in *Count Zero*: 'Specifically, the Finn said, the Wig had become convinced that God lived in cyberspace, or perhaps that cyberspace was God, or some new manifestation of same. The Wig's ventures into theology tended to be marked by major paradigm shifts, true leaps of faith' (Gibson 1986: 121). This concept is unambiguously revisited in *Mona Lisa Overdrive*, but in a far more liminal understanding:

"That the matrix is God?" "In a manner of speaking, although it would be more accurate, in terms of the mythform, to say that the matrix has a God, since this being's omniscience and omnipotence are assumed to be limited to the matrix."

"If it has limits, it isn't omnipotent." "Exactly. Notice that the mythform doesn't credit the being with immortality, as would ordinarily be the case in belief systems positing a supreme being, at least in terms of your particular culture. Cyberspace exists, insofar as it can be said to exist, by virtue of human agency"

(Gibson 1988: 129).

The last of the Sprawl novels suggests that cyberspace is a god, not because it can propel humanity towards its limits, but because it has the power to transcend humans, allowing them to further expand their limits.

In *Ghost in the Shell*, there seems to be a gap between the cyborgian body and the "ghost" or "soul" contained within it; this gap is a human aspect that seems to be impossible to clone or replicate and allows for an awareness of both individuality and humanity, a penetrating conflict on which the series philosophy is based. Nonetheless, the notion of cyberspace seems to be a liminal sphere caught between these two binaries, for although it is an extension of the technological aspect of the cyborg, the ghost is often found within cyberspace rather than within the mechanized body (Endo 2011: 233). Major Motoko Kusanagi conceptually dives into cyberspace and virtually coexists within it, making the ghost something far more than a spirit encased in a cyborgian shell. This atypical relationship between the ghost and cyberspace, however, does make Major existentially question her own self and humanity, as she asks her partner BatÙ: 'What if a cyber-brain could possibly generate its own ghost, create a soul all by itself? And if it did, just what would be the importance of being human then?' (Oshii 1995: 00:42:53–00:43:01). Major's ghost is all that is left of her human self, and if a ghost could be generated artificially, as could a human body, where does that leave humanity? A similar question is raised when someone's cyber-brain is hacked—as the Puppet Master does, or the Laughing Man in the *Stand Alone Complex* series—where essentially one is able to hack one's ghost or soul. In *Innocence*, the cyber-hacker Kim suggests that mind and soul are no different, since both are interconnected with the matrix: 'Humans are nothing but the thread from which the dream of life is woven. If dreams, consciousness, even ghosts are no more than rifts and warps in the uniform weave of the matrix' (Oshii 2004: 01:11:00–01:11:11).

In both Gibson's novels and *Ghost in the Shell*, there is a sense of amalgamation and formation of a unitary self, although the form of this amalgamation differs with each story. The unification of Wintermute and Neuromancer once again leads to further fragmentation; while in the case of Major and Puppet Master, the amalgamation serves to achieve more of a concept of the unitary self, but one that still does not seem to be fixed within a single shell. However, cyberspace occupies a more optimistic or God-like position in *Ghost in the Shell* than in the Sprawl trilogy. Whereas Gibson ultimately flirts with the idea of transcendence in cyberspace, transcendence also seems to be slightly Sisyphean as a form of resacralization in *Mona Lisa Overdrive*. In Oshii's *Ghost* films, Major is able to transcend her physical body, gaining both omnipotence and omniscience, becoming a soul in a computer program.[9] Although borrowing heavily from Western and Christian ideals, the notion of the soul in the series goes beyond these traditions, in that the spirit is not confined to one "shell" but rather is able to travel or coexist with another in a single vessel (Hasegawa 2002: 136), allowing it an even more liminal freedom than in Gibson's novels. Whereas cyberspace has limits in the Sprawl novels, being simply an extension of human capabilities, the internet is 'vast and limitless' (Oshii 1995: 01:17:35–01:17:37) for Major. Like God, Major tells BatÙ, '[a]lways remember … Whenever you enter the Net, I'll be by your side' (Oshii 2004: 01:32:00–01:32:09). Cyberspace can be a spiritual place, like when one prays to a God, or a liminal space existing between heaven and earth. This is not to say that cyberspace in these cyberpunk works does not contain dangers, as both works deal with the serious threat of cyber-hackers—although most of the time these cyber-hackers tend to be far more multifaceted than traditional villains. As Pesce states, '[a]ny discussion of cyberspace is a discussion about believing; if cyberspace is the imagination, then cyberspace contains what we believe it contains, nothing more, nothing less. Put another way, the only things we take into cyberspace are our preconceptions. These preconceptions can come in the form of prejudices, tastes, or even spiritual beliefs' (1995: 287). Possibly due to the technology's infancy, cyberspace in cyberpunk tends to take on the uncanny role of being a secular place of the sacred, either as a spiritual place to reach humanity's limits, or one that can even outstrip them.

Strangers in Cyberspace

The matrix in cyberpunk is a habitation for liminal characters and modern strangers alike. The emblematic removal of the physical body in cyberspace, a symbolic representation of the instability of the unitary self, allows it to be a perfect place where the alienated and powerless modern stranger can become powerful and controlling, a liminal space where one can challenge both the boundaries and authority of the overshadowing culture. In the spirit of Baudelaire's *flâneur* or the hard-boiled detective—who, as Benjamin argued, shared a sort of metaphorical relationship[10]—the cyberpunk criminal "hackers" or "cowboys" are active observers that describe the uncanny reality of their liminal surroundings. Their backdrop is the globalized technological metropolis, where the reason, order, and law that run through the futuristic city streets are juxtaposed with the uncanny shadow cast on its disenfranchised 'low-lifes,' drug addicts, criminals, and cyborgs.[11] As Lance Olsen describes in relation to Gibson's work, cyberspace provides a variable utopian space for societal outsiders:

> ... the definition of cyberspace, the virtual area that manifests Gibson's idea of termite art, a realm on the others side of the computer keyboard ... that both exists and does not exist, opens up in expectation, chance, burning bushes, voodoo gods ... a zone where anything can happen, everything is possible, all fences are down, the dead can dance, the living can die ... A narratological region that continually chews away at its own boundaries and hence the reader's, problematizing everything from place to gender, identity to its own position in the "world." Cyberspace is the symbolic territory of termite art (1995: 296).

Cyberpunk's cyberspace is both a representation of the alienated Western individual of modernity and a reflection of the physical world around him (or her), but equally it offers itself as a place where alienation can thrive as a positive element. In the first *Ghost in the Shell* film, Major originally associates and also contrasts the comforting alienation of being underwater. Similar to cyberspace, Major feels an optimistic alienation, where the feelings of being fearful, cold, and alone allow for feelings of hope. Within her cybernetic body, Major still feels 'confined, only free to expand ... within boundaries' (Oshii 1995: 00:32:20–00:32:25), whereas the alienating aspect of cyberspace comes from its vast and endless opportunities, something she ultimately chooses. What cyberspace offers the modern stranger in cyberpunk fiction is a place where alienation and fragmentation are embraced as part of a continuous process of becoming rather than a form of alienation that occurs when the unitary self is unachievable. Case, for example, rejects the Wintermute-Neuromancer proposal of living in cyberspace without the constraints of the physical body. It seems Case is unwilling to accept an either/or binary of 'meat' and cyberspace, finally coming to terms with the fact that *'cyberspace is not the end of the human body'* (Pesce 1995: 285). With a total removal of the physical flesh, cyberspace lacks the liminal sphere of alienation, and therefore the possibility of resacralizing, for 'the concrete is always presented through manifestation rather than through evocation' (ibid.). In the technological, fragmented world, life exists somewhere between reality and cyberspace. After Case rejects the "heaven" of cyberspace, this liminal state is metaphorically used to describe the transitional point of jacking out. It is at this moment, when Case is in between cyberspace and reality, that Gibson perfectly illustrates his and even our own world:

> There was a gray place, an impression of fine screens shifting, moire, degrees of half tone generated by a very simple graphics program. There was a long hold on a view through chainlink, gulls frozen above dark water. There were voices. There was a plain of black mirror, that tilted, and he was quicksilver, a bead of mercury, skittering down, striking the angles of an invisible maze, fragmenting, flowing together, sliding again ... (1984: 244).

While society's fragmentation constantly battles a progression from transcendence to wholeness, Gibson ironically uses liminal language to describe Case's genuine moment of clarity, a phase when he is caught between the "meat" and the digital.

It was unproblematic for Gibson and Oshii to view the internet as both liminal and optimistic in the early 1980s and even 1990s, as it still was a form of technology that was more or less undetermined. Like much groundbreaking science fiction, *Neuromancer* was both highly prophetic and erroneous in its vision of the future. Gibson's concept of the internet is not necessarily what we have today, in that it may not be the 'consensual hallucination' (ibid. 5) we jack all our senses into, as he described it—although advances in virtual reality have been influenced by Gibson's work (Walker 1989; Walser 1989; Hayles 1999) and its potential amalgamation with AI may still prove him to be even more accurate than once thought. Nonetheless, it is something that is omnipresent in our society.[12] We are all interconnected through it, and in practice it is a construct on which we store our memories and experiences. In another sense, the internet may be far more liminal than Gibson imagined, as we do not "jack in and out" of cyberspace; rather, it has become something that never goes away in our lives. We are continuously "jacked in" even if we are not directly engaging with it. The internet has become too canny in many ways, as it uninterruptedly lives alongside our reality, and as a result is far more colourless than Gibson's literary interpretation. Due to the fact that the current generation has lived only knowing the internet, a world in which an aspect of themselves lives constantly in cyberspace, the worlds of *das Heimliche* and *Unheimliche* tend to overlap.

Although she was centering on the uncanny as a sexual threat, Cixous argues in "Fictions and its Phantoms" for an instance of overlap between the canny and uncanny that the internet seems to share, in that 'the word joins itself again, and *das Heimliche* and *Unheimliche* join together, pair up ...' (1976/2011: 20). Due to its permanent liminal characteristics, cyberspace no longer has the ability to dislocate someone from the physical world, since being in a state of dislocation has become commonplace. Life online has become more of a reality for many people than the reality of their physical world, which has become increasingly illusory. When people spend the majority of their time in liminal cyberspace, a sense of perpetual or permanent liminality, or an endless performance, can overcome the individual. Many individuals are using the internet to experiment with their identity, either by imagining themselves as completely different people living a different life, even possibly in a different world, or by presenting their "real" self as something they may not actually be offline. What the Internet Age has done is transform the notion of the self, essentially removing it from the physical body. By being an omnipresent and undetectable reality, technology dominated by the internet is able to subversively control one's perception or attitude towards life without allowing for any sacred space.

Cyberspace: Heaven or Hell?

Comparing works from the 80s and 90s with more contemporary literature, there seem to be a couple major shifts in works that deal with cyberspace. One is the obvious shift from science fiction to a fiction far more grounded in reality that evidently arose from the fact the internet plays a much more significant role in our lives. The other is that there seems to be a genuine shift from enthusiasm, or at the very least a reserved optimism, to a far more pessimistic interpretation of cyberculture. This is evident in the most recent live-action *Ghost in the Shell* film (2017), in which cyberspace is viewed much more negatively at the film's conclusion than in the anime original. In the 2017 film, even Major refuses amalgamation with the film's Puppet Master-esque villain on those same dystopic grounds. The negative aspects of the internet were always present: risk of being hacked, infringements on security and privacy; however, these threats have become more realized in an individual's life, thereby shifting the corresponding fears from peripheral to commonplace. Although there are still some romantic depictions of hackers as being anti-capitalist anti-heroes, as in the show *Mr. Robot*, internet culture and the 'cowboys' riding through it have grown ominous and alarming in a lot of contemporary literature and film.[13] Moreover, more and more contemporary authors are writing about the shortcomings and consequences of the Information Age and social media. In Gibson's cyberpunk universe, as in our own contemporary world, information is everything; but unlike our current reality, information remains largely secretive in Gibson's worlds.

A world without secrets has the ability to govern itself perfectly, as Dave Eggers' *The Circle* argues, or rather the novel's eponymous multinational technology company argues. Eggers' book tends to borrow heavily from what have become clichéd tropes of prototypical totalitarian dystopian novels such as *1984* (1949/1961) and *Brave New World* (1932/2007). Nonetheless, with some fundamental changes in this dystopian society, it resembles contemporary reality more closely than it does science fiction. The society's lack of individualism and privacy arise not necessarily from governmental tyranny, thought control or social and biological engineering, but rather from the people themselves. Yes, The Circle is a powerful, internet-based corporation in the mould of Google or Facebook. But rather than any in serious form of propaganda, brainwashing, or torture, the company's power resides in giving the people the technological full disclosure they desire. The Circle is a community that, although walled off from the outside world, creates the apparatus for how people throughout the world communicate. Through the narrator, protagonist Mae Holland describes her opinions between The Circle and the rest of society: '[o]utside the walls of the Circle, all was noise and struggle, failure and filth. But here, all had been perfected. The best people had made the best systems and the best systems had reaped funds, unlimited funds that made possible this, the best place to work. And it was natural that it was so, Mae thought. Who else but utopians could make utopia?' (Eggers 2013: 31). The Circle's goal is to communicate its utopian values to the rest of the world via the internet, to integrate or make whole the fragmented and disconnected world outside, to make the world as "perfect" as the community of The Circle. As one of its founders argues, The Circle's logo, a giant C, represents the incompleteness or fractured state of modern life, as well as the company's goal to connect everything through the information highway, '[s]o any information that eludes us, anything that's not accessible, prevents us from being perfect' (ibid. 289). The project begins when politicians' lives migrate completely online, resulting in their around-the-clock accountability. This mission soon spreads to everyone. The Big Brother of the past is no longer needed; people will watch themselves, confirming the transition from the panoptical gaze to that of the cyborgian (Vidler 1992; Willet 1996). Unlike Vidler, who argues that the cyborgian gaze is based upon fragmented and 'refracted lines' (1992: 160), Eggers' take on the cyborgian gaze is far more totalitarian. We have become a society of the AIs we once feared; we have become the new Wintermutes and Puppet Masters. To not join means to be hiding something, and therefore, according to the people of The Circle, to be stealing something from the rest of society. To not join means you do not belong and therefore are shamed, a major concern for Mae—and The Circle itself—when she first joins the community. Mae quickly finds out that fitting in and communicating with everyone about herself is far more important than the actual work she is doing. As the uncanny is removed from cyberspace, secrets have either become monotonous in reality or, as in The Circle, regarded as dangerous.

The removal of the uncanny in cyberspace seems to also remove the element of the sacred from it, but not necessarily the religious fundamentalism. Some of The Circle's most zealous and faithful followers see the movement as one that that fulfills the established Christian crusade of regaining a wholeness previously lost in the Fall:

> "You connected it all. You found a way to save all the souls. This is what we were doing in the church—we tried to get them all. How to save them all? This has been the work of missionaries for millennia ... Now all humans will have the eyes of God. You know this passage? 'All things are naked and opened unto the eyes of God.' Something like that. You know your Bible?" Seeing the blank looks on the faces of Mae and Francis, he scoffed and took a long pull from his drink. "Now we're all God. Every one of us will soon be able to see, and cast judgment upon, every other. We'll see what He sees. We'll articulate His judgment. We'll channel His wrath and deliver His forgiveness. On a constant and global level. All religion has been waiting for this, when every human is a direct and immediate messenger of God's will (Eggers 2013: 398–399).

The secularizing process of modernity's mission to replace God is complete. Mae and her colleagues at The Circle react by ridiculing the fan, making him the reverse of Nietzsche's madman, one who comes not to tell us that we have killed God, but that we have instead reestablished God.[14] Although Mae thought the fan to be ridiculous, the opening line of the novel, 'MY GOD, MAE thought. It's heaven' (ibid. 1), shows that she subconsciously believes the sentiment to be true, at some level. The hybridity, liminality, and uncanniness that once defined the sacred aspects of cyberspace have now been eliminated. The internet is no longer a space of infinite possibility, but a space of closed perfection and regulation, and has become a tool to conceal the liminal aspects of life that in its inception it validated. Although outlandish at times, a novel like *The Circle* is not alone in seeing the Internet Age as a newly forming dystopia. The expression of individuality that cyberspace and social media once fostered is beginning to transform into something regulated, ubiquitous, homogeneous—and as a result, begins to lose any liminal and utopian spirit.

Notes: Chapter V

[1] This chapter will focus on the three novels, although the Sprawl universe was introduced as early as 1981 in some of Gibson's short stories that were later complied in the collection *Burning Chrome* (1986).

[2] Foucault argued that unlike a utopia's characterization of being a space that is an ordered, coherent whole, a heterotopia is a state organized 'in sites so very different from one another that it is impossible to find a place of residence for them, to define a common locus beneath them all.' These are disturbing and disquieting textual spaces 'because they secretly undermine language … dissolve our myths and sterilize the lyricism of our sentences' (1970/2005: xix).

[3] Other cyberpunk films such as *Blade Runner* and *The Matrix* series are extremely transparent when using positive Christian metaphors and allusions.

[4] 'I die soon, in one sense. As does Wintermute' (Gibson 1984: 259).

[5] 'I got no idea at all what'll happen if Wintermute wins, but it'll *change* something!' (ibid. 260).

[6] 'For now we see through a glass, darkly' (Oshii 1995: 00:32:39–00:32:40).

[7] 'When I was a child, my speech, feelings, and thinking were all those of a child. Now that I am a man, I have no more use for childish ways' (Oshii 1995: 01:16:48–01:17:00).

[8] According to Rudy Rucker (2016), the concepts of "meatware" or "wetware" are used in cyberpunk literature to define both an organic computer system, such as the human brain, and humans in general. Gibson uses the term 'meat' in *Neuromancer*, as the term 'wetware' was not used in cyberpunk literature until Michael Swanwick's *Vacuum Flowers* (1987/2016), and not popularized until Rucker's novel *Wetware* (1988).

[9] 'She's gone. Somewhere beyond that 'rift in the uniform weave of the matrix.' She's definitely alive. Merging somewhere on the vast net, or with the entire domain' (Oshii 2004: 01:13:14–01:13:28).

[10] See Walter Benjamin's "On Some Motifs in Baudelaire" (1939/2007).

[11] Among other sources, Acker uses Gibson's *Neuromancer* as a basis in creating the characters in *Empire of the Senseless*, as a disenfranchised cyborg subculture of the future (Clune 2010: 116; Houen 2012: 181).

[12] 'Cyberspace. A consensual hallucination experienced daily by billions of legitimate operators, in every nation' (Gibson 1984: 51).

[13] *Super Sad True Love Story* by Gary Shteyngart (2010), Thomas Pynchon's *Bleeding Edge* (2013), Jennifer Egan's *A Visit from the Goon Squad* (2011), Nikesh Shukla's *Meatspace* (2014), Tim Maughan's *Infinite Detail* (2019),

and Lin's *Taipei* are just some of the novels that showcase a rising skepticism of not just the actualization of cyber threats that hackers produce, but our dependence on our online, socially mediated lives. Likewise, many episodes of the popular television series *Black Mirror* examine the dark side of humanity's relationship with the internet and technology as a whole.

14 Although not exclusive to cyberspace, the recent forming of "The Way of the Future" by Silicon Valley pioneer Anthony Levandowski, a new church/religion that worships artificial intelligence, shows that this concept is not as implausible as one may think. Levandowski argues that '[w]hat is going to be created will effectively be a god,' while insisting that '[t]he church is how we spread the word, the gospel. If you believe [in it], start a conversation with someone else and help them understand the same things' (Harris 2017).

VI

Strange Gender and Post-Humanism

You only have to look at the Medusa straight on to see her. And she's not deadly. She's beautiful and she's laughing.
—Hélène Cixous, "The Laugh of Medusa"

The body is not a site on which a construction takes place; it is a destruction on the occasion of which a subject is formed.
—Judith Butler, *The Psychic Life of Power: Theories in Subjection*

The cyborg is a creature in a post-gender world; it has no truck with bisexuality, pre-oedipal symbiosis, labour, or other seductions to organic wholeness through a final appropriation of all the powers of the parts into a higher unity.
—Donna Haraway, "A Cyborg Manifesto: Science, Technology, and Socialist-Feminism in the Late Twentieth Century"

"She decided that since she was setting out on the greatest adventure any person can take, that of the Holy Grail, she ought to have a name (identity). She had to name herself."
—Kathy Acker, *Don Quixote, which was a dream*

Much like history itself, the history of the modern stranger has been dominated by the masculine gaze. Things slowly began to change after WWII, when second-wave feminism rose out of the chaotic world like *Canticle*'s Rachel, looking to create social change from the leftover ashes. Simone de Beauvoir's groundbreaking *Le Deuxième Sexe* (*The Second Sex*) (1949/1989) was the first to wage war against the biological determinism of Freud's declaration that '[a]natomy is destiny' (de Beauvoir 1989: 46), which governed and enforced gender roles

---

How to cite this book chapter:
Beghetto, R. G. 2022. *Monstrous Liminality; Or, The Uncanny Strangers Of Secularized Modernity*. Pp. 145–167. London: Ubiquity Press. DOI: https: //doi.org/10.5334/bcp.g. License: CC-BY-NC

in a patriarchal society. Not only did critiques of the patriarchy arise through more self-reflective men like Antonioni; by the 1960s, the ascent of gender studies further challenged the phallocentric stance of society. While Antonioni's critical representations are essentially limited, since they themselves are still confined to the perspective of the male gaze, the works of intellectuals such as Hélène Cixous, Luce Irigaray, and Julia Kristeva redefined gender classifications on their own terms. Donna Haraway pushed the boundaries even further by integrating the liminal and uncanny cyborg with the rising post-gender, technocratic world, questioning the biological or natural principles of both body and gender. Haraway looks to the biotechnological age to deconstruct the natural/artificial, human/machine, masculine/feminine binaries in an attempt to help usher in a rising post-gender world, through reinventing gender, politics, and identity. Regardless of technology's negative aspects, Haraway understands that we are not able to look backwards, since technology is part of our lives whether we want it to be or not. Her "A Manifesto for Cyborgs" (1985/2004) looks towards a hybrid utopian vision that is able to exist in the present world by locating the beauty within the monstrous aspects of the present. As Jeanine Thweatt-Bates argues,

> [p]osthuman has become a way of naming the unknown, possible, (perhaps) future, altered identity of human beings, as we incorporate various technologies into our human bodies and selves. It therefore functions as an umbrella term, covering a span of related concepts: genetically enhanced persons, artificial persons or androids, uploaded consciousness, cyborgs and chimeras (mechanical or genetic hybrids). Thus, the posthuman is not any one particular thing; it is an act of projection, of speculation about who we are as human beings, and who we might become. Posthuman is inherently plural, a disturbing ambivalence (2016: 1).

In order for the cyborg to display its utopian characteristics, it must be seen not as something to be feared, but rather something to be embraced. As Rod Giblett argues, '[w]hereas we can refuse to be Terminators, we are already cyborgs' (2008: 148). Haraway's cyborg represents an open-mindedness, a flexible device for an egoless and genderless world that dissolves hegemonic binaries and oppression. The cyborg represents the entity that is fully connected but removed from the outside world, blurring the lines of subjective and objective, reimagining the Oedipal and Christian narratives of Western society.

Nonetheless, this new movement in feminist studies elaborates on what already exists in the modern stranger, as argued from the beginning of this work: being an uncanny individual in liminal modernity positions the stranger in a paradoxical situation where secularization and resacralization incessantly orbit one another. Many of the liminal and uncanny factors of the modern stranger found in *Frankenstein* were discussed in the opening chapter. However, I have reserved the discussion of gender specifically for this section, which assesses the question within the subject of the modern stranger at its birth. Despite lacking any really strong female characters, Shelley's novel may well be the origin of gender and posthumanist critique of the male-dominated, secularized world. Critics such as Sandra M. Gilbert and Susan Gubar argue that *Frankenstein* embodies 'woman's helpless alienation in a male society' (1979: 247), while Daniel Cottom states that 'the repression of women and, specifically, of female sexuality contributes to the novel's monstrousness. Victor's refusal to create a female reveals the erogeneity of the science of that first creation' (1980: 69). However, the main struggle concerning gender in the novel has more to do with authorship and language. Cecilia A. Feilla claims a direct connection between the Creature's liminality and hybridity and Shelley as a female author:

> Mary Shelley presents the women writer as self-possessed … rather than imitating or rejecting men's writing, she accepts her position, her text and her creature as monster and thus founds a place for women's writing in the liminal space of the monstrous. Like a Romantic daemon, the monster exists within the in-between, an intermediary between human and divine worlds, angel and devil, and, in the case of *Frankenstein*, opens a breach in the canon of literature through which the monsters were let in (2008: 171).

Language, monstrosity, and posthumanism are all tied to gender in *Frankenstein* through a female author and her literary and symbolic creations. The Creature, as modern stranger, uncannily points to not only the hybridity of the modern world, but also the material and social constructs of both body and gender. *Frankenstein* has influenced gender theorists to take the monstrous, abject qualities of the female body and resacralize them within the confines of secularized modernity. Critics such as Anne Kull (2001; 2003; 2016), Elaine Graham (2002), and Jennifer Thweatt-Bates ascertain a theological and sacred notion to Haraway's anti-essentialist cyborg alongside the essay's feminist argument. According to Thweatt-Bates,

> [t]he theological conclusions generated by [the] appreciation of the cyborg's embeddedness within material creation are significant, and provide a foundation for an ethics of relationship that is radically inclusive, positing as it does hybrid kinship with both the "natural" and the "technological" creatures we inhabit the world with. These theological engagements with the cyborg, therefore, turn to the ecotheological implications of the cyborg's hybridity, materiality, and interconnectedness (2016: 142).

Like many things in secularized modernity, posthumanismand and transhumanism may at first seem to be anti-religious and secular, but they paradoxically allows for the return of the sacred, for '[s]o long as religious motifs continue to inform visions of technological sublime then discourses of transcendence and re-enchantment must be directly confronted as part of an enduring symbolic of representation' (Graham 2002: 16). Existing in liminal space, the posthumanist cyborg blurs the boundaries of the sacred and profane through the distortion of human/machine and male/female dichotomies, by undressing natural identity symbols while simultaneously establishing technological new ones.

A flowing link between Frankenstein's Creature and Haraway's cyborg is Hélène Cixous' use of Medusa (Clayton 2003: 136–137), which seems to connect the cyborg and Medusa in the liminal space of the abyss.[1] Just as Shelley gave a revolutionary voice to the Creature, Cixous in "The Laugh of Medusa" bestows Medusa with a voice, to speak against the illusions and myths that men have created in an attempt to control females through fear. By re-examining the myth of Medusa, Cixous wants us to invert the uncanny monstrousness of the female gender to understand that it is merely a deception, developed from an uncanny fear of women by men who have historically 'riveted [women] between two horrifying myths: between the Medusa and the abyss' (1975/1976: 885). Although society has displaced women into the liminal sphere of the monstrous and the unknown, Cixous, like Haraway, looks to an uncanny process of 'extend[ing] ourselves without ever reaching an end' (ibid. 878). Cixous removes the horrifying fear that has enveloped the myth of Medusa and replaces it with the ironic laugh of the (post)modern stranger: 'Rewriting the horrifying Medusa of a masculist mythology, Cixous creates a laughing Medusa who, in the role of the hysteric, resists the male view of her sexuality in becoming incomprehensible, unclassifiable, as one finds her only "in the divide"' (Aneja 1999: 58). Questioning these myths by looking 'at the Medusa straight on,' women will see through the masculine veil and realize that 'she's not deadly. She's beautiful and she's laughing' (Cixous 1976: 885). Important to this study of post-gender and posthumanism is the correlation between the posthuman and the concept of the abyss. Through the lens of Paul Tillich's theological understanding of the abyss, and alongside more secular ideas of the concept from thinkers such as Luce Irigaray, Diane Elam, and Linda M. G. Zerilli, I will look to establish a connecting point of the modern stranger discussed up to now with the more posthuman, post-gender, and (post)modern version found in the latter half of 20th-century feminist writings.

After establishing the connection between language, gender, liminal posthumanism, and the abyss, I will analyze these interconnecting ideas in two works by Kathy Acker, *Don Quixote, which was a dream* (1986) and *Empire of the Senseless* (1988). The liminal act of resacralization, although not initially transparent, is an important aspect of Acker's writing, as is the notion of hybridity. Since her novels consist of a rewriting or appropriation of various famous novels, hybridity is visible in language and genre, alongside a style that jumps from fiction to autobiography to essay to journal; furthermore, hybridity and liminality are also focal points in regard to many of her characters. In *Empire* and especially *Don Quixote*, 'dichotomies like male/female, white/black, human/animal, master/slave do not exist as such but collide in a carnivalesque universe' (Garrigós González 1996: 116). In these novels, Acker simultaneously supports and critiques the ability to create one's own language and identity outside the boundaries of gender, while also attempting the modern stranger's inadvertent task of finding the sacred in a world of liminality.

From Shelley's 'Hideous Progeny' to Haraway's Cyborg

Mary Shelley alluded to the fact that gender was an underlining issue in both *Frankenstein*'s narrative and authorship, responding 'to the question, so frequently asked [her]', how she, 'then a young girl, came to think of, and to dilate upon, so very hideous an idea' (5). Shelley was praised for her groundbreaking novel, but judging from the interrogative questioning as exemplified above, the novel's subject matter was deemed to be inappropriate, or at the very least shocking, for any woman to be writing about during the 19th century. The issue of gender as an absence is an integral theme of the novel. Leaving out the female voice is a deliberate act that critiques women's status in society, both public and private, even going to the lengths of stripping away women's traditional role as child-bearers. Mother figures are non-existent, both for Victor and his Creature, while most of the female characters are marginalized, ignored, or simply disposed of.[2] Victor seeks to not only replace God with the discovery of immorality but also, by creating life without a female counterpart, seeks to establish a world operated peerlessly by man. Victor's misogynist inclinations become apparent through his act of not creating a partner for the Creature, supported by a rationale based essentially on his opinion that a female creature would be far more horrifying: '... she might become ten thousand times more malignant than her mate and delight, for its own sake, in murder and wretchedness' (Shelley 2003: 170).

This is not to suggest that the novel entirely lacks a female voice. While Victor is the author or creator of the Creature, Shelley is the creator of her own 'hideous progeny' (10), the novel itself. It is through authorship that the female voice continues to exist. As Barbara Johnson maintains, in *Frankenstein* 'the monstrousness of selfhood is intimately embedded within the question of female autobiography' (Johnson 1992: 10). Shelley correlates imaginative creation and the notion of the female genius with that of monstrosity and the demonic symbolism through the Creature.[3] While the female voice is not wholly transparent in the male-dominated plot, Shelley paradoxically enforces it through composition, thereby exposing the dread of the 'monstrous' female gender as an uncanny feature that clouds the novel, rather than unveiling it in a more unequivocal manner:

> Like the monster, woman in a patriarchal society is defined as an absence, an enigma, mystery, or crime, or she is allowed to be a presence only so that she can be defined as a lack, a mutilated body that must be repressed to enable men to join the symbolic order and maintain their mastery ... Her difference places her outside culture, and her abominable presence places her within it. Mary Shelley, because she writes from this paradoxical position, has been accused of artistic failure ... But her representation of the liminal position of women—and the relation of that position to sexual categories of a patriarchal culture—is precisely her achievement (Hodges 1983: 162–163).

Through the connection of the two hideous progenies, Shelley is able to address gender and the patriarchal society. The Creature's realization of its ugliness, or rather the ugliness projected onto it by a male-dominated society,[4] correlates to the female identity/body, in that women tend to see themselves as monstrous and unnatural because that is how society views them, due to the impossibility of living up to existing conventional associations with purity (Gilbert & Gubar 1979: 240). Patriarchal history has positioned women as goddess or vamp, but never as an equal, which ultimately situates them within an abject void. When faced with the possibilities of a potential female creature's ability to reinvent social norms, Victor Frankenstein sees only the impending danger the female represents and disposes of the dismembered female body parts. By doing so, he solidifies the boundaries of the patriarchal and structured society, leaving the female body abject, fragmented, incomplete. The correlation between cultural boundaries and those of the physical body is found everywhere in civilization, for 'the human body is always treated as an image of society' (Douglas 1966: 74). Similar to cultural and social bodies that create boundaries to keep out what is 'out of place,' the physical body likewise produces margins, in order to produce a division between dirt and purity, since 'boundaries can represent any boundaries which are threatened or precarious' (ibid. 82). Contamination exists where there are ambiguities and contradictions in social systems, as well as within ambiguities of the corporeal body, though sex "pollution" does not tend to 'flourish' within male-organized societies (ibid. 143).[5] The completion of the female counterpart leaves too many uncertainties for Frankenstein; consequently, he fears that he is unable to control the discharges from the margins of the body and society, the dirt that threatens order and control. Both sexes in the novel are victims of their own preordained gender: the female characters are casualties because of their passivity; the male characters suffer due to their excessive determination.

The only character that encompasses both genders is the Creature, whose feminine gender representationally presides alongside the masculine traits inherited by Frankenstein, which intensifies its liminal, post-gender, cyborgian stature. The cyborg fittingly incorporates an ambiguous notion of gender, whose cyborgian and liminal nature challenges the aspects of the masculine/feminine binary, ultimately destroying any illusions of the unitary self. If Frankenstein's Creature is 'pre-sexual,' gender does not account for the basis of its identity, although 'that is not to say that sexual aberration is missing from Shelley's definition of monstrosity: simply, sexuality is always a part of the other identifying traits' (Halberstam 1995: 42). Despite this, in an attempt to become "normalized," the Creature pleads with Frankenstein to repair society's shattered gender binary that continues to exist within it: 'You must create a female for me with whom I can live in the interchange of those sympathies necessary for my being' (Shelley 2003: 147). Here we can see Bruno Latour's argument that, although secularized modernity continuously maintains a world apportioned into binaries, it still refuses to acknowledge society's cumulative 'hybridization,' which ironically increases as a result of this 'purification' (1991/1993: 11–12). As a result, Latour argues that we were never modern.[6] Since society comprises a collective of humans and non-humans, representing society in a series of binaries (such as natural/artificial), hybridity paradoxically clashes against modernity's constant attempt to rationalize everything. As Latour contends:

> By rendering mixtures unthinkable, by emptying, sweeping, cleaning and purifying the arena that is opened in the central space ... the moderns allowed the practice of mediation to recombine all possible monsters without letting them have any effect on the social fabric, or even any contact with it. Bizarre as these monsters may be, they posed no problem because they did not exist publicly and because their monstrous consequences remained untraceable. What the premoderns have always ruled out the moderns can allow, since the social order never turns out to correspond, point for point, with the natural order (1993: 42).

Frankenstein's Creature wishes to destroy its hybrid and liminal characteristics through the creation of a female counterpart, thereby reaffirming modernity's neat binary.

By attempting to purify society through the destruction of the female companion, Victor in reality solidifies the hybridization and taboo, unwilling to create an opposite binary for the Creature, and as a result retains and coagulates the Creature's liminal nature. The Creature's female companion remains dismembered and dispensable, while the Creature itself still exists as an illusory whole that is fundamentally a stitched up hybrid of body parts. The Creature, the female companion, and even *Frankenstein* as a text all express this artificial uncanny fragmentation or mutilation of the body (Favret 1987; Salotto 1994) that is often credited to Haraway's cyborg. As Julie Clarke points out, '[b]oth Frankenstein's monster and the cyborg solicit the uncanniness associated with body mutilation and fragmentation' (2002: 39), while Margret Owens sees the Creature as 'the most enduring nightmare of that age' and a fundamental illustration and exploration of the fragmented body that would lead to fascination of the dismembered body found in 20th-century avant-garde art (2005: 12), as seen in Beckmann's *The Night*. This creates a predicament in which secularized modernity's act of purification is paradoxically in conflict with its tendency to resacralize itself within its perpetual liminal space.

Jane Bennett sees Latour's concept of hybridization 'as a modern form of magic and a potential site of enchantment,' since 'the essence of such magic was mobility and morphing transformations from one state, space, or form to another' (2016: 98). Although I agree with her statement, the same can be said of the sacred, and since Latour's thesis revolves around a constant purification, his sense of hybridization fits more within a secular society that tends to continuously search for the sacred; as a result, the concept of the cyborg can also be considered an element of resacralization in the modern world. The cyborg that was born in Shelley's novel in order to transgress forbidden borders has become more difficult to repress in modern society where 'the proliferation of monsters is indeed getting completely out of control. The processes of purification, which in Latour's opinion have always been illusory, can no longer disguise the fact' (Lykke 1996: 17).

Nonetheless, Frankenstein's Creature as cyborg is seriously questioned by Donna Haraway in her canonical "Cyborg" essay. Haraway defines the cyborg as 'a creature in a post-gender world' that is able to break down rigid binaries but, according to her, goes beyond Frankenstein's Creature, since 'the cyborg has no origin story in the Western sense' and '[u]nlike the hopes of Frankenstein's monster, the cyborg does not expect its father to save it through a restoration of the garden; ... the fabrication of a heterosexual mate, through its completion in a finished whole, a city and cosmos' (2004: 9). To Haraway, a cyborg is only a cyborg once it extinguishes its historical weight, its unwinnable Oedipal battle and its hope for unity. Apprehensive of, or in contradiction to, the ideas of reproduction and (re)birth that are part of the network of what she refers to as 'informatics of domination' (ibid. 22, 30), Haraway's cyborg looks to go beyond the creator/created dichotomy and even the anti-technological reading that many originally attributed to Shelley's novel. Thweatt-Bates explains that there seems to be a division between the common portrayal of 'cyborgs and other posthuman hybrids ... as figures of the monstrous, moral abominations resulting from the transgression of ontological boundaries' and the heroic 'defiance of categorical identities' that 'is the source of powerful action' (Thweatt-Bates 2016: 24–25). Haraway's post-gender cyborg is therefore closer to Frankenstein's Creature than Haraway would prefer, as it exists between the liminal plain of both characterizations of the cyborg. The two liminal symbols also share a convincing connection as being 'outside the pale of human limitations' (Feilla 2008: 170), particularly because *Frankenstein* is not the anti-technological novel many have labeled it as, and the Creature, as Gilbert and Gubar claim, 'may really be a female in disguise' (1979: 237). The three texts[7] from which the Creature gains its knowledge link the Creature's plight with that of women through 'the unattainable glamour of male heroism,' along with 'all the masculine intricacies' that have been denied them due to their "monstrous" births (ibid. 238). Furthermore, Susan Stryker takes the Creature's liminal gendering even further by connecting the monstrousness of Shelley's literary Creature to that of a transgender, whose 'embodiment, like the embodiment of the monster, places its subject in an unassimilable, antagonistic, queer relationship to a Nature in which it must nevertheless exist,' a condition that Stryker argues ultimately leads to rage (1994/2006: 248). Still, Stryker does not see the two related simply by a comparable, problematic struggle of identity, but rather sees between the Creature and the transgender an optimistic and utopian element of constructing one's identity that 'exceeds and refutes the purpose of the master' (ibid.). For Catherine Waldby, this is where both the cyborg and Frankenstein's Creature are interchangeable, in that both represent 'ways to think about human becoming. To reject them is to reject possible human futures, to refuse to engage with the consequences of shifting modes of embodiment, reproduction, and living process' (2004: 36).

It is correct that in the story the Creature aspires to 'organic wholeness through a final appropriation of all the powers of the parts into a higher unity' (Haraway 2004: 9), but ultimately its desire is never realized, and it remains a liminal entity even when its fictional male creator dies. The Creature's search for reproduction and redemption is never fulfilled and altogether abandoned at the novel's end, ushering in the spectre of the cyborg that preternaturally 'birthed' a culture of cyborgian hybridity. This entity would have to go through transition, for the process of hybridization can be considered as cyborgian as its outcome, and as a result, one cannot appraise the first cyborg[8] in the same way as the contemporary cyborg, for it has been assembled slowly over time.

A Spiral Dance in the Abyss

In jettisoning the past, Haraway's cyborg world nonetheless retains the aspect of resacralization of the female gender through the uncanny, the hybrid, and the monstrous. Haraway admits that the cyborg is the uncanny *doppelgänger* to the goddess, standing against but also alongside the image of the spiritual deity. The difference between the two is that the cyborg's paradoxical "perfection" is closer to the artificial and monstrous than the idealistic or beautiful natural perfection of the goddess. Initially, the cyborg may seem to lack or reject the spirituality or sacredness of the natural body by accepting the artificial into it. Even though Haraway chooses the cyborg over the "sacred" goddess, she does acknowledge that they are both 'bound in the spiral dance" (2004: 39).

Could this spiral dance entangling them be situated in the liminal abyss of the resacralization? For instance, the cyborg's transgression of boundaries and 'regeneration' (ibid.) of the body forces one to expand 'the spiritual practice of listening to and caring for one's own body' (Mercedes &Thweatt-Bates 2009:

73). The cyborg merely develops the technological and spiritual hybridity of the body, and the more one understands that the cyborg uncannily resembles the natural human body, the simpler it is to see the spiritual potential of the cyborg's 'broken boundaries' that are able to 'recraft the world' (ibid. 77). As a technological stranger, the cyborg pushes the boundaries of sacred/secular by relocating, though not necessarily negating, transcendence beyond traditional hierarchical and horizontal constructs into a 'nonbinary model of interrelation' (Braidotti 2011: 205). Haraway's cyborg, therefore, rejects not transcendence but rather essentialism (ibid. 83) and 'totalizing narratives of ultimate resolution and closure' (Graham 2002: 211). The spiral dance[9] between goddess and cyborg becomes a 'transgressive boundary crossing' between the disembodied soul and 'embodied reality' (Graham 2016: 67), creating a liminal coil between two liminal figures, one sacred and one profane.

The cyborg likewise opens up possibilities in regard to gender that were once restricted due to its strangeness. Just as the cyborg lives in the posthuman abyss between human and machine, it likewise lives in the abyss between genders. Through the rejection of biological reproduction, the cyborg uncannily and paradoxically opens up a space for (re)birth of societal resacralization. Likewise, by reimagining the "goddess" of second-wave feminism, Haraway does not necessarily discard the ascribed spirituality and sacredness, but rather seems to remodel it for the contemporary technological world that no longer wishes to command gender essentialism. Through a rebirth, the cyborg therefore allows for what Judith Butler calls the 'passive medium' (1999: 12) of the body to once again occur, allowing for it to inscribe a post-gender and anti-Oedipal culture or society onto the body. Butler connects this *tabula rasa* of the body to the Christian and Cartesian notion of the body as 'inert matter' or a 'profane void' (ibid.) that can allow for a liminal space of resacralizing. We see this secularized sacredness in Butler's approach to the ritual of gender performance, where she understands Turner's theory of ritual performance almost in Kierkegaardian terms of repetition, being both 'a reenactment and re-experiencing' (ibid. 178). By emphasizing the repeating facet of Turner's concept of the sacred ritual, Butler liminalizes the theory by stressing the profane, therefore allowing us to see ritual as both a 'transgressive and normative performance' (McKenzie 1998: 222).

Equally, Haraway's techno-feminist cyborg does not entirely dissolve the Judeo-Christian narratives of Western society that it challenges, with which it still seems to be, at least symbolically, interconnected, Thweatt-Bates points out a divine/human hybridity that exists within Christology and which survives in the complex relationship between the posthumanism and spirituality of Haraway's cyborg thesis. The cyborg is essentially neither secular nor sacred, for the secular cyborg dances with both the goddess and the 'Catholic sacramentality'[10] in Haraway's work, 'a perspective in which the material becomes the sacred' (Thweatt-Bates 2016: 82). The cyborg, therefore, disrupts the boundaries of the sacred and secular just as it does with nature and technology, as well as with gender. Not being confined to either binary, the cyborg is forced to live in the midst of these often violent borders. Kull, for instance, sees a connection between Tillich's argument for 'place of the mythos of technology' (2003: 240) and Haraway's cyborg. In comparing Tillich's vision of "the technical city" to the cyborg, Kull sees both as being modern symbols of understanding 'our time, our technologies, and ourselves' (ibid. 241). Modern technology, for Tillich, seems to rest with the liminal space of the abyss and ambiguity, between the creative human spirit of autonomy that propels us further in becoming and the soulless, lifeless technological structure that looks to remove that freedom. Yet for Tillich, paradoxically, the divine and sacred are located liminally and symbolically in 'the ground and abyss of being' (1988: 147) where, in the creative and destructive ambiguity of the holy void, every form disappears and re-emerges within these boundaries. Boundaries are not just for crossing, but are spaces upon which to oscillate and exist. "Living on the boundaries" of the abyss, although difficult, allows for both the sanctioning and rupturing of the existing language and culture 'to create new events of divine presence' (Gudmarsdottir 2016: 22, 59). As Eugene Taylor argues, Tillich's vision of 'the abyss is a realm of creative chaos that transcends values. It is transmoral. It is mystic illumination—the holy void, the tolerance of ambiguity, the attraction to the gray areas of life because of their hidden possibilities' (2009: 237). While academics (Althaus-Reid 2000; Daly 1973/1985; Gudmarsdottir 2016; Ulanov 1999/2005) have pointed out some aspect of the untidy relationship between Tillich's theology and gender, sexuality, and the feminine,[11] the notion of the abyss itself is nonetheless a strong element in feminist thought.

Feminism 'opens unto the abyss' (Elam 2006: 24) and is about 'keeping sexual difference ... open as the space of radical uncertainty' (ibid. 55). In this sense, the abyss should be seen as a symbolic representation of the infinite, of the unreachability of the limits. Diane Elam (1994/2006) defines the liminality of the female abyss as a space of creation and destruction, of support and rupture:

> On the one hand, the abyss fills up with representations of women. What it means to be or act as a woman is continually more determined ... On the other hand, however, the abyssal operation is infinite. The very filling up leaves one "full of abyss." The series of images in the *mise en abyme* is without end; each additional image changes all the others in the series without ever completely filling up the abyss, which gets deeper with each additional determination (Elam 2006: 29–30).

For Irigaray (1987/1993b), the abyss exists in the space between men and women.[12] Irigaray argues for maintaining this otherness, otherwise the possibility of coasting back towards the image of the woman in terms of the language and gaze of the man returns.[13] For women to become subjects and free individuals outside of the patriarchal construct, Irigaray expresses the need for the female divine: 'If women have no God, they are unable either to communicate or commune with one another. They need ... an infinite if they are to share a little' (1993b: 62). The lack of the female divine 'paralyzes the infinite of becoming a woman' (ibid.). This female divine that Irigaray calls for goes beyond notions of feminine and motherhood that have become part the male hegemonic definition of the female. This new female divine incorporates the infinite and ambiguity of being a woman, and consequently a woman's potential to become a subject of her own. While it may be possible for one to transcend the self through encountering the other, the female subject must begin with cultivating the self in order to return to the self. Therefore, Irigaray sees the divine in similar terms as Bloch's spirit of utopia, in that the self needs to burn through the other, simultaneously being inside and outside the boundaries of the abyss.

In more secular terms, although still allied with the idea of resacralization, Zerilli in *Feminism and the Abyss of Freedom* (2005) takes Hannah Arendt's theory of 'the abyss of freedom' and applies it to feminism's call for social revolution. For Arendt, 'the abyss of freedom' is when there is a moment of pause or a 'legendary hiatus between end and beginning, between a no-longer and a not-yet' (Arendt 1963: 205). As we have seen with other intellectuals, Zerilli perceives the abyssal liminal space as a liberating realm of transcendence and becoming, in an attempt to locate and recapture what she and Arendt call feminism's 'lost treasure,' the radical imagery of political, social, and thereby gender freedom. Zerilli demands '[a] freedom-centered feminism' that 'would strive to bring about transformation in normative concepts of gender without returning to the classical notion of freedom as sovereignty' (2005: 180), looking to escape and surpass an idea of autonomy and equality still situated in patriarchal etymology.

Haraway's spiral dance traverses the same abyssal tensions of finite and infinite, between the imaginary and the realistic. Living on the borders of the abyss between profane cyborgian and sacred goddess symbolism, the cyborg simultaneously maintains and destroys Western and Christian symbiotic elements, thus creating a more complex relationship between the two. The "sacramentality" in Haraway's work is an uncanny residue that allows for reforming, becoming, and resacralizing the notions of gender and the body. Through the liminal gaze of the stranger, the cyborg traverses the liminal space of utopian dreams and dystopian nightmares. The infinite possibilities that the technological 'female divine' generates must do so in the uncertain hope of technological autonomy, while ultimately still battling the patriarchal and capitalist society it exists in:

> The disruption of boundaries that the cyborg myth foregrounds is always, and necessarily, ambiguous with respect to its promise. And this ambiguity signals a kind of playful daring of the cyborg. Haraway's cyborg signals not a collapse into some variant of a return but

an advance into the zone of greatest danger. Haraway's wager is that the cyborg can find the weak points, the points that offer political possibilities for more pleasurable modes of life from within planetary grid of technological domination (Kull 2003: 243).

The cyborg as stranger inevitability must move through this liminal chaotic zone of uncertainty and danger; however, empowered by Medsua's ironic gaze of monstrous beauty, the posthuman and androgynous cyborg looks to unfasten new ways of understanding the symbolic qualities of gender and body, while navigating its own abyssal vanguard, its "no (wo)man's land.

Cyborgs, Dogs, and Abortions: The Abject of Gender in Kathy Acker's Don Quixote and Empire of the Senseless

The (post)modern strangers that exist in Kathy Acker's novels—anarchist punks, feminists, transvestites, even pirates—belong not only to the fringes of society, but also to the fringes of reality and fiction. From cyborgs to anthropomorphic and shapeshifting dogs, Acker constantly blurs both gender and natural/artificial lines of humanity's dichotomy. Moreover, her characters are existentially homeless, struggling with a constant search for a better place, for '[e]ven freaks need homes, countries, language, communication' (1986: 202). Speaking through her female protagonist in *Don Quixote*, she states, '[i]t is for you, freaks my loves, I am writing and it is about you' (ibid.). Language plays an integral part in shaping both reality and fiction, and Acker uses fiction as a means of reversing the "myths of reality". Alex Houen claims that '[i]n writing herself other, Acker frequently questions the fictionality of her allobiographies by tempering her creativity with plagiarism. Rather than simply willing wholesale belief in her fictional world, then, she often suspends the fictionality in order to consider how the writing relates to contexts of power' (2012: 176). However, Acker takes an innovative approach in 'writing herself other' by playing with gender binaries through language, inducing a desire to capture a post-gender society. Rather than tackling a new world in similar language, Acker challenges the old world with new language, trying to escape the history of 'books' and 'nature' (1986: 14). Renowned novels and stories originally about male development or perseverance are reinterpreted by Acker's use of a female voice and female struggle. By placing women in celebrated men's roles, Acker blurs gender binaries rather than upholding them, more so than the recognized lens of the marginalized other could. In order to achieve this, she must battle with the socio-political phallocentric language by simultaneously reversing it, yet still being a part of it: 'she was both a woman therefore she couldn't feel love and a knight in search of Love. She had had to become a knight, for she could solve this problem only by becoming partly male' (ibid. 29).

Don Quixote is a non-linear, surrealist tale about an originally nameless woman who, after coping with the ordeal of an abortion, sets out on a series of imaginary adventures that range between socio-political and philosophical ponderings, dreams, and even madness. Searching endlessly for love and freedom, Don Quixote strives to transform herself beyond what a patriarchal and capitalist America is able to offer her. Acker's virtually androgynous reinterpretation of Miguel de Cervantes' famous character repurposes the myth of the quixotic knight in the secularized modern world of nihilistic and capitalist urges. It also allows for a woman to take on the role of the hero and knight who takes on the symbolic enemies of society instead of the illusory ones in Cervantes' tale (Worthington 2000: 245). Although it may seem an impossibility to accomplish in a consumer and nihilistic society, the 'night-knight' (1986: 10) of Acker's *Don Quixote* foolishly searches for her 'Holy Grail' (ibid. 9): love. Don Quixote pursues a form of love in which a woman is a subject and not an object, for according to her, 'objects can't love' (ibid. 28). This quest for ultimate love that Don Quixote embarks on is a utopian pursuit of a love that is not produced or controlled by men.

Like most liminal journeys of the modern stranger, Don Quixote's quest is shrouded not only 'in language that veers wildly between the sacred and the profane' (O'Donnell 2013: 528), but also in language that is violent or abhorrent. As a female character, Don Quixote is especially a witness to and victim of the language of sexual violence. By embracing 'the traditional oedipal narrative structure and the misogynist violence inherent in it,' Acker is able 'to explore that structure for sites of feminine agency' (Worthington 2000: 244), where violence opens up the liminal world of resacralization and becoming through a form of anguish. The originally nameless protagonist of Acker's *Don Quixote* is "born again" after she goes through the procedure of an abortion. Paradoxically, through death she is able to live again. Her death and subsequent rebirth allow her the freedom to resist the social confines of the female and her maternal role as a woman, what Ellen G. Friedman describes as 'a precondition for surrendering the constructed self' (1989: 42). Don Quixote's abortion places her on the road to secular "knighthood" because it allows her to become a 'hole-ly' (Acker 1986: 13) subject while still allowing for the transcendent act of reclaiming her body, thereby 'aborting' her past identity. By naming herself, Don Quixote has the opportunity to become her own creator and authority over her identity. Here, Don Quixote takes in her own hands the symbolic power God had gifted to Adam. In the creation story of *Genesis*, God gives Adam the power and authority over the creatures around him, including Eve, through the act of naming (Leonard 1990; Schimmel 1989; Thwaites 2017), since 'by naming the world we impose a pattern and a meaning which allows us to manipulate the world' (Spender 163). In order to take back the power over her own life, identity, and body, take it away from the external monstrousness placed on her by the male gaze and a phallocentric society, Don Quixote must name herself.

In "The Laugh of Medusa," Cixous argues that '[b]y writing her self, woman will return to the body which has been more than confiscated from her, which has been turned into the uncanny stranger on display—the ailing or dead figure, which so often turns out to be the nasty companion, the cause and location of inhibitions' (1976: 880). A comparable revolutionary Medusa briefly appears in Acker's novel. Unlike Cervantes' protagonist, who is symbolic of Medusa's slayer Perseus, Acker's Don Quixote is more closely linked with Medusa. As '[h]er snakes writhe around nails varnished by the Blood of Jesus Christ' (1986: 28), virtually appropriating or resacralizing the power of the messianic, Medusa quickly interchanges with Don Quixote as a formidable force of the feminine. In the face of man, represented as a dog, Medusa shouts: 'I'm your desire's object, dog, because I can't be a subject ... What you name 'love', I name 'nothingness' ... as long as you cling to a dualistic reality, which is a reality molded by power, women will not exist with you ... When you love us, you hate us, because we have to deny you' (ibid.). This "dualistic reality" that Medusa argues women are trapped within reinforces the gender hierarchy, places the female gender as other, and relegates the feminine to the realm of animals. Nonetheless, Acker's representation of man as dog uncannily places them on an equal plane, maintaining that the animal or monstrous qualities, if they exist in humanity, represent a hybridity that exists in both genders. Acker's Medusa reflects the abject back towards the social order, exposing its fragmentation, hybridity, and more importantly its hypocrisy. Acker's Medusa, however, is more liminal than Cixous', in that while its gaze reflects the monstrousness back on male-dominated society, therefore keeping it in the context of Cixous' revolutionary interpretation, Acker does not invert Medusa as a representation of beauty like Cixous does. Instead, Acker retains Medusa's monstrous terror as an uncanny gaze reflected back at patriarchal society, thus rejecting Cixous' female essentialism and ubiquitousness.

Similarly, one of the main protagonists in *Empire of the Senseless* is the mixed-race cyborg named Abhor. Abhor is an outcast, a 'construct cunt' (Acker 1988: 37) that represents a liminal or symbolic 'site of gender conflict' (Pitchford 2002: 98). At the beginning of the novel, Abhor's tragic Oedipal story of being raped by her father is told by her male lover, Thivai, through his language and not hers. Acker is not subtle in naming her protagonist; disgust and violence have defined her, while her identity has been fashioned by language that is not her own, a language that creates a myth that confines those to the monstrosity with which they historically have been labeled. While raping her, Abhor's father gives her sacred power by calling her his God but instantly removes it by referring to himself as God's creator, and asserts that he both 'made' and is 'making' her.[14] Abhor's father takes away her power by controlling her body, in order to punish her for believing that she was in control of it as well as of her sexuality. By creating God, he thereby controls her past, present, and future identities. Because of this and her mother's passivity, Abhor is disgusted by the word *mother* (Acker 1988: 15) and cannot help but see all heterosexual love as resembling rape to some degree. While it is a misconception that Andrea Dworkin or Catherine MacKinnon state that "all heterosexual love is rape,"[15] Dworkin does argue that '[v]*iolation* is a synonym for intercourse' (1987/2007: 163), while MacKinnon claims that in a patriarchal society, heterosexuality 'institutionalizes male sexual dominance and female sexual submission' (1989: 113). As Irigaray argues, all heterosexual love is not rape, but it is outside the realm transcendence: 'when a male lover loses himself in the depths of the beloved woman's sensual pleasure, he swells within her as in an abyss, an unfathomable depth. Both of them are lost, each in the other, on the wrong side, or the other side, of transcendence' (1993a: 194). This lack of autonomy similarly forces Don Quixote to experience lesbian sex, for she argues, 'when I make love to a woman or myself, I'm controlling the body. Loving a woman is controlling. Whereas, when I make love to a man, I'm the opposite' (Acker 1986: 127). This inability or lack of control in society is at its most abject when it is endorsed during an act of love between two people.

Paradoxically, it is this abjection that spurs Don Quixote's quest to find this 'taboo' or impossible notion of love. When it comes to the abject, Kristeva and Butler both emphasize the necessity of trauma, internally and externally, between self/other and subject/object, as trauma uncannily discloses what is hidden or repulsive about the self just as much as it does with society. As Butler argues, '[t]he "abject" designates that which has been expelled from the body, discharged as excrement, literally rendered "Other"' (1999: 168). This appears as an expulsion of alien elements, but the alien is effectively established through this expulsion. The construction of the '"not me" as the abject establishes boundaries which are also the first contours of the subject' (ibid. 169). Through abjection, the destruction or blurring of boundaries allows for the abject subject to create individual and newly formed boundaries of the self. As Abhor's lover argues, 'GET RID OF MEANING. YOUR MIND IS A NIGHTMARE THAT HAS BEEN EATING YOU: NOW EAT YOUR MIND' (Acker 1988: 38). Although Thivai's message is accurate, he is also a significant part of the constructed 'meaning' that is causing these nightmares. Abhor only begins to gain her freedom when she goes off on her own adventure without Thivai, when she is able to gaze into the abject monstrousness and write her own story.

Acker's Resacralization of the Symbolic

The problem Acker and her gender-defying protagonists face is difficult: despite the fact they deconstruct the language and boundaries of society, they are confined to using the language and binaries given to them. As Acker states in the epigraph to the second part of *Don Quixote*, '[b]eing dead, Don Quixote could no longer speak. Being born into and part of a male world, she had no speech of her own. All she could do was read male texts which weren't hers'

(1986: 39). This has led many critics (Friedman 1989b; Hume 2001; Muth 2011) to question Acker's linguistic goal, even calling her work "a triumphal failure" (Redding 1994: 301) or, at the very least, problematic in that her work 'attests to a prior system of order still very much operational' (Hume 2001: 486). Acker herself acknowledges this through the voice of Abhor:

> Ten years ago it seemed possible to destroy language through language: to destroy language which normalizes and controls by cutting that language. Nonsense would attack the empire-making (empirical) empire of language, the prisons of meaning. But this nonsense, since it depended on sense, simply pointed back to the normalizing institutions (1988: 134).

Ultimately, it is difficult to think one can simply "get rid of meaning" or separate language from its connotation, especially through the medium of literature. Acker's imaginative utopia clashes with constructed reality, resulting in Acker and her protagonists ultimately collapsing under the weight of their utopian values being resisted and eventually pushed down on them. For instance, Abhor shares many attributes with Haraway's conception of the cyborg; however, she does not reach any "utopian" status because of it. Technology has not changed her standing as a male object or a commodity, but instead has strengthened it. The blurring of natural and artificial has not dissolved Abhor's Oedipal-constructed past, since it is consonant with the capitalistic society that surrounds her. With *Don Quixote*, the protagonist's rebirth does not culminate in equality in the outside world, and by the novel's end, Don Quixote, like Cervantes' character, is swayed back to reality, and the genderless identifying of the character slowly fades back towards gender-specific pronouns.

However, to deem Acker's mission—and that of her protagonists—a failure misses the entire hybrid and liminal scope of the novels, especially since both *Don Quixote* and *Empire* acknowledge this "failure" to some degree. Her novels take place in the liminal sphere of utopian dream and harsh reality, resulting in the characters' constant oscillation and alienation both internally and externally. Acker's Don Quixote evokes the spirit of Cervantes' original character, who himself was displaced and alienated from the world around him; however, the chief distinction is that although Acker's Don Quixote and Abhor are displaced, they are modern strangers and not just marginalized others, because they are uncanny and symbolic representations of the fragmented and liminal society that created and house them. New York City is a paradoxical place that fosters the ability to find one's identity as well as, simultaneously, the ability to deny it. With 'its neon and street lights' that give 'out an artificial polluted light' (1986: 18), New York allows for an artificially constructed emptiness where one's expectations can be born. But, as Cristina Garrigós González points out, *Don Quixote* 'is a novel about love and violence, but it is also about the power of a city, New York, over a woman' (1996: 114). One of the novel's outcasts discourages Don Quixote when she realizes that the city is a hellish capitalist space, which only amplifies the strangeness or abnormality she feels from the home she previously ran away from (Acker 1986: 115). Don Quixote's quest to find love is therefore even more absurd 'in the materialistic, machist and sexist world in which we live. A city like New York represents all the western values carried to an extreme' (Garrigós González 1996: 116).

Equally, the landscape of *Empire*'s dystopian Paris is itself hellish, suffering from disease, capitalist nihilism, crime, and poverty, while the Algerian revolution that sought to bring about a transformation in the end 'changed nothing' (1988: 110). Abhor recognizes her liminal and fragmented identity reflected by the city: '... in this Paris death and life were fucking. Just like my father gave birth to me and wanted to kill me. In Paris, death smelled like life and vice-versa, especially in human beings' (ibid. 82). For a male outcast like Thivai, Paris is still '[t]he true city of dreams ... a city in which a person could do anything' (ibid. 147). On the other hand, for Abhor, the city is far uncannier in its utopian spirit. Abhor sees herself stuck between the otherness of both men and women, leaving her with a fragmented and liminal identity. The men that controlled the city, 'the dead,' were never seen, while the women, 'the mutants,' were the only ones visible: 'The urban areas of the Western world were now composed of dead and mutants. I was confused to the point of psychosis because I wasn't sure what I was' (ibid. 110). Unable to locate her identity in these binaries, her liminal existence once again brings up gender ambiguity, an ambiguity that is reflected in the glass buildings of the Parisian cityscape:

> Since I was a mutant from outer space who was living in exile in Paris, Paris looked as if it was made up of glass. Glass cuts through the flesh. Paris was a bloody city. Rectangular blocks of mirrored glass intersected tall buildings of black glass about a quarter way down their lengths ... Under the bank, there was a building of opaque grey glass which was nameless. 'Nameless' meant 'useful'; there was no end to the depth of the building (ibid.).

Paris' violent nature, which symbolically cuts through the physical body, unveils the indistinctness of both body and city. Although one could become anything within this emptiness, Acker conveys emptiness as an uncertainty and seriously questions whether any utopian reflections can grow from it. Abhor doubts the notion of being 'useful' as a distinguishing feature of utopia, since usefulness is a sign of a commodity culture and objectification. According to Henri Lefebvre, space is never neutral, nor is it an empty container waiting to be filled by social human activity. Space in a capitalist and phallocentric society is always produced from the ideologies that control it. Argues Lefebvre, 'the space thus produced also serves as a tool of thought and of action" and "in addition to being a means of production it is also a means of control, and hence of domination, of power' (1991: 26). However, these spaces for Lefebvre produce more than a means of control. They also have 'strange effects' (ibid. 97), which seem to blur the lines between the external and internal worlds of the individual. Lefebvre states, '[t]he space of the dream is strange and alien, yet at the same time as close to us as is possible"; but nonetheless "it still has a sensual-sensory character. It is a theatrical space even more than a quotidian or poetic one: a putting into images of oneself, for oneself' (ibid. 208–209).

The space of the dream is analogous to the space of the city, strange and alien but also recognizable due to its recurring elements. Acker's novels exist within physical and imaginative space, yet are forced to operate and 'adhere to the oedipal rules in an endeavor to examine the narrative possibilities for empowerment in death' (Worthington 2000: 244). By obeying while also resisting these narratives, Acker's modern strangers exist in a liminal zone of reality and dream, horror and beauty. Just as '[h]er father's transgression introduces her to a complexity in the world, which is both more painful and more truthful' (Conte 1999: 16), the city also offers a similar backdrop for a world of experience and suffering that releases harsh reality from dream or illusion, and vice versa.

Despite Acker's association of utopian thinking with the act of suffering, the torment her characters go through does not necessarily offer them any sort of transcendence or elucidation. Just as her characters' liminal identities bring about no equality of the sexes, suffering likewise results in no utopian outcome. Instead, she problematizes the idea of suffering as a tool of transcendence. Throughout *Don Quixote*, Acker associates Catholicism with madness because of its belief that surrendering to suffering is the pathway to being healed. Although Don Quixote, like a Jesus figure, is attracted to "sinners" and loves others who suffer, thereby linking suffering and her quest for love, the characters are not healed by this suffering but instead continue to endure more. Suffering is not a requirement to reach a different plane of spiritual consciousness but is something one must go through, simply because to love and to be human are acts grounded in suffering. Her conversation with God at the end of the novel allows her to realize that a quest in search of any idealism was doomed from the beginning. The genderless God she encounters is a self-proclaimed 'mealy mouthed hypocrite, dishonest … 'whore', who points out Its monstrous imperfections and tells the 'night' to look inwards: 'God continued condemning Him- or Herself: "So now that you know I'm imperfect, night, that you can't turn to Me: turn to yourself"' (Acker 1986: 207). The 'Me' that God refers to seems to be the idealistic and essential representation of God or love that Don Quixote chases after, concepts which she acknowledges are unattainable after she realizes that she actually *is* made in God's monstrous and fragmented image. In this sense, she maintains the Christian doctrine of God's omnipresence, but deconstructs the idealism that has held God as superior and perfect.

Acker not only deconstructs the sacred into the secular, but also reconstructs and resacralizes it through the sacred self and the liminal act of becoming. Suffering and torment do not lead to a healed or unified self, but continue in reaffirming estrangement from the fractured self. While the transcendence that exists in the beginning of the novel is one of gender, Don Quixote's transcendence at the end is one of perception, making the quest for essentialism, her 'sickness,' (ibid. 18) fade away. Don Quixote neither fulfills nor abandons her quest, nor does she awaken from her dream and return to reality. In the end, she awakens to a hybrid of the two, invoking Baudelaire's axiom of '[b]e drunk always' (ibid. 73).[16] Don Quixote breaks another set of chains and once again begins her life anew: 'I thought about God for one more minute and forgot it. I closed my eyes, head drooping, like a person drunk for so long she no longer knows she's drunk, and then drunk, awoke to the world which lay before me' (1986: 207). The message of *Don Quixote* might be summed up by Acker herself speaking about creating one's own values: '[p]eople are searching for their centers (be they centers of pleasure, pain, whatever) but really, in a way, it's a search for "God"' (2018: 147). Don Quixote's search ends with finding God, but that ultimately leads to her realizing the ugly truth that perfect love, with another human or even with God, does not really exist, that love is a complicated, flawed, monstrous emotion. Yet despite Don Quixote's repetitive cycle of failures in her quest for love, her utopian spirit is not diminished. The utopian fragments and residue from her quest still linger, although reformed outside the realm of ideals, residing in a hybrid but symbolic place. For example, Don Quixote romanticizes the notion of the musician Prince, an artist famous for blurring the lines of gender, race, and morality, as being the perfect president of the United States of America (Acker 1986: 21). Furthermore, despite what may be seen as failure, Don Quixote and Acker may have been triumphant in what Cixous maintains as 'writing her self,' although in a more liminal understanding of what constitutes the female self, and therefore arriving much closer to Haraway's claim to 'live on the boundaries, to write without the founding myth of original wholeness' (2004: 33).

In *Empire*, Abhor correspondingly ends the novel in an ambiguous state. She learns to ride a motorcycle, which acts as both a gender-abolishing act and mode of personal freedom. Not only does Abhor reject the Oedipal and capitalist culture surrounding her, she also refuses to join its antagonistic other in Thivai's terrorism or the typical rebellious outfit of the motorcycle gang (Horn 2015: 142). By refusing to be a slave to Thivai's violent cause or join a gang consisting solely of men, she substitutes these options with her own cause: that is, becoming her own gang and, as a result, allowing herself hope despite not knowing what that hope actually is outside of existing within disgust:

> "I stood there, there in the sunlight, and thought that I didn't as yet know what I wanted. I now fully knew what I didn't want and whom I hated. That was something.
>
> And then I thought that, one day, maybe, there I'd *[sic]* be a human society in a world which is beautiful, a society which wasn't just disgust (Acker 1988: 227).

Since she is unable to put utopian ideals into words, Acker moves away from trying to blur binary divisions through language in exchange for the use of symbolic representations. Tattoos become the underlining symbol of the novel due to their 'ambiguous social value' (ibid. 130). According to Acker, they are the 'most positive thing in the book' since they concern 'taking over, doing your own sign-making... The meeting of body and, well, the spirit' (Friedman 1989a: 17–18). Abhor maintains this stance when claiming that early Christian tattoos were seen as stigmata indicating exile and tribal identity (Acker 1988: 130). Acker uses the tattoo's sacred and 'defamatory' (ibid.) essence as the liminal and resacralized symbol of the stranger, for it instantaneously represents the sacred/profane, masculine/feminine, dream/taboo hybridity of modern secularized life that can only be expressed through symbolic and liminal representations, representations she can live within. In *On Revolution*, Arendt suggests that the best way to navigate through the abyss of freedom is to locate a freedom that is a 'visible, tangible reality' (1963: 33), or freedom is at risk of collapsing under itself. To write oneself female is to exist in the abyssal and liminal space between iconoclastic ambiguity and tangible reality.

Notes: Chapter VI

[1] Although Medusa is never mentioned in *Frankenstein*, in the posthumous poem "On the Medusa of Leonardo Da Vinci in the Florentine Gallery," Percy Shelly captures a similar revolutionary beauty in Medusa's monstrous gaze as Cixous does. Both Mary Shelley and her husband use the symbol of 'monstrous ... eyes, whose strength lies in seeing as much as in being seen' (Clayton 2003: 132).

[2] The character Safie may be the exception to this argument. See '"They Will Prove the Truth of My Tale": Safie's Letters as the Feminist Core of Mary Shelley's *Frankenstein*' (1991) by Joyce Zonana.

[3] Feilla expands on this notion, arguing that during Shelley's time, 'women either *possess* (male) genius and thus are monsters or *are possessed* by genius (divine spirits) ... Moreover, the description of the creature as a *daemon* throughout the 1818 edition of *Frankenstein* further underscores its associations with the figure of genius ... Belonging neither to the world of humans nor of the gods, daemons were outside the pale of human limitations—moral, physical, social or legal—and were generally considered to be neither good nor bad, neither moral nor immoral' (2008: 168–170).

[4] Freud's projection theory and the theory of the Oedipus complex have been adapted and expanded by a feminist psychoanalyst critique. In her book *The Interpretation of the Flesh: Freud and Femininity*, Teresa Brennan argues that women sometimes take on the physical and psychological manifestations of men's projected femininity where '[t]he desire of the other, in short,

embodies an image and attention that can enhance or diminish one's capacities' (1992: 226).

[5] Building on Douglas' pollution boundaries, Judith Butler uses her work in relation to homosexuality:

> Since anal and oral sex among men clearly establishes certain kinds of bodily permeabilities unsanctioned by the hegemonic order, male homosexuality would, within such a hegemonic point of view, constitute a site of danger and pollution, prior to and regardless of the cultural presence of AIDS. Similarly, the "polluted" status of lesbians, regardless of their low-risk status with respect to AIDS, brings into relief the dangers of their bodily exchanges. Significantly, being "outside" the hegemonic order does not signify being "in" a state of filthy and untidy nature. Paradoxically, homosexuality is almost always conceived within the homophobic signifying economy as both uncivilized and unnatural (1999: 168).

[6] Katherine Hayles (1999) develops this idea further when taking into account 'the seriated history of cybernetics', expanding on Latour's claim by adding that 'we have always been posthuman' (1999: 291).

[7] Milton's *Paradise Lost*, Plutarch's *Lives*, and Johann Wolfgang von Goethe's *The Sorrows of Werther*.

[8] While the question of what the first cyborg or prototype truly is may be debatable, I agree with the many scholars (Botting 2013; Fuller 2003; Gray, Mentor & Figueroa-Sarriera 1995) who argue that, due to the biological and technological orientation of the Creature, Shelley's novel contains the first cyborg.

[9] Following van Genep's classification of the rite of passage, Omofolalabo Soyinka Ajayi states the importance of dancing as a liminal journey of 'uniting the spiritual with the earthly' (1996: 187).

[10] Like her cyborg, Haraway herself is caught in a spiral dance of the sacred and profane. While claiming she is 'a committed atheist and anti-Catholic' (2004: 334), she still acknowledges the influence that her Catholic upbringing has had on her work: 'But I am also deeply formed by theology, and particularly by Roman Catholic theology and practice. I learned it. I studied it. It is deep in my bones' (ibid. 333). In *Manifestly Haraway*, although reiterating her hatred for the Catholic Church, Haraway likes to see herself 'as a secular Catholic' (2016: 267–269). Relatedly, using Butler's understanding of gender as performance, Alison Webster (1998) similarly argues that the Christian faith has become something performed and created rather than something obtained in the modern world.

[11] Exploring Tillich's ideas of abyssal boundaries, Ann Belford Ulanov notes that in his extensive work on the subject, gender is never discussed; she does, however, argue that '[l]atent in Tillich's doctrine of symbols is the meeting, mixing and exchanging of masculine and feminine modes of being' (2005: 232).

12. 'Between man and woman a strangeness must subsist that corresponds to the fact that they dwell in different worlds. Perceiving such a difference is more difficult than perceiving biological or social differences. It remains invisible, as subjectivity itself, but, without respecting it, we cannot meet each other as humans' (Irigaray 2004: xii).
13. 'To include the other in my universe prevents meeting with the other, whereas safeguarding the obscurity and the silence that the other remains for me aids in discovering proximity' (ibid. 29).
14. 'I Know you're mine!!!...I made you!!!...I'm making you...My father explained again, 'I am fucking God and I made God' (Acker 1988: 15).
15. Dworkin rejects this interpretation of her work, stating, '[w]hat I think is that sex must not put women in a subordinate position. It must be reciprocal and not an act of aggression from a man looking only to satisfy himself. That's my point' (cited in Kelso 2018: 89). Moreover, in *Intercourse*, Dworkin argues that sex is also 'a communion, a sharing, mutual possession of an enormous mystery', and therefore 'has the intensity and magnificence of violent feeling transformed into tenderness' (1987/2007: 81).
16. 'Be drunk always. Nothing else matters; there are no other subjects. Not to feel the grim weight of Time breaking your backs and bending you double, you must get drunk and stay drunk' (Baudelaire 2010a: 73).

CONCLUSION

Spectral Monsters and Modern Strangers

In the beginning there is ruin. Ruin is what remains or returns as the spectre from the moment one first looks at oneself and a figuration is eclipsed. The figure, the face, then sees its visibility being eaten away.
—Jacques Derrida, *Memoirs of the Blind*

Monsters are our children. They can be pushed to the farthest margins of geography and discourse, hidden away at the edges of the world and in the forbidden recesses of our mind, but they always return.
—Jeffrey Jerome Cohen, "Monster Culture (Seven Theses)"

The phantom is therefore also a metapsychological fact: what haunts are not the dead, but the gaps left within us by the secrets of others.
—Nicholas Abraham, "Notes on the Phantom"

Thus strangely are our souls constructed, and by such slight ligaments are we bound to prosperity or ruin.
—Mary Shelley, *Frankenstein*

Spectres and Monsters

Monstrosity has been discussed, and relatedly Shelley's Creature, throughout this book as a sort of hauntological theme or thread connecting many of the modern stranger figures mentioned. This haunting quality is why, when examining *Frankenstein* in the opening chapter, I allocated the Creature—modernity's first mythological monster—more to Derrida's concept of the spectre than to that of monstrosity. In most cases, the philosophical uses of spectre versus monster are not always distinguishable, but I believe they exist within the same liminal and preternatural plane. The differences, if any, and similarities

---

How to cite this book chapter:
Beghetto, R. G. 2022. *Monstrous Liminality; Or, The Uncanny Strangers Of Secularized Modernity*. Pp. 169–178. London: Ubiquity Press. DOI: https://doi.org/10.5334/bcp.h. License: CC-BY-NC

between the two may conceivably be as subtle and equivocal as Derrida's estimation of spirit and spectre.[1] Historically, what chiefly distinguished monsters and spectres from one another were corporeal and ethereal divisions. Where the monster exemplified something that is alive and physical, the spectre was an imaginary, supernatural representation of the return of the dead. 'A Specter, or Apparition,' argues Catholic demonologist Pierre Le Loyer in his *Treatise of Specters*, 'is an Imagination of a Substance without a Bodie, the which presenteth itself sensibly unto men, against the order and course of Nature, and maketh them afraid' (1605: 1).[2] This distinction between the two did not drastically change during the Gothic era. Gothic monsters represent 'violence, sadism, and unsavory appetite' that live on the edges of reason, whereas Gothic spectres are predominantly seen as representations of the human imagination or illusory supernaturalism that ultimately become discredited as fabrications (Brittan 2017: 30). While one entity appears to question reason from its own liminal surroundings, the other exists to eventually restore order and reason through the dispelling of superstition. It is with *Frankenstein* that these binary, though delicate, distinctions become radically intertwined, giving us a modern experiment that results in creating the first spectral-monster that, as we have seen, both haunts and embodies secularized modernity and its uncanny strangers. Consequently, I would like to bring the discussion back to *Frankenstein*, monstrosity, and the spectral, in an attempt to 'return to the dead,' as it were.

One way to argue the Creature, and accordingly the modern stranger, is both monster and spectre is to say that it goes through its own liminal *Bildungsroman*, advancing from a teratological to hauntological entity, originating with the monstrous and unnatural birth that eventually culminates in the spectral after the Creature's development and assumed death. However, this reading can be somewhat misleading, since it depicts a linear progression or transformation from monster to spectre, which can be problematic for two reasons. First, the Creature in *Frankenstein* is continuously both spectre and monster from birth, something even Victor Frankenstein addresses: 'I then reflected, and the thought made me shiver, that the creature whom I had left in my apartment might still be there, alive, and walking about. I dreaded to behold this monster ... I threw the door forcibly open, as children are accustomed to do when they expect a spectre to stand in waiting for them on the other side; but nothing appeared' (Shelley 2003: 88). Secondly, in isolation this interpretation suggests the spectral is superior to the monstrous, indicating a progression or transcendence from latter to former. Rather, Shelley's revolutionary influence on the subject is achieved by making the two interchangeable by forming the spectre into flesh, something Derrida also acknowledges by arguing, 'Mary Shelley brought our attention to the anagram that makes the spectre in respect visible again' (1994/2005: 288). By making the spectre corporeal, Shelley paradoxically brings the spectre into the monstrous and vice versa, thereby symbolically bringing it from the realm of superstition into the uncanny and liminal edges of reason to stand alongside its uncanny cousin. It is with *Frankenstein* that both spectre and monster are spoken and listened to,[3] and more importantly, also possibly respected.[4]

Returning to Derrida's language concerning monster and spectre, it is obvious that they share many fundamental characteristics. Both operate in uncanny territories of liminality, exploring the unknown and indefinable, and thereby are seen as symbolic warnings or threats that continuously haunt us. More importantly, they are also entities we may be able to see but which nonetheless, through an abject absence, interrogate and question the notion of the self, otherness, and the concept of being present. To Derrida (1992/1995) and other scholars such as Jeffrey Cohen (1996), monsters are alive and fully realized, and if they exist within our imagination, they do so predominantly within, though not limited to, a realm of hybridity. Spectres, on the other hand, seem to be even more liminal to Derrida, in that they seem to go beyond the 'hybridization' of monstrosity (1995: 386). A spectre is something that is neither present nor real, but nonetheless is still able to insinuate itself into our present and real worlds. Although ghostly in nature, spectres still to some degree exist within the visible, corporeal, and material world, presenting themselves as images of individuals from our past.

The fundamental difference between the two may well centre on a negligible variation of paradox, where the spectre operates in disjunction, residing within the neither/nor category while the hybrid monster exists within the conjunction of both/same. However, if examined closely, there seems to be little degree of separation between the two uncanny forces; yet although having previously contemplated the subject in a 1990 interview published in *Points*, Derrida never really brings up monsters in *Specters'* hauntological narrative, although others (Ganteau 2015; Shildrick 2002) have written on the obvious connection. The purely monstrous is thus, for Derrida, an impossibility.

Derrida must have seen Shelley's Creature as more in line with the spectre than with monstrosity, especially since true monstrousness for Derrida is unable to sustain itself, while his reluctance to connect the two could be accorded to the fact that monsters lose their monstrosity, potency, and strength over us once they are perceived or recognized as monsters (1995: 386) and, as a result, vanquished. Regardless of its initial monstrosity and abjection, the uncanny monster, even though it helps alter culture, slowly dilutes itself into a canny familiarity, into the very thing it once threatened.[5] This is what Derrida calls 'the movement of culture' (ibid. 387), a relationship akin to the secularization/resacralization process. Ironically, the Creature is always regarded as a monster by the humans it interacts with, a projection that the monster itself is forced to embody, yet this does not remove the threat it poses to us. What the monster is never given by Victor is an identity. If to name something is to have power over it, the Creature may well have retained its power over Victor because it was never named and, as a result, remained unknown and haunting even to its creator, despite it being perceived by Frankenstein, and thus by itself, as a monster. Still, notwithstanding, the Creature never loses its hauntological threat, and therefore is never tamed.[6]

Spectres and Phantoms

One discernible reason for the omission of the monster in *Specters* is that Derrida's spectre is largely tied to his definition of messianic time. The spectre is neither past nor future for Derrida, and consequently allows the 'spectral moment' to 'no longer belong to time' (2006: xix). Since the spectre is simultaneously *revenant* and *arrivant*, the past is just as ambiguous or unknown as the future, and therefore 'must carry beyond present life' (ibid.). Time for Derrida, as for Benjamin, is a crucial aspect of the messianic; there seems to be a difference between the "monstrous moment" and that of the 'messianic moment' that the spectre embodies. While the monster does represent an *arrivant*, a warning or threat of a possible future,[7] and even a questioning of humanity's traditional values, Derrida ironically does not seem to allocate any sort of past, and therefore any messianic character, to it. The spectre is messianic in that it disrupts time, epitomized by Derrida's use of the *Hamlet* quote, 'time is out of joint,' thereby blurring the lines between past, present, and future. The spectre is simultaneously an inheritance from the past and future, which precedes any experience 'beyond the living present in general' (ibid. xix). Time for Derrida is a series of 'modalized presents' (ibid.), therefore messianic time cannot exist in the present but rather outside of it. The monstrous moment, on the other hand, seems to exist in instances, in the abruption of time directly associated with the present/future but not the past/present/future of disjointed time.

Frankenstein itself, both in structure and genre, also refuses to be confined to a certain moment in time, but nonetheless captures a moment where time has been disrupted; it simultaneously captures the monstrous living in the messianic. Derrida must have accepted a spectral element in Shelley's Creature specifically due to its being a hybridization of dead body parts. Frankenstein's Creature also contains a history and represents "a return of the dead," as does the spectre, only one that is more fragmented, uncanny, and subconscious. Even though it is not originally weighed down by history, at least until it develops an obsession with its creator, the Creature still carries the dead with it at birth in ways that may not be so easily recognized or decipherable as the image of a spectre, but nonetheless conveys a culturally miscellaneous past. If the spectre is an image of an individual that translates to the collective, the monster is an image of the collective that channels itself unknowingly into the individual; to borrow Bloch's utopian symbolism, one is Kant burning through Hegel, while the other is Hegel burning through Kant.

For Cohen, however, all monsters—not just Shelley's—are 'a cultural body' even in origin (1996: 4), as the monster is part of a larger cultural perspective and is neither born nor exists entirely in isolation. To say the Creature in *Frankenstein* is free of history, and therefore completely free to cultivate itself (Armitt 2012; Gilbert & Gubar 1979), is a half-truth. Because it is made up of parts and not a solitary body, the Creature is tied to nothing specific, such as a spectre of communism, the French Revolution, or messianism, and therefore is autonomous to some extent; but nonetheless it carries the ruins of the past that haunt it in secrecy and silence.

Accordingly, we could argue that the Creature is haunting in a language far more reminiscent of Nicolas Abraham and Maria Torok's psychoanalytic concept of the 'transgenerational phantom'[8] than of Derrida's spectre. Abraham first raised the issue in "Notes on the Phantom" (1975/1994), before further developing the concept of cryptonymy during his collaboration with Torok. Abraham and Torok's phantom may be more applicable to *Frankenstein*'s Creature for a few reasons. A side—though overarching—argument is that the notion of the phantasmagorical goes beyond an illustration of the fantastic, referring to 'a bizarre or fantastic combination, collection, or assemblage,'[9] efficiently summing up the Creature's multifarious makeup. Moreover, in the introduction to Abraham and Torok's *The Shell and the Kernel*, Nicholas T. Rand describes the phantom as an 'unfelt mourning, unassimilated trauma, the unwitting psychical inheritance of someone else's secrets—drive a wedge between us and our society' (1987/1994: 22). Similar to Derrida's spectre, the phantom is a product of displacement, and moreover a symbol of the return of the dead.[10] Yet despite these eerie similarities to Derrida's spectre, Colin Davis maintains that the main separation of Abraham and Torok's phantom from Derrida's specter lies in the problem of secrecy:

> The crucial difference between the two ... is to be found in the status of the secret. The secrets of Abraham and Torok's lying phantoms are unspeakable in the restricted sense of being a subject of shame and prohibition. It is not at all that they cannot be spoken; on the contrary, they can and should be put into words so that the phantom and its noxious effects on the living can be exorcised. For Derrida the ghost and its secrets are unspeakable in a quite different sense. Abraham and Torok seek to return the ghost to the order of knowledge; Derrida wants to avoid any such restoration and to encounter what is strange, unheard, other, about the ghost ... The secret is not unspeakable because it is taboo, but because it cannot (yet) be articulated in the languages available to us. The ghost pushes at the boundaries of language and thought" (2007: 13).

While discussing secrecy in Chapter 1, I mentioned how secrecy lies between two liminal worlds, and how the responsibility of modernity's monstrous secret sits on the shoulders of the human creator in *Frankenstein*. The Creature may well be Victor's, as well as our, spectre; but in regard to the Creature, the unconscious and historical secret resides silently within its own body. Frankenstein instantly acknowledges the secret of secularized modernity's monstrous ambiguity when he witnesses the spectre's 'watery eyes'. However, this secret ambiguity, this transgenerational phantom, haunts the Creature unknowingly from within. While it tries to cultivate itself in a secularized, "technological," and unrestricted rising world, the sacred past soundlessly haunts the Creature. The Creature's attempt to exorcise this phantom of the abyss through resacralization is extinguished when Frankenstein refuses its wish for love and companionship, ensuring the Creature's permanently liminal state. Ultimately, it may always have been a false hope, since even the Creature acknowledges this outcome would not exorcise its monstrosity but rather solidify it: 'It is true, we shall be monsters, cut off from all the world; but on that account we shall be more attached to one another' (Shelley 2003: 148). The Creature wishes for a utopia of monstrosity and strangerhood, completely removed from the rest of normal society, though it is fated to manifest itself through secularized modernity's movement of culture, as a monster, phantom, spectre, and modern stranger.

Addressing the Monster in the Spectral Room

Derrida's hauntology has taken precedence over Abraham and Torok's cryptonymy in contemporary criticism; and if Davis' distinction is correct, it may be that Derrida's deconstruction theory is more influential due to its 'rehabilitation of ghosts' (Davis 2007: 8) and its insistence that we should in fact let the dead speak and not exorcise them. This, however, does not explain why Derrida was silent on Abraham and Torok's theory. Friends with Abraham, Derrida was also very much informed on their theory, since he wrote the foreword to *The Wolf Man's Magic Word: A Cryptonymy* (1977/2005), the first time that Abraham and Torok collaborated on the subject.[11] Unlike Davis, Zoltán Dragon sees little difference between their works, arguing that the two hauntological 'trends … do not exclude each other' (2005: 257). Dragon goes on to argue that Derrida's spectre is in fact haunted by Abraham and Torok's silent phantom:

> Derrida thus incorporates the pivotal concepts of cryptonymy, and utilizes them to a deconstructive end—thus silencing the psychoanalytic background or inheritance. This forms an uncanny kernel in his own discourse that gains its final formulation … in his program of *hauntology*, being present via its very absence. Thus, the very program of hauntology or spectropoetics is already haunted by a silent and effective phantom, whose effect is the transmission of the Derridean crypt on and on (ibid. 269).

I bring this up in order to re-address the monster hiding in Derrida's spectre/messianic theory. By saying Shelley is the first to make the spectre visible, Derrida must downplay the monstrousness within Frankenstein's Creature, and subsequently, his own secular idea of messianism. Derrida does not shy away from connecting the monster to deconstructionism (1997: 5), conceivably even connecting it 'to the critique of a tradition deformed by a humanist view' (Johnson 1993: 261). Though by questionably ignoring the *revenant* characteristics of the monster, Derrida, like Victor Frankenstein, does seem to 'turn his eyes away'[12] from the monstrous act that leads to the ruin, and instead focuses on the ruins that make up the spectre/messianic. In this sense, for Derrida, the spectre as spectator undermines the actor that is monster, since actions can themselves be monstrous, as seen with both Frankenstein and his Creature, and can be difficult to extrapolate from one another.

From this perspective, a comparison might be Ernst Bloch removing the horrors of WWI from his utopian spirit. Although the horrors of the Great War, or any horrific event, are not something anyone would encourage, it would be impossible to build Bloch's utopian spirit without the monstrous event. Yet, as mentioned in Chapter 3, we run into problems when we base our utopian and secularized messianism around such horrific events of destruction. Derrida cannot 'domesticate' (1995: 386) his monsters just as he understood we could not exorcise our phantoms and spectres. In evaluating Eliade's traditional idea that monsters are a threat to the religious and sacred order, Timothy K. Beal blurs these divine binaries of sacred and monstrous, arguing that 'what [monsters] often reveal is a divinity or a sacredness that is like many of our religions and like many of ourselves, caught in endless, irreducible tensions between order and chaos, orientation and disorientation, self and other, foundation and abyss. Religion is never without its monsters' (2002: 10). Like the uncanny that it is so closely associated with, 'the *monstrum* is a message that breaks into this world from the realm of the divine' (ibid. 7). The monster might well be the human liminal kernel that balances the flawlessness of the human spirit, as Leopardi believed.

Consequently, the modern stranger can be the true spectral-monster or *spect-actor*, and therefore its uncanny role in secular messianism becomes challenging. Even though it is born on the ruins of the sacred and attempts in various ways to resacralize the spiritual gaps that secularized modernity instigated, it may not be the most ideal archetype of the messianic, something it probably does not desire to be associated with anyway; or more appropriately, we need to finally address the uncanny and chilling warning (because that is what both monsters and spectres do) that our messianic impulses, as both individuals and collectives, can sometimes in fact be monstrous.

Adaptation and the Future of the Modern Stranger—A Coda

The uncanny spectres of modernity have left a liminal underpinning to our contemporary world, while its cultural monsters are still being challenged.

Like humans themselves, traditions and cultures, whether well-established or loosely connected concepts, must adapt to the changing world. Just as Baudelaire, who despised the destruction of the Arcades and the Paris he knew and loved, adapted his poetry to find beauty in the new "ugliness" of the modern metropolis, traditions should also adapt. While Adorno's argument that 'those who want to adapt must learn increasingly to curb their imagination' (1991: 192) rings true to some degree, adaptation does not necessarily mean conforming to societal conventions and expectations. Society also must adapt to include strangers, whose feelings of boredom, alienation, *ennui*, and marginalization are largely ignored or dismissed. Inclusion is an important aspect of the modern stranger, as despite being closely related, strangers are not necessarily outsiders; they have not rejected or abandoned modern society but rather have chosen to be immersed within it, becoming an intrinsic part of secularized modernity itself, even if it means residing in the uncanny shadows and voids that modernity has created within itself. Baudelaire's *flâneur*, for example, is the quintessential symbol of simultaneously being both physically and spiritually engaged and detached within modern society, though this modern/anti-modern sentiment is likewise realized in Acker's experimentation with language being a part of, yet instantaneously disconnected from, the society she lives in. The absence of a complete rejection of traditional and modern societal norms and customs, despite one's disinclination towards them, leaves the modern stranger almost in a love/hate relationship with secularized modernity and its discontents. This liminal perspective allows the modern stranger to criticize from within; a panoptical gaze that allows for a reimagining or resacralizing of the past, creating a viewpoint that is extremely beneficial and valuable to any society, if heeded. Yet we must ask ourselves, does further adapting the modern stranger to society put an end to the concept of the modern stranger, and moreover, should it be the goal of a society to end strangerhood once and for all? There is a danger of excessive liminality, to be sure, though there is a greater danger in removing the liminality of the stranger. Making the outlook of the stranger the new status quo dissolves the constructive aspects that made the modern stranger such a valuable figure in both defining, redefining, and resacralizing secularized modernity in the first place; consequently, it is imperative to listen to the voices of modern strangers while they adapt to society, something always attempted, though ultimately never truly achieved.

Yet despite retaining a common uncanny strangeness and the same spiritual and physiological principle, the contemporary stranger has changed into more of a visible and geographical entity that makes up a big part of what Ahmed (2014) refers to as 'affect aliens'. In many ways, the modern stranger has become more complicated and challenging, as its more traditional definition of binary and fully marginalized "outsider" seems to be in conflict with Simmel's more modern and liminal meaning, encompassing people who go beyond simply a psychological or even spiritual inability to blend in with society, as does the modern stranger. This raises questions as to whether modernity is truly over or whether it is simply continuing its process of change. It remains to be seen whether we have completely exhausted modernity and, as a result, the idea of the stranger, or whether modernity itself has become the spectre. If modernity is indeed over, it may well be because the stranger has changed; modernity's monster, its spectre, its resacralizing spirit, may finally have transformed beyond what modernity entails, thus ultimately changing it into something new. Or are we still caught in liminal modernity, since many aspects of our recent past seem to be repeating? Are the spectres of 20th-century totalitarianism and fascism being renewed? Or are we witnessing the chaotic colliding of alternate ideas that existed at the turn of the century, as presented in Musil's *Qualities*, where meaning and truth are constantly being questioned? Not to mention, the Covid-19 pandemic that is currently invading all our lives. How will strangerhood be transformed by new forms of alienation; by a society too afraid to leave their homes and too anxious to return to "normal" society after self-alienating for such a long period? More importantly, how will the stranger be effected by the conflict ignited by the people who want vaccines and those who do not? Our current and unruly times may be pushing us towards something totally diffrerent, like millions of "New Angels"/ "Angels of History" being carried away with our backs turned toward a chaotic and unkown future. Nevertheless, whether we are still in a modern era or one that is completely beyond modernity, the uncanny stranger must nonetheless resist the urge to faithfully conform to new status quos or binaries, even those based on the stranger itself. If we want to acclimatize in nourishing and introspective ways to an ever-evolving society, the liminality of the stranger is too important to lose—strangerness should be always protected, not abolished.

Notes: Conclusion

[1] 'The spirit, the specter are not the same thing, and we will have to sharpen this difference; but as for what they have in common, one does not know what it is, what it is presently. It is something that one does not know, precisely, and one does not know if precisely it is, if it exists, if it responds to a name and corresponds to an essence' (Derrida 2006: 5).

[2] The first time the word "spectre" (or "specter") appeared in English was actually in Zacharie Jones' 1605 English translation of Le Loyer's treatise (Chesters 2011: 146, n18).

[3] 'He should learn to live by learning not how to make conversation with the ghost but how to talk with him, with her, how to let them speak or how to give them back speech, even if it is in oneself, in the other, in the other in oneself: they are always there, specters, even if they do not exist, even if they are no longer, even if they are not yet' (Derrida 2006: 221).

4. 'Respect for the spectre, as Mary Shelley would say' (Derrida 2005: 73).
5. '... from the moment they enter into culture, the movement of acculturation, precisely, of domestication, of normalization has already begun' (Derrida 1995: 386).
6. This reading focuses on Shelley's novel; however, through popular culture, such as the Universal "Frankenstein" films (1931–39), the Creature/Monster slowly becomes tamed. While James Whale's 1931 film did not name the Creature—this is something that developed over time—it does begin to diminish the Creature's intelligence, empathy, individualism, and, as a result, its uncanniness.
7. A future that would not be monstrous would not be a future' (Derrida 2006: 387).
8. The transgenerational phantom is a phenomenon whereby horrifying secrets are silently passed down from previous generations to their offspring through the unconscious. However, as Rand maintains, '[a]spects of this concept have the potential to illuminate the genesis of social institutions and may provide a new perspective for inquiring into the psychological roots of cultural patterns and political ideology' (1994: 169).
9. https://www.merriam-webster.com/dictionary/phantasmagoria.
10. '... the phantom which returns to haunt bears witness to the existence of the dead buried within the other' (Abraham 1994: 175).
11. The only time Derrida mentions them is when he references his foreword, "Fors," in *Specters of Marx*, but not their actual work.
12. 'I employ these words, I admit, with a glance toward the business of childbearing—but also with a glance toward those who, in a company from which I do not exclude myself, turn their eyes away in the face of the as yet unnameable, which is proclaiming itself and which can do so, as is necessary whenever a birth is in the offing, only under the species of the non-species in the formless, mute, infant, and terrifying form of monstrosity' (Derrida 1978: 370).

References

Abe K. *The Ruined Map.* (Translated by Saunders ED.) New York: Vintage Books; 2001.
Abraham N. Notes on the Phantom: A Compliment to Freud's Metapsychology. (Translated by Rand NT.) In: Abraham N & Torok M (Eds.) *The Shell and the Kernel: Renewals of Psychoanalysis, Volume 1.* Chicago; London: University of Chicago Press; 1994. pp. 171–176.
Abraham N, Torok M. *The Shell and the Kernel: Renewals of Psychoanalysis, Volume 1.* (Translated by Rand NT.) Chicago; London: University of Chicago Press; 1994.
Abraham N, Torok M. *The Wolf Man's Magic Word: A Cryptonymy.* (Translated by Rand NT.) Minneapolis: University of Minnesota Press; 2005.
Acker K. *Don Quixote: Which Was a Dream.* New York: Grove Press; 1986.
Acker K. *Empire of the Senseless.* New York: Grove Press; 1988.
Acker K. *Kathy Acker: The Last Interview: and Other Conversations.* Brooklyn: Melville House Publishing; 2018.
Acquisto J. *The Fall Out of Redemption: Writing and Thinking Beyond Salvation in Baudelaire, Cioran, Fondane, Agamben, and Nancy.* New York: Bloomsbury Publishing; 2015.
Adorno TW. *The Culture Industry: Selected Essays on Mass Culture.* London: Routledge; 1991.
Adorno TW, Horkheimer M. *Dialectic of Enlightenment.* (Translated by Cumming J.) New York: Continuum; 1982.

Agamben G. *Homo Sacer: Sovereign Power and Bare Life.* (Translated by Heller-Roazen D.) Stanford CA: Stanford University Press; 1998.
Agamben G. *The Time That Remains: A Commentary on the Letters to the Romans.* Stanford CA: Stanford University Press; 2005.
Ahmed S. Not in the Mood. *New Formations*: A Journal of Culture, Theory, Politics. 2014; 82: 13–28. DOI: https://doi.org/10.3898/NeWF.82.01.2014
Ahmed S. *The Promise of Happiness.* Durham (NC): Duke University Press; 2010.
Ajayi OS. In Contest: The Dynamics of African Religious Dances. In: Welsh-Asante K (Ed.) *African Dance: An Artistic, Historical, and Philosophical Inquiry.* African World Press; 1996. pp. 183–202.
Alighieri D. *The Divine Comedy.* (Translated by Sisson CH.) Oxford: Oxford University Press; 1998.
Althaus-Reid M. *Indecent Theology: Theological Preservations in Sex, Gender and Politics.* London: Routledge; 2000.
Anderson LM. *German Expressionism and the Messianism of a Generation.* Amsterdam; New York: Rodopi; 2011.
Aneja A. The Medusa's Slip: Hélène Cixous and the Underpinnings of Écriture Feminine. In: Jacobus LA and Barreca R (Eds.) *Hélène Cixous: Critical Impressions.* Amsterdam: Gordon and Breach; 1999. pp. 58–75.
Antonioni M, Leprohon P. *Michelangelo Antonioni: An Introduction.* (Translated by Sullivan S.) New York: Simon and Schuster; 1963.
Appiah KA. There Is No Such Thing As Western Civilisation. *The Guardian* (9 Nov. 2016). www.theguardian.com/world/2016/nov/09/western-civilisation-appiah-reith-lecture. Accessed: 15-09-2019.
Arendt H. *On Revolutions.* New York: Penguin; 1963.
Armitt L. *Where No Man Has Gone Before: Essays on Women and Science Fiction.* London: Routledge; 2012.
Artz L. *Global Entertainment Media: A Critical Introduction.* Chichester; Malden MA: John Wiley & Sons; 2015.
Asad T. *Formations of the Secular: Christianity, Islam, Modernity.* Standord CA: Stanford University Press; 2003.
Asad T. Reading a Modern Classic: W. C. Smith's 'The Meaning and End of Religion'. *History of Religions.* 2001; 40(3): pp. 205–222. DOI: https://doi.org/10.1086/463633
Auerbach E. *Dante: Poet of the Secular World.* (Translated by Manheim R.) Chicago: University of Chicago Press; 1961.
Avalon (2001). Directed by **Oshii M.** Miramax Home Entertainment: 2003.
Bader VM. Post-Secularism or Liberal-Democratic Constitutionalism? *Erasmus Law Review.* 2012; 5(1): pp. 5–26. DOI: https://doi.org/10.5553/ELR221026712012005001002
Badiou A. *Saint Paul: The Foundation of Universalism.* Standord CA: Stanford University Press; 2003.

Baer U. *Remnants of Song: Trauma and the Experience of Modernity in Charles Baudelaire and Paul Celan.* Stanford CA: Stanford University Press; 2000.
Baker Jr. JM. Vacant Holidays: The Theological Remainder in Leopardi, Baudelaire, and Benjamin. *MLN.* 2006; 121(5): pp. 1190–1219. DOI: https://doi.org/10.1353/mln.2007.0000
Barricelli JP. *Giacomo Leopardi.* Boston: Twayne; 1986.
Baudelaire C. *Baudelaire as a Literary Critic.* (Translated by Hyslop LB and Hyslop Jr. FE.) University Park: Pennsylvania State University Press; 1964.
Baudelaire C. *Curiosités Esthétiques.* Paris: Calmann-Lévy; 1935.
Baudelaire C. *Intimate Journals.* (Translated by Isherwood C.) Mineola NY: Courier Corporation; 2006.
Baudelaire C. *Journaux Intimes: Fusees.* Paris: J. Corti; 1949.
Baudelaire C. *L'art Romantique.* Paris: Michel Lévy Frères; 1869.
Baudelaire C. *Le Spleen De Paris: Suivi De, La Fanfarlo.* Lausanne: Rencontre; 1968.
Baudelaire C. *Paris Spleen.* (Translated by Sorrell M.) London: Oneworld Classics; 2010a.
Baudelaire C. *Selected Writings on Art and Artists.* Cambridge University Press; 1981.
Baudelaire C. *The Flowers of Evil, bilingual edition.* (Translated by McGowan J.) Oxford University Press; 2008.
Baudelaire C. The Painter of Modern Life. In: *Painter of Modern Life and Other Writings.* (Translated by Mayne J.) New York: Phaidon Press; 2010b.
Baudrillard J. *Symbolic Exchange and Death.* (Translated by Grant IH.) Thousand Oaks CA: Sage Publications; 1993.
Bauman Z. *Modernity and Ambivalence.* Cambridge, Cambridgeshire: Polity Press; 1991.
Beal TK. *Religion and Its Monsters.* New York: Routledge; 2002.
Beckett W. *Max Beckmann and the Self.* Munich; New York: Prestel; 1997.
Beckford JA. SSSR Presidential Address Public Religions and the Postsecular: Critical Reflections. *Journal for the Scientific Study of Religion.* 2012; 51(1): pp. 1–19. DOI: https://doi.org/10.1111/j.1468-5906.2011.01625.x
Beckmann M. *Self-Portrait in Words: Collected Writings and Statements, 1903–1950.* (Translated by Heller R and Britt D.) Chicago: University of Chicago Press; 1997.
Beckmann M. *Self-Portrait of a Clown.* Wuppertal: Museum von der Haidt; 1921.
Beckmann M. *The Night.* Düsseldorf: Kunstsammlung Nordrhein-Westfalen; 1919.
Bellman B.L. *The Language of Secrecy: Symbols and Metaphors in Poro Ritual.* New Brunswick: Rutgers University Press, 1984.
Benjamin W. Critique of Violence. In: *Reflections: Essays, Aphorisms, Autobiographical Writings.* (Translated by Jephcott E.) New York: Schocken Books; 1986. pp. 277–300.

Benjamin W. On Some Motifs in Baudelaire. In: *Illuminations: Essays and Reflections*. (Translated by Zohn H.) New York: Schocken Books; 2007a. pp. 155–200.

Benjamin W. *The Arcades Project*. (Translated by Eiland H and McLaughlin K.) Cambridge MA: Belknap Press; 1999.

Benjamin W. Theses on the Philosophy of History. In: *Illuminations: Essays and Reflections*. (Translated by Zohn H.) New York: Schocken Books; 2007b. pp. 253–264.

Bennett J. *The Enchantment of Modern Life: Attachments, Crossings, and Ethics*. Princeton: Princeton University Press; 2016.

Berg IC. *Irony in the Matthean Passion Narrative*. Minneapolis: Fortress Press; 2014.

Berger A. *The Portable Postmodernist*. Walnut Creek CA: Altamira Press; 2003.

Berman J. *Narcissism and the Novel*. New York: New York University Press; 1990.

Berman M. *All that is Solid Melts into Air: The Experience of Modernity*. New York: Penguin Books; 1988.

Bersani L. *Baudelaire and Freud*. Berkeley: University of California Press; 1977.

Best S. Introduction: Pathologies of Power and the Rise of the Global Industrial Complex. In: Best S, Kahn R, Nocella AJ (Eds). *The Global Industrial Complex: Systems of Domination*. Lanham: Lexington Books; 2011.

Biles J. *Ecce Monstrum: Georges Bataille and the Sacrifice of Form*. New York: Fordham University Press; 2007.

Binni W. *Nuova Poetica Leopardiana*. Firenze: Sansoni; 1978.

Black Mirror. Created by **Brooker C**. Netflix, 2019.

Blade Runner: The Final Cut (1982). Directed by **Scott R**. Warner Home Video: 2007.

Bloch E. *The Spirit of Utopia*. (Translated by Nassar AA.) Stanford CA: Stanford University Press; 2000.

Bloch M. *Prey into Hunter: The Politics of Religious Experience*. Cambridge: Cambridge University Press; 1992.

Blom P. *The Vertigo Years: Change and Culture in the West, 1900–1914*. Toronto: McClelland & Stewart; 2008.

Blood S. *Baudelaire and the Aesthetics of Bad Faith*. Stanford CA: Stanford University Press; 1997.

Blumberg J. *Mary Shelley's Early Novels: This Child of Imagination and Misery*. New York: Palgrave Macmillan; 1993.

Bondanella P, **Bondanella JC**. *Cassell Dictionary Italian Literature*. London: Cassell; 2001.

Booth WC. The Empire of Irony. *The Georgia Review*. 1983; 37(4): pp. 719–737.

Bordwell D. *Figures Traced in Light: On Cinematic Staging*. Berkeley: University of California Press; 2005.

Botting F. *Limits of Horror: Technology, Bodies, Gothic*. Manchester; New York: Manchester University Press; 2013.

Botting F. *Making Monstrous: Frankenstein, Criticism Theory.* Manchester; New York: Manchester University Press; 1991.
Botting F. "Monsters of the Imagination": Gothic, Science, Fiction. In: Seed D (Ed.) *A Companion to Science Fiction.* Malden MA: Blackwell Publishing; 2005.
Botting F. *The Gothic.* Cambridge: Boydell & Brewer; 2001.
Botz-Bornstein T. *Films and Dreams: Tarkovsky, Bergman, Sokurov, Kubrick, and Wong Kar-Wai.* Lanham: Lexington Books; 2007.
Bovey A. *Monsters and Grotesques in Medieval Manuscript.* Toronto; Buffalo: University of Toronto Press; 2002.
Braidotti R. *Nomadic Subjects: Embodiment and Sexual Difference in Contemporary Feminist Theory (Second edition).* New York: Columbia University Press; 2011.
Braidotti R. *The Posthuman.* Cambridge: Polity; 2013.
Brennan T. *The Interpretation of the Flesh: Freud and Femininity.* London; New York: Routledge; 1992.
Brittan F. *Music and Fantasy in the Age of Berlioz.* Cambridge UK; New York: Cambridge University Press; 2017.
Brockmann S. *A Critical History of German Film.* Rochester: Camden House; 2010.
Brunette P. *The Films of Michelangelo Antonioni.* Cambridge; New York: Cambridge University Press; 1998.
Buck-Morss S. *The Dialects of Seeing.* Cambridge MA: MIT Press; 1991.
Bukatman S. *Terminal Identity: The Virtual Subject in Postmodern Science Fiction.* Durham: Duke University Press; 1993.
Burke E. *Reflections on the Revolution in France.* Oxford: Oxford University Press; 1999.
Burton RDE. *Baudelaire and the Second Republic: Writing and Revolution.* New York: Oxford University Press; 1991.
Butler J. *Gender Trouble: Feminism and the Subversion of Identity.* New York: Routledge; 1999.
Butler J. *Parting Ways: Jewishness and the Critique of Zionism.* New York: Columbia University Press; 2012.
Butler J. *Precarious Life: The Powers of Mourning and Violence.* London; New York: Verso; 2004.
Călinescu M. *Five Faces of Modernity: Modernism, Avant-garde, Decadence, Kitsch, Postmodernism.* Durham: Duke University Press; 1987.
Calvino I. *Six Memos for the Next Millennium.* Cambridge MA: Harvard University Press; 1988.
Camilletti FA. *Leopardi's Nymphs: Grace, Melancholy, and the Uncanny.* Abingdon: Routledge; 2017.
Camus A. *The Myth of Sisyphus and Other Essays.* (Translated by O'Brien J.) New York: Vintage Books; 1991.
Camus A. *The Rebel: An Essay on Man in Revolt.* (Translated by Bower A.) New York: Vintage Books; 1991.

Camus A. *The Stranger.* (Translated by Ward M.) New York: Vintage Books; 1989.
Caputo JD. Hospitality and the Trouble With God. In: Kearney R, Semonovitch K (Eds.) *Phenomenologies of the Stranger: Between Hostility and Hospitality.* New York: Fordham University Press; 2011. pp. 83–97.
Carchia G. *L'Amore del Pensiero.* Macerata: Quodlibet; 2000.
Carlorosi S. *A Grammar of Cinepoiesis: Poetic Cameras of Italian Cinema.* Lanham: Lexington Books; 2015.
Casanova J. A Secular Age: Dawn or Twilight? In: Warner M (Ed.) *Varieties of Secularism In a Secular Age.* Cambridge MA: Harvard University Press; 2010. pp. 265–281.
Castle T. *The Female Thermometer: Eighteenth-Century Culture and the Invention of the Uncanny.* New York: Oxford University Press; 1995.
Chatman S. *Antonioni, Or, The Surface of the World.* Berkeley: University of California Press; 1985.
Chatman S, Duncan P. *Michelangelo Antonioni: The Investigation.* Köln; London: Taschen; 2004.
Chesters T. *Ghost Stories in Late Renaissance France: Walking by Night.* Oxford; New York: Oxford University Press; 2011.
Chun WHK. *Control and Freedom: Power and Paranoia in the Age of Fiber Optics.* Cambridge MA: MIT Press; 2006.
Cixous H. Fictions and Phantoms: A Reading of Freuds's Das Unheimliche (The 'Uncanny'). In: *Volleys of Humanity: Essays 1972-2009.* (Translated by Denomme R, Prenowitz E.) Edinburgh: Edinburgh University Press; 2011. pp. 15–40.
Cixous H. The Laugh of the Medusa. (Translated by Cohen K, Cohen P.) *Signs.* 1976; 1(4): pp. 875–893. DOI: https://doi.org/10.1086/493306
Clair J. *The Great Parade: Portrait of the Artist as Clown.* (Translated by Couëlle M.) New Haven: Yale University Press; 2004.
Clarke J. The Human/Not Human in the Work of Orlan and Sterlac. In: Zylinska J (Ed.) *The Cyborg Experiments: The Extensions of the Body in the Media Age.* London; New York: Continuum; 2002. pp. 33–55.
Clayton J. *Charles Dickens in Cyberspace: The Afterlife of the Nineteenth Century in Postmodern Culture.* New York: Oxford University Press; 2003.
Clément C, Kristeva J. *The Feminine and the Sacred.* (Translated by Todd JM.) New York: Columbia University Press; 2001.
Clune MW. *American Literature and the Free Market, 1945-2000.* Cambridge; New York: Cambridge University Press; 2010.
Cohen J. *Monster Theory: Reading Culture.* Minneapolis: University of Minnesota Press; 1996.
Cole-Turner R. Science, Technology and the Mission of Theology in a New Century. In: Boesak A, Hansen L (Eds.) *God and Globalization, Vol. 2.* Gauteng: African Sun Media; 2010. pp. 139–165.

Connolly WE. Belief, Spirituality, and Time. In: Warner M, VanAntwerpen J, Calhoun C (Eds.) *Varieties of Secularism in a Secular Age*. Cambridge MA: Harvard University Press; 2010. pp. 126–144.
Connolly WE. *Pluralism*. Durham: Duke University Press; 2005.
Cooper JC, Skrade C. *Celluloid and Symbols*. Philadelphia: Fortress Press; 1970.
Conte J. Discipline and Anarchy: Disrupted Codes in Kathy Acker's Empire of the Senseless. *Revista Canaria de Estudios Ingleses*. 1999; 32: pp. 13–31.
Cottom D. Frankenstein and the Monster of Representation. *SubStance*. 1980; 9(28): pp. 60–71. DOI: https://doi.org/10.2307/3683905
Covino WA. Cyberpunk Literacy; or Piety in the Sky. In: Taylor TW, Ward I (Eds.) *Literacy Theory in the Age of the Internet*. New York: Columbia University Press; 1998. pp. 34–46.
Cristaudo W. *Religion, Redemption and Revolution: The New Speech Thinking of Franz Rosenzweig and Eugen Rosenstock-Huessy*. Toronto; Buffalo: University of Toronto Press; 2012.
Croce B. *Poesia e non poesia: note sulla letteratura europea del secolo decimonono*. Rome: Laterza; 1935.
Culler J. Introduction. In: *The Flowers of Evil* by Baudelaire C. (Translated by McGowan J.) Oxford; New York: Oxford University Press; 2008. pp. xxi–xxxvii.
Curtin DW. *Environmental Ethics for a Postcolonial World*. Lanham: Rowman & Littlefield; 2005.
Cusset F. *French Theory: How Foucault, Derrida, Deleuze, & Co. Transformed the Intellectual Life of the United States*. (Translated by Fort J, Berganza J, Jones M.) Minneapolis: University of Minnesota Press; 2008.
Dahlbom B. Going to the Future. In: Berleur JJ, Whitehouse D (Eds.) *An Ethical Global Information Society: Culture and Democracy Revisited*. Boston: Springer; 2013. pp. 83–95. DOI: https://doi.org/10.1007/978-0-387-35327-2_8
Daly M. *Beyond God the Father: Toward a Philosophy of Women's Liberation*. Boston: Beacon Press; 1985.
Davis C. *Haunted Subjects: Deconstruction, Psychoanalysis and the Return of the Dead*. New York: Springer; 2007.
Davis E. *TechGnosis: Myth, Magic, and Mysticism in the Age of Information*. Berkeley: North Atlantic Books; 2015.
de Beauvoir S. *Second Sex*. (Translated by Parshley HM.) New York: Vintage Books; 1989.
de Certeau M. *The Practice of Everyday Life*. (Translated by Rendall S.) Berkeley: University of California Press: 1984.
de la Durantaye L. *Giorgio Agamben: A Critical Introduction*. Stanford CA: Stanford University Press; 2009.
Deleuze G. *Cinema 2: The Time-Image*. (Translated by Tomlinson H and Galeta R.) Minneapolis: University of Minnesota Press; 1989.

Deleuze G, Guattari F. *A Thousand Plateaus: Capitalism and Schizophrenia*. (Translated by Massumi B.) Minneapolis: University of Minnesota Press; 1987.

Deleuze G, Guattari F. *Anti-Oedipus: Capitalism and Schizophrenia*. (Translated by Hurley R, Seem M, Lane HR.) Minneapolis: University of Minnesota Press; 1983.

de Man P. *Blindness and Insight: Essays in the Rhetoric of Contemporary Criticism*, 2nd ed. New York: Oxford University Press; 1971.

Derrida J. *Of Grammatology*. (Translated by Spivak GC.) Baltimore: Johns Hopkins University Press; 1997.

Derrida J. *Points...: Interviews, 1974–1994*. (Translated by Kamuf P.) Stanford CA: Stanford University Press; 1995.

Derrida J. *Politics of Friendship*. (Translated by Collins G.) London: Verso; 2005.

Derrida J. *Specters of Marx: The State of the Debt, the Work of Mourning and the New International*. (Translated by Kamuf P.) New York: Routledge; 2006.

Derrida J. The Force of Law: The "Mystical Foundation of Authority". In: Cornell D (Ed.) *Deconstruction and the Possibility of Justice*. New York: Routledge; 1992. pp. 3–67.

Derrida J. *Writing and Difference*. (Translated by Bass A.) London: Routledge; 1978.

Dery M. *Flame Wars: The Discourse of Cyberculture*. Durham: Duke University Press; 1994.

Di Tomasso L. Apocalypticism and Popular Culture. In: Collins JJ (Ed.) *The Oxford Handbook of Apocalyptic Literature*. New York: Oxford University Press; 2014. pp. 473–510.

Dolar M. 'I Shall Be with You on Your Wedding-Night': Lacan and the Uncanny. October. 1991; 58: pp. 5–23. DOI: https://doi.org/10.2307/778795

Donald J. *Imagining the Modern City*. Minneapolis: University of Minnesota Press; 1999.

Donawerth J. *Frankenstein's Daughters: Women Writing Science Fiction*. Syracuse: Syracuse University Press; 1997.

Dorman A. *Paradoxical Japaneseness: Cultural Representation in 21st Century Japanese Cinema*. London: Springer; 2016.

Douglas M. *Purity and Danger: An Analysis of Concepts of Pollution and Taboo*. New York: Praeger; 1966.

Douglas M. *Natural Symbols: Explorations in Cosmology*. London; New York: Routledge; 1996.

Dragon Z. Derrida's Specter, Abraham's Phantom: Psychoanalysis as the Uncanny Kernel of Deconstruction. *The AnaChronisT*. 2005; 11: pp. 253–269.

Dunn RJ. Narrative Distance in *Frankenstein*. *Studies in the Novel*. 1974; 6(4): pp. 408–417.

Durkheim E. *Durkheim on Religion: A Selection of Readings with Bibliographies*. (Translated by Redding J and Pickering WSF.) London; Boston: Routledge & K. Paul; 1975.
Dworkin A. *Intercourse, 20th anniversary edition*. New York: BasicBooks; 2007.
Egan J. *A Visit From the Goon Squad*. New York: Anchor Books; 2011.
Eggers D. *The Circle*. New York: Knopf Canada; 2013.
Eksteins M. *Rites of Spring: The Great War and the Birth of the Modern Age*. Toronto: Key Porter Books; 1989.
Elam D. *Feminism and Deconstruction*. London; New York: Routledge; 2006.
Elger D. *Expressionism: A Revolution in German Art*. London: Taschen; 2007.
Eliade M. *The Quest: History and Meaning in Religion*. Chicago: University of Chicago Press; 2013.
Eliade M. *The Sacred and the Profane: The Nature of Religion*. (Translated by Trask WR.) New York: Harcourt, Brace & World; 1959.
Eliot TS. *Essays Ancient and Modern*. New York: Harcourt, Brace and Company; 1936.
Eliot TS. *Selected Essays, 1917–1932*. New York: Harcourt, Brace and Company; 1932.
Elkin L. *Flaneuse: Women Walk the City in Paris, New York, Tokyo, Venice and London*. London: Random House; 2016.
Endo Y. Women and Science in Japanese *Anime*: A Challenge to the Traditional Construction of the Female Identity. In: Andréolle DS and Molinari V (Eds.) *Women and Science, 17th Century to Present: Pioneers, Activists and Protagonists*. Newcastle upon Tyne: Cambridge Scholars Publishing; 2011. pp. 227–240.
Favret MA. The Letters of *Frankenstein*. Genre. 1987; 20: pp. 3–24.
Featherstone M, Burrows R. *Cyberspace/Cyberbodies/Cyberpunk: Cultures of Technological Embodiment*. London: Sage; 1996.
Feilla CA. Literary Monsters: Gender, Genius, and Writing in Denis Diderot's 'On Women' and Mary Shelley's *Frankenstein*. In: Baumgartner HL, Davis R (Eds.) *Hosting the Monster*. New York: Rodopi; 2008. pp. 163–177.
Ferguson H. *The Lure of Dreams: Sigmund Freud and the Construction of Modernity*. New York: Routledge; 1996.
Fondane B. *Baudelaire Et L'experience Du Gouffre*. Paris: Seghers; 1947.
Forster EM. *The Machine Stops (Golden Deer Classics)*. Oregan Publishing; 2017.
Foucault M. *The Order of Things: An Archaeology of the Human Sciences*. London: Routledge; 2005.
Foucault M. What is Enlightenment? In: Rabinow P (Ed.) *The Foucault Reader*. New York: Pantheon Books; 1984. pp. 32–50.
Freud S. Future Prospects of Psychoanalytic Therapy. In: *Collected Papers, Vol. 2*. (Translated by Strachey J.) New York: Basic Books; 1959. pp. 285–296.

Freud S. *The Interpretation of Dreams.* (Translated by Strachey J.) New York: Avon; 1965.

Freud S. The Uncanny. In: *The Standard Edition of the Complete Psychological Works of Sigmund Freud, vol. 17 (1917–1919).* (Translated by Strachey J.) London: The Hogarth Press; 1955. pp. 217–256.

Friedan B. *The Feminine Mystique.* New York: W. W. Norton & Company; 2010.

Friedman EG. A Conversation with Kathy Acker. *The Review of Contemporary Fiction.* 1989a; 9(3): pp. 12–22.

Friedman EG. 'Now Eat Your Mind': An Introduction to the Works of Kathy Acker. *The Review of Contemporary Fiction.* 1989b; 9(3): pp. 37–49.

Frosini F. Absolute and Relative Perfection of the "Monsters": Politics and History in Giacomo Leopardi. *Philosophy Today.* 2016; 60(1): pp. 107–123. DOI: https://doi.org/10.5840/philtoday2015121196

Frueh J. *Monster/Beauty: Building the Body of Love.* 2001.

Frye N. *Northrop Frye's Writings on the Eighteenth and Nineteenth Centuries, Volume 17.* Toronto: University of Toronto Press; 2005.

Fuller SC. Reading the Cyborg in Mary Shelley's "Frankenstein". *Journal of the Fantastic in the Arts.* 2003; 14(2): pp. 217–227.

Fussell P. *The Great War and Modern Memory.* New York: Oxford University Press; 1975.

Gaggi S. The Cyborg and the Net: Figures of the Technological Subject. In: Erben DL (Ed.) *Adrift in the Technological Matrix.* Lewisburg: Bucknell University Press; 2003. pp. 125–139.

Galassi J. Introduction. In: *Canti: Poems/A Bilingual Edition.* (Translated by Galassi J.) New York: Farrar, Straus and Giroux; 2014.

Ganteau JM. *The Ethics and Aesthetics of Vulnerability in Contemporary British Fiction.* New York: Routledge; 2015.

Garrigós González C. What is it to be a Woman in a Postmodern World? Or Kathy Acker's *Don Quixote,* Lost in the City of Nightmares. *Revista de Estudios Norteamericanos.* 1996; 4: pp. 113–119.

Ghadessi T. *Portraits of Human Monsters in the Renaissance: Dwarves, Hirsutes, and Castrati as Idealized Anatomical Anomalies.* Kalamazoo: Medieval Institute Publications, Western Michigan University; 2018.

Ghost in the Shell (1995). Directed by **Oshii M.** Manga Entertainment: 1998.

Ghost in the Shell (2017). Directed by **Sanders R.** Paramount: 2017.

Ghost in the Shell 2: Innocence (2004). Directed by **Oshii M.** Paramount Pictures: 2004.

Ghost in the Shell: Stand Alone Complex (2002). Written and directed by **Kamiyam K.** Manga Entertainment: 2005.

Giblett R. *The Body of Nature and Culture.* Basingstoke; New York: Springer; 2008.

Gibson W. *Burning Chrome.* New York: Ace Books; 1986.

Gibson W. *Count Zero.* New York: Ace Books; 1986.

Gibson W. *Mona Lisa Overdrive.* Toronto; New York: Bantam Books; 1988.
Gibson W. *Neuromancer.* New York: Ace Books; 1984.
Giddens A. *The Consequences of Modernity.* Stanford CA: Stanford University Press; 1990.
Gilbert SM. Preface: "Unreal City": The Place of the Great War in the History of Modernity. In: Mackaman D, Mays M (Eds.) *World War I and the Cultures of Modernity.* Jackson: University Press of Mississippi; 2000. pp. ix–xv.
Gilbert SM, Gubar S. *The Madwoman in the Attic: The Woman Writer and the Nineteenth-Century Literary Imagination.* New Haven: Yale University Press; 1979.
Gleber A. *The Art of Taking a Walk: Flanerie, Literature, and Film in Weimar Culture.* Princeton: Princeton University Press; 1999.
Goddu TA. *Gothic America: Narrative, History, and Nation.* New York: Columbia University Press; 1997.
Goethe JW. *The Sorrows of Young Werther.* London: Penguin; 1989.
Goll I. Der Expressionismus stirbt. *Zenit.* 1921; 1(8): pp. 8–9.
Goodstein ES. *Experience Without Qualities: Boredom and Modernity.* Stanford CA: Stanford University Press; 2005.
Graham EL. Manifestations of the Posthuman in the Postsecular Imagination. In: Hurlbut JB, Tirosh-Samuelson H (Eds.) *Perfecting Human Futures: Transhuman Visions and Technological Imaginations.* Wiesbaden: Springer; 2016. pp. 51–72.
Graham EL. *Representations of the Post/human: Monsters, Aliens and Others in Popular Culture.* Manchester: Manchester University Press; 2002.
Gramsci A. *Gramsci's Prison Letters.* (Translated by Henderson H.) London: Zwan; 1988.
Gray CH, Mentor S, Figueroa-Sarriera HJ. Cyborgology: Constructing the Knowledge of Cybernetic Organisms. In: *Cyborg Handbook.* New York: Routledge; 1995. pp. 1–14.
Gray EI. *The Poetry of Indifference: From the Romantics to the Rubáiyát.* Amherst: University of Massachusetts Press; 2005.
Greenspan A. *Shanghai Future: Modernity Remade.* New York: Oxford University Press; 2014.
Grill G. *The World as Metaphor in Robert Musil's The Man Without Qualities: Possibility as Reality.* Rochester: Camden House; 2012.
Gudmarsdottir S. *Tillich and the Abyss: Foundations, Feminism, and Theology of Praxis.* New York: Springer; 2016.
Habegger HR. *Mysteries of the Universe and Planet Earth: Revealing the Absolute Convergence of Modern Science Discoveries and Biblical Creation History.* WestBow Press; 2013.
Habermas J. *Between Naturalism and Religion: Philosophical Essays.* (Translated by Cronin C.) Cambridge; Malden: Polity Press; 2008.

Habermas J. *The Philosophical Discourse of Modernity: Twelve Lectures*. (Translated by Lawrence F.) Cambridge: MIT Press; 1990.

Haggerty GE. *Gothic Fiction/Gothic Form*. University Park: Pennsylvania State University Press; 1989.

Haggerty GE. The Failure of Heteronormativity in the Gothic Novel. In: Boe ADF, Coykendall A (Eds.) *Heteronormativity in Eighteenth-Century Literature and Culture*. Farnham; Burlington: Ashgate; 2015. pp. 131–150.

Hagner M. Enlightened Monsters. In: Clark W, Golinski J (Eds.) *The Sciences in Enlightened Europe*. Chicago: University of Chicago Press; 1999. pp. 175–217.

Halberstam J. *Skin Shows: Gothic Horror and the Technology of Monsters*. Durham: Duke University Press; 1995.

Hammond K. Monsters of Modernity: Frankenstein and Modern Environmentalism. *Cultural Geographies*. 2004; 11(2): pp. 181–198. DOI: https://doi.org/10.1191/14744744004eu301oa

Hanson M. *Building Sci-fi Moviescapes: The Science Behind the Fiction*. Gulf Professional Publishing; 2005.

Haraway D. A Manifesto for Cyborgs: Science, Technology, and Socialist Feminism in the Late 1980s. In: *The Haraway Reader*. New York: Routledge; 2004. pp. 7–45.

Haraway D. *Manifestly Haraway*. Minneapolis: University of Minnesota Press; 2016.

Harris M. Inside the First Church of Artificial Intelligence. *Wired*. 15 Nov. 2017; https://www.wired.com/story/anthony-levandowski-artificial-intelligence-religion/. Accessed: 03-20-2018.

Hasegawa Y. Post-identity Kawaii: Commerce, Gender and Contemporary Japanese Art. In: Lloyd F (Ed.) *Consuming Bodies: Sex and Contemporary Japanese Art*. London: Reaktion Books; 2002. pp. 127–141.

Hayles K. *How We Became Posthuman: Virtual Bodies in Cybernetics, Literature, and Informatics*. Chicago: University of Chicago Press; 1999.

Healy SD. *Boredom, Self, and Culture*. Cranbury, N.J.: Fairleigh Dickinson University Press; 1984.

Heidegger M. *The Fundamental Concepts of Metaphysics: World, Finitude, Solitude*. (Translated by McNeill W, Walker N.) Bloomington: Indiana University Press; 1995.

Henderson C. The Internet as a Metaphor for God? *CrossCurrents*. 2000; 50(1/2): pp. 77–83.

Henthorne T. *William Gibson: A Literary Companion*. Jefferson: McFarland & Company, Inc.; 2011.

Hermans T. *The Conference of the Tongues*. London: Routledge; 2007.

Hiddleston JA. *Baudelaire and the Art of Memory*. Oxford: Clarendon Press; 1999.

Hodges D. Frankenstein and the Feminine Subversion of the Novel. *Tulsa Studies in Women's Literature*. 1983; 2(2): pp. 155–164.

Hoeveler DL. Frankenstein, Feminism, and Literary Theory. In: Schor E (Ed.) *The Cambridge Companion to Mary Shelley*. Cambridge: Cambridge University Press; 2003. pp. 45–62.

Hoeveler DL. *Gothic Riffs: Secularizing the Uncanny in the European Imaginary, 1780–1820*. Columbus: Ohio State University Press; 2010.

Hogle JE. "Frankenstein" as Neo-Gothic: From the Ghost of the Counterfeit to the Monster of Abjection. In: Rajan T, Wright, J (Eds.) *Between Cultures: Transformations of Genre in Romanticism*. Cambridge: Cambridge University Press; 1998. pp. 176–210.

Holt A. 'The Terrorist in My Home': Teenagers' Violence Towards Parents—Constructions of Parent Experiences in Public Online Message Boards. *Child & Family Social Work*. 2011; 16(4): pp. 454–463. DOI: https://doi.org/10.1111/j.1365-2206.2011.00760.x

Horn M. *Postmodern Plagiarisms: Cultural Agenda and Aesthetic Strategies of Appropriation in US-American Literature (1970–2010)*. Boston; Berlin: De Gruyter Mouton; 2015.

Horvath A. *Modernism and Charisma*. Basingstoke; New York: Palgrave Macmillan; 2013.

Houen A. *Powers of Possibility: Experimental American Writing Since the 1960s*. Oxford; New York: Oxford University Press; 2012.

Huet MH. *Monstrous Imagination*. Cambridge: Harvard University Press; 1993.

Hume K. Voice in Kathy Acker's Fiction. *Contemporary Literature*. 2001; 42(3): pp. 485–513. DOI: https://doi.org/10.2307/1208993

Hutcheon L. *A Poetics of Postmodernism: History, Theory, Fiction*. New York: Routledge; 2003.

Hutcheon L. *Double Talking: Essays On Verbal and Visual Ironies in Canadian Contemporary Art and Literature*. Toronto: ECW Press; 1992.

Hutcheon L. *Irony's Edge: The Theory and Politics of Irony*. New York: Routledge; 2003.

Huxley A. *Brave New World*. Toronto: Vintage Canada; 2007.

Indick W. *The Digital God: How Technology Will Reshape Spirituality*. Jefferson: McFarland & Company, Inc.; 2015.

Irigaray L. *An Ethics of Sexual Difference*. (Translated by Burke C, Gill GC.) Ithaca: Cornell University Press; 1993a.

Irigaray L. *Luce Irigaray: Key Writings*. (Translated by Irigaray L, Harrington L.) A&C Black; 2004.

Irigaray L. *Sexes and Genealogies*. (Translated by Gill GC.) New York: Columbia University Press; 1993b.

Irigaray L. *This Sex Which is Not One*. (Translated by Porter C.) Ithaca: Cornell University Press; 1985.

Jaeggi R. *Alienation*. (Translated by Neuhouser F.) New York: Columbia University Press; 2014.

Jager C. *Unquiet Things: Secularism in the Romantic Age*. Philadelphia: University of Pennsylvania Press; 2015.

Jaspers K. *Man in the Modern Age*. (Translated by Paul E, Paul C.) London: Routledge & K. Paul; 1951.

Jauß HR. *Toward an Aesthetic of Reception*. (Translation by Bahti T.) Minneapolis: University of Minnesota Press; 1982.

Johnson B. My Monster/My Self. *Diacritics*. 1992; 12(2): pp. 2–10. DOI: https://doi.org/10.2307/464674

Johnson B. The Last Man. In: Fisch AA (Ed.) *The Other Mary Shelley: Beyond Frankenstein*. New York: Oxford University Press; 1993. pp. 258–266.

Jonsson S. Neither Inside nor Outside: Subjectivity and the Spaces of Modernity in Robert Musil's "The Man Without Qualities". *New German Critique*. 1996 (68): pp. 31–60. DOI: https://doi.org/10.2307/3108663

Jung CG. *Essays on Contemporary Events: 1936–1946*. (Translated by Hull RFC.) Psychology Press; 2014.

Kafka F. "Prometheus." In: *The Complete Stories*. (Translated by Muir W, Muir E.) New York: Schocken Books; 1971. p. 432.

Kearney R. *Strangers, Gods and Monsters: Interpreting Otherness*. London; New York: Routledge; 2003.

Kelso J. Andrea Dworkin on the Biblical Foundations of Violence Against Women. In: Blyth C, Colgan E, Edwards KB (Eds.) *Rape Culture, Gender Violence, and Religion: Biblical Perspectives*. Springer; 2018. pp. 83–102.

Ketterer D. Frankenstein's "Conversion" from Natural Magic to Modern Science—and a Shifted (and Converted) Last Draft Insert. *Science Fiction Studies*. 1997; 24(1): pp 57–78.

Kierkegaard S. *Either/Or, Part I*. (Translated by Hong HV, Hong EH.) Princeton: Princeton University Press; 1987.

Kierkegaard S. Repetition. In: Hong HV, Hong EH (Eds.) *Fear and Trembling/Repetition*. Princeton: Princeton University Press; 1983. pp. 125–187.

Kierkegaard S. *The Concept of Irony, With Continual Reference to Socrates*. (Translated by Hong HV, Hong EH.) Princeton: Princeton University Press; 1989.

Kilgour M. *The Rise of the Gothic Novel*. London; New York: Routledge; 1995.

Kristeva J. *Powers of Horror: An Essay on Abjection*. (Translated by Roudiez LS.) New York: Columbia University Press; 1982.

Kristeva J. *Strangers to Ourselves*. (Translated by Roudiez LS.) New York: Columbia University Press; 1991.

Kristeva J. *This Incredible Need to Believe*. (Translated by Brahic BB.) New York: Columbia University Press; 2009.

Kubiak S. Why Is Kwame Antony Appiah's Proposal to Dismiss the Concept of "The West" Premature. *Crossroads*. 4th July 2017; http://www.crossroads.uwb.edu.pl/kwame-anthony-appiahs-proposal/. Accessed: 20-09-2019.

Kalyvas A. The Complexities of Sovereignty. In: Calarco M, DeCaroli S (Eds.) *Giorgio Agamben: Sovereignty and Life.* Stanford CA: Stanford University Press; 2007. pp. 23–42.

Kendrick J. *Hollywood Bloodshed: Violence in 1980s American Cinema.* Carbondale: Southern Illinois Press; 2009.

Kosari M, Abbas A. Thirdspace: The Trialectics of the Real, Virtual and Blended Spaces. *Journal of Cyberspace Studies.* 2018; 2(2): pp. 163–185. DOI: https://doi.org/10.22059/jcss.2018.258274.1019

Krueger O. The Internet as Distributor and Mirror of Religious and Ritual Knowledge. *Asian Journal of Social Science.* 2004; 32(2): pp. 183–197. DOI: https://doi.org/10.1163/1568531041705077

Kuhn RC. *The Demon of Noontide: Ennui in Western Literature.* Princeton NJ: Princeton University Press; 2017.

Kull A. Cyborg and Religious? Technonature and Technoculture. *Scientia et Fides.* 2016; 4(1): pp. 295–311. DOI: http://dx.doi.org/10.12775/SetF.2016.016

Kull A. Cyborg Embodiment and the Incarnation. *Currents in Theology and Mission.* 2001; 28(3/4): pp. 279–284.

Kull A. Exploring Technonature with Cyborgs. In: Drees WB (Ed.) *Is Nature Ever Evil?: Religion, Science, and Value.* London; New York: Routledge; 2003. pp. 236–243.

Lacan J. *Écrits.* (Translated by Sheridan A.) New York; London: W.W. Norton and Company; 1977.

Lacan J. *The Seminar of Jacques Lacan: Book 2: The Ego in Freud's Theory and in the Technique of Psychoanalysis 1954–1955.* (Translated by Tomaselli S.) Cambridge: Cambridge University Press; 1988.

La Dolce Vita (1960). Directed by **Fellini F.** Criterion Collection: 2014.

La Notte (1961). Directed by **Antonioni M.** Criterion Collection: 2013.

Latour B. *We Have Never Been Modern.* (Translated by Porter C.) Cambridge: Harvard University Press; 1993.

L'Avventura (1960). Directed by **Antonioni M.** Criterion Collection: 2001.

Lebowitz N. *Italo Svevo.* New Brunswick NJ: Rutgers University Press; 1978.

L'Eclisse (1962). Directed by **Antonioni M.** Criterion Collection: 2014.

Leed EJ. *No Man's Land: Combat and Identity in World War 1.* Cambridge; New York: Cambridge University Press; 1979.

Lefebvre H. *The Production of Space.* (Translated by Nicholson-Smith D.) Oxford UK; Cambridge MA: Blackwell; 1991.

Le Loyer P. *A Treatise of Specters or Straunge Sights, Visions and Apparitions Appearing Sensibly Unto Men: Wherein is Delivered, the Nature of Spirites, Angels, and Divels. Their Power and Properties: as Also of Witches, Sorcerers, Enchanters, and Such Like...* (Translated by Jones Z.) London: Val. S.[immes]; 1605.

Leonard J. *Naming in Paradise: Milton and the Language of Adam and Eve.* Oxford: Clarendon Press; 1990.

Leopardi G. *Canti: Poems/A Bilingual Edition.* (Translated by Galassi J.) New York: Farrar, Straus and Giroux; 2014.

Leopardi G. *Moral Tales: Operette Morali.* (Translated by Creagh P.) Manchester: Carcanet New Press; 1983.

Leopardi G. *Pensieri.* (Translated by Di Piero WS.) Baton Rouge: Louisiana State University Press; 1981.

Leopardi G. *Zibaldone.* (Translated by Baldwin K et al.) New York: Farrar, Straus and Giroux, 2013.

Leopardi G. *Zibaldone di Pensieri: Scelta.* Milano: A. Mondadori; 1983.

Liceti F. *De monstrorum caussis, natura, et differentiis libri duo ....* Germany: Apud Paulum Frambottum, 1634.

Lewis AZ. *Read Him Again and Again: Repetitions of Job in Kierkegaard, Vischer, and Barth.* Eugene OR: Wipf and Stock Publishers; 2014.

Lewis MG. Postscript to The Castle Spectre. In: Clery EJ, Miles R (Eds.) *Gothic Documents: A Sourcebook 1700–1820.* Manchester; New York: Manchester University Press; 2000. p. 198.

Lewis MG. *The Monk: A Romance.* Peterborough ON; Orchard Park NY: Broadview Press; 2004.

Lewis W. *A Battery Shelled.* London: Imperial War Museum; 1919.

Lin T. *Bed: Stories.* Hoboken: Melville House; 2007.

Lin T. *Eeeee Eee Eeee: A Novel.* Hoboken: Melville House; 2007.

Lin T. *Shoplifting from American Apparel.* Brooklyn: Melville House; 2009.

Lin T. *Taipei.* New York: Knopf Doubleday Publishing Group; 2013.

Lo and Behold, Reveries of the Connected World (2016). Directed by **Herzog W.** Netfilx.

Lundin R. *Beginning with the Word (Cultural Exegesis): Modern Literature and the Question of Belief.* Grand Rapids MI: Baker Academic; 2014.

Luporini C. *Leopardi Progressivo.* Nuova. Roma: Editori Riuniti; 1993.

Lykke N. Between Monsters, Goddesses, and Cyborgs: Feminist Confrontations with Science. In: Lykke N, Braidotti R (Eds.) *Between Monsters, Goddesses, and Cyborgs: Feminist Confrontations with Science, Medicine, and Cyberspace.* London; Atlantic Highlands NJ: Zed Books; 1996. pp. 12–29.

Lyotard JF. *The Postmodern Condition: A Report on Knowledge.* (Translated by Bennington G, Massumi B.) Minneapolis: University of Minnesota Press; 1984.

M (1931). Directed by **Lang F.** Criterion Collection: 2004.

MacKinnon CA. *Toward a Feminist Theory of the State.* Cambridge MA; London: Harvard University Press; 1989.

Madge C, O'Connor H. Mothers in the Making? Exploring Liminality in Cyber/Space. *Transactions of the Institute of British Geographers, New Series.* 2005; 30(1): pp. 83–97. DOI: https://doi.org/10.1111/j.1475-5661.2005.00153.x

Malchow HL. Frankenstein's Monster and Images of Race in Nineteenth-Century Britain. *Past & Present.* 1993(139): pp. 90–130.

Mann S. *The Science of Boredom: The Upside (and Downside) of Downtime*. London: Little, Brown Book Group; 2017.

Manolopoulos M. A Thinking Otherwise: With Kevin Hart. In: *With Gifted Thinkers: Conversations with Caputo, Hart, Horner, Kearney, Keller, Rigby, Taylor, Wallace*. Bern: Peter Lang; 2009. pp. 75–100.

Mao D. Blasting and Disappearing. In: Antliff M, Klein SW (Eds.) *Vorticism: New Perspectives*. Oxford: Oxford University Press; 2013. pp. 235–255.

Marsh N. *Mary Shelley: Frankenstein*. Basingstoke; New York: Palgrave Macmillan; 2009.

Marx K. *Capital: A Critique of Political Economy, Volume 1*. (Translated by Fowkes B.) London: Penguin; 1976.

Marx K. *Economic and Philosophic Manuscripts of 1844*. (Translated by Milligan M.) Mineola NY: Dover Publications; 2007.

Marx K, Engels F. *The Communist Manifesto*. (Translated by Moore S.) Penguin UK; 2005.

Maughan T. *Infinite Detail: A Novel*. New York: Farrar, Straus and Giroux; 2019.

McCarthy VA. *Kierkegaard as Psychologist*. Evanston: Northwestern University Press; 2015.

McConnell FD. *The Science of Fiction and the Fiction of Science: Collected Essays on SF Storytelling and the Gnostic Imagination*. Jefferson NC: McFarland; 2009.

McHale B. *Constructing Postmodernism*. Psychology Press; 1992.

McKenzie J. Genre Trouble: (The) Butler Did It. In: Phelan P, Lane J (Eds.) *The Ends of Performance*. New York; London: New York University Press; 1998. pp. 217–235.

McLennan G. Postsecularism: A New Global Debate. In: Hayden P, el-Ojeili C (Eds.) *Globalization and Utopia: Critical Essays*. Basingstoke; New York: Palgrave Macmillan; 2009. pp. 82–98.

McMahon JL. The Existential Frankenstein. In: Sanders SM (Ed.) *The Philosophy of Science Fiction Film*. Lexington: University Press of Kentucky; 2007. pp. 73–88.

Mellor AK. *Mary Shelley: Her Life, Her Fiction, Her Monsters*. New York: Methuen; 1988.

Mercedes A, Thweatt-Bates J. Bound in the Spiral Dance: Spirituality and Technology in the Third Wave. In: Klassen CA (Ed.) *Feminist Spirituality: The Next Generation*. Lanham; Boulder; New York; Toronto; Plymouth: Lexington Books; 2009. pp. 63–83.

Metropolis (1927). Directed by Lang F. Kino International Corporation: 2002.

Michie EB. Frankenstein and Marx's Theories of Alienated Labor. In: Behrendt SC (Ed.) *Approaches to Teaching Mary Shelley's "Frankenstein"*. New York: MLA; 1990. pp. 93–98.

Miller Jr. GA. *Understanding William Gibson*. Columbia SC: University of South Carolina Press; 2016.

Miller Jr. WM. *A Canticle for Leibowitz*. New York: Bantam Dell; 2007.
Milton J. *Paradise Lost*. 2nd ed. London: Pearson Longman; 2007.
Minghelli G. *In the Shadow of the Mammoth: Italo Svevo and the Emergence of Modernism*. Toronto: University of Toronto Press, 2002.
Modern JL. *Secularism in Antebellum America: With Reference to Ghosts, Protestant Subcultures, Machines, and Their Metaphors; Featuring Discussions of Mass Media, Moby-Dick, Spirituality, Phrenology, Anthropology, Sing Sing State Penitentiary, and Sex with the New Motive Power*. Chicago; London: University of Chicago Press; 2011.
Modern Times (1936). Directed by **Chaplin C**. Criterion Collection: 2010.
Moloney B. Psychoanalysis and Irony in "La Coscienza di Zeno". *The Modern Language Review*. 1972; 67(2): pp. 309–318. DOI: https://doi.org/10.2307/3722314
Monod J. *Chance and Necessity*. (Translated by Wainhouse A.) New York: Vintage Books; 1972.
Moreno BG, Moreno FG. Beyond the Filthy Form: Illustrating Mary Shelley's Frankenstein. In: Davison CM, Mulvey-Roberts M (Ed.) *Global Frankenstein*. New York: Palgrave Macmillan; 2018.
Moretti F. The Dialectic of Fear. *New Left Review*. 1982; 136(1): pp. 67–85.
Morson GS. *Narrative and Freedom: The Shadows of Time*. New Haven; London: Yale University Press; 1994.
Morton T. *A Routledge Literary Sourcebook on Mary Shelley's Frankenstein*. London: Routledge; 2002.
Mr. Robot. Created by **Esmail S**. Universal Pictures Home Entertainment, 2018.
Muecke DC. *The Compass of Irony*. London: Methuen; 1969.
Musil R. *A Man Without Qualities: Volume 1*. (Translated by Pike B.) New York: Vintage Books; 1995.
Musil R. *Der Mann ohne Eigenschaften*. Hamburg: Rowohlt; 1967.
Muth KR. Postmodern Fiction as Poststructuralist Theory: Kathy Acker's Blood and Guts in High School. *Narrative*. 2011; 19(1): pp. 86–110.
Nancy JL. *Dis-enclosure: The Deconstruction of Christianity*. (Translated by Bergo B, Malenfant G, Smith MB.) Fordham University Press; 2008.
Nash P. *The Void*. Ottawa: National Gallery of Canada; 1918.
Nasr V. Lessons from the Muslim World. *Daedalus*. 2003; 132(3): pp. 67–72.
Nathan E, Topolski A. *Is There a Judeo-Christian Tradition?: a European Perspective*. Berlin: De Gruyter; 2016.
Neale S. *Genre and Hollywood*. New York: Psychology Press; 2000.
Negri A. *Diary of an Escape*. (Translated by Emery E.) Cambridge; Malden: Polity; 2010.
Negri A. *Flower of the Desert: Giacomo Leopardi's Poetic Ontology*. (Translated by Murphy TS.) Albany: SUNY Press; 2015.
Ngai S. *Ugly Feelings*. Cambridge MA; London: Harvard University Press; 2009.
Nietzsche F. Eternal Recurrence. In: *Complete Works of Friedrich Nietzsche, Volume 16*. (Translated by Ludovici AM.) Edinburgh: T.N. Foulis; 1911a.

Nietzsche F. *On the Genealogy of Morals; Ecce Homo*. (Translated by Kaufmann W.) New York: Vintage Books; 1967.
Nietzsche F. *The Birth of Tragedy and Other Writings*. (Translated by Speirs R.) Cambridge: Cambridge University Press; 1999a.
Nietzsche F. *The Gay Science: With a Prelude in Rhymes and an Appendix of Songs*. (Translated by Kaufmann W.) Knopf Doubleday Publishing Group; 2010.
Nietzsche F. *Thus Spake Zarathursta*. (Translated by Common T.) New York: Dover Publications; 1999b.
Nietzsche F. Twilight of the Idols. In: *Complete Works of Friedrich Nietzsche, Volume 16*. (Translated by Ludovici AM.) Edinburgh: T.N. Foulis; 1911b.
Nietzsche F. *Untimely Meditations*. (Translated by Hollingdale RJ.) Cambridge; New York: Cambridge University Press; 1997.
O'Donnell P. Modernism and Postmodernism. In: Matthews TJ (Ed.) *A Companion to the Modern American Novel, 1900-1950*. Malden MA: Wiley-Blackwell; 2013. pp. 518-534.
Olsen L. Virtual Termites: A Hypotextual Technomutant Explo(it)ration of William Gibson and the Electronic Beyond(s). *Style*. 1995; 29(2): pp. 287-313.
Origo I. *Leopardi: A Study in Solitude*. Books & Company, Helen Marx Books; 1999.
Orwell G. *1984: A Novel*. New York: New American Library; 1961.
Owens ME. *Stages of Dismemberment: The Fragmented Body in Late Medieval and Early Modern Drama*. Newark: University of Delaware Press; 2005.
Paliwoda D. *Melville and the Theme of Boredom*. Jefferson NC; London: McFarland; 2010.
Pamerleau WC. The Search for Meaning in Tillich and Antonioni. In: Morefield KR (Ed.) *Faith and Spirituality in Masters of World Cinema: Volume II, Volume 2*. Newcastle upon Tyne: Cambridge Scholars Publishing; 2011. pp. 42-58.
Parsons DL. *Streetwalking the Metropolis: Women, the City and Modernity: Women, the City and Modernity*. Oxford: Oxford University Press; 2000.
Patty JS. Baudelaire's Knowledge and Use of Dante. *Studies in Philology*. 1956; 53(4): pp. 599-611.
Payne P. *Robert Musil's "A Man Without Qualities": A Critical Study*. New York: Cambridge University Press; 1988.
Pease A. *Modernism, Feminism and the Culture of Boredom*. Cambridge: Cambridge University Press; 2012.
Perez G. *The Material Ghost: Films and Their Medium*. Baltimore: Johns Hopkins University Press; 1998.
Pesce M. *VRML Browsing and Building cyberspace, Volume 1*. New Riders Publishing; 1995.
Pike DL. *Metropolis On the Styx: The Underworlds of Modern Urban Culture, 1800-2001*. London: Cornell University Press; 2007.
Pimenova D. Fan Fiction: Between Text, Conversation, and Game. In: Hotz-Davies I, Kirchhofer A, Leppänen S (Eds.) *Internet Fictions*. Newcastle upon Tyne: Cambridge Scholars Publishing; 2009. pp. 44-61.

Piper K. Inuit Diasporas: *Frankenstein* and the Inuit in England. *Romanticism.* 2007; 13(1): pp. 63-75. DOI: https://doi.org/10.1353/rom.2007.0017

Piser C. Dreaming Moosbrugger: The Other Versus Modernity in Musil's *The Man Without Qualities. More than Thought.* November 2010; pp. 1-10.

Pitchford N. *Tactical Readings: Feminist Postmodernism in the Novels of Kathy Acker and Angela Carter.* Lewisburg: Bucknell University Press; 2002.

Plutarch. *Plutarch's Lives.* (Translated by Perrin B.) London: William Heinemann; 1914.

Poggi C. *Inventing Futurism: The Art and Politics of Artificial Optimism.* Princeton; Oxford: Princeton University Press; 2009.

Popper KR. *Utopia and Violence.* London: Hibbert Trust; 1950.

Puissant SC. *Irony and the Poetry of the First World War.* Basingstoke: Palgrave Macmillan; 2009.

Pynchon T. *Bleeding Edge.* Random House; 2013.

Rabaté JM. *1913: The Cradle of Modernism.* Malden MA: Blackwell; 2007.

Radcliffe AW. On the Supernatural in Poetry. *New Monthly Magazine.* 1826; 16(1): pp. 145-152.

Radcliffe AW. *The Italian: Or, the Confessional of the Black Penitents.* Oxford University Press; 1968.

Radcliffe AW. *The Mysteries of Udolpho: A Romance.* London: Folio Society; 1987.

Rainey LS, editor. *Modernism: An Anthology.* Malden MA: Blackwell; 2005.

Rajan T. Introduction. In: Shelley M. *Valperga: Or, The Life and Adventures of Castruccio, Prince of Lucca.* New York; Oxord: Oxford University Press; 1997. pp. 7-42.

Rand NT. Introduction: Renewals of Psychoanalysis. In: Abraham N, Torok M. *The Shell and the Kernel: Renewals of Psychoanalysis, Volume 1.* (Translated by Rand NT.) Chicago; London: University of Chicago Press; 1994. pp. 1-22.

Ranisch R, Sorgner SL. Introducing Post- and Transhumanism. In: Ranisch R, Sorgner SL (Ed.) *Post- and Transhumanism: An Introduction.* New York: Peter Lang; 2014. pp. 8-27.

Rapatzikou TG. *Gothic Motifs in the Fiction of William Gibson.* Amsterdam; New York: Rodopi; 2004.

Raposa M. *Boredom and the Religious Imagination.* Charlottesville: University of Virginia Press; 1999.

Ray M. L'Inquiétude. In: Caws MA (Ed.) *Manifesto: A Century of Isms.* Lincoln: University of Nebraska Press; 2001. pp. 335-339.

Redding AF. Bruises, Roses: Masochism and the Writing of Kathy Acker. *Contemporary Literature.* 1994; 35(2): pp. 281-304. DOI: https://doi.org/10.2307/1208840

Remarque EM. *All Quiet on the Western Front.* (Translated by Wheen AW.) New York: Ballantine Books; 1958.

Remarque EM. *Im Westen nichts Neues.* London: Routledge; 1984.

Remarque EM. *The Road Back*. (Translated by Wheen AW.) Boston: Little, Brown; 1931.
Reichardt J. Artificial Life and the Myth of Frankenstein. In: Bann S (Ed.) *Frankenstein, Creation and Monstrosity*. London: Reaktion; 1994. pp. 136–157.
Rennie N. *Speculating on the Moment: The Poetics of Time and Recurrence in Goethe, Leopardi, and Nietzsche*. Göttingen: Wallstein Verlag; 2005.
Rheiner W. Expressionismus und Schauspiel. *Die neue Schaubühne*. 1919; 1: pp. 14–17.
Rice S. *Parisian Views*. Cambridge: MIT Press; 1999.
Rosengarten F. *Giacomo Leopardi's Search for a Common Life Through Poetry: a Different Nobility, a Different Love*. Madison NJ: Fairleigh Dickinson University Press; 2012.
Ross A. *Strange Weather: Culture, Science, and Technology in the Age of Limits*. London; New York: Verso; 1991.
Royle N. *The Uncanny*. Manchester: Manchester University Press; 2003.
Rucker R. *Wetware*. New York: Avon Books; 1988.
Rucker R. "What is Wetaware?" *Rudy's Blog*; 2016. http://www.rudyrucker.com/blog/2007/08/25/what-is-wetware/. Accessed: 05-10-2019.
Ruh B. *Stray Dog of Anime: The Films of Mamoru Oshii, Second Edition*. New York: Palgrave Macmillan; 2014.
Russell B. *The Conquest of Happiness*. London; New York: Routledge; 2015.
Rutherford J. The Third Space: Interview with Homi Bhabha. In: *Identity: Community, Culture, Difference*. London: Lawrence & Wishart; 1990. pp. 207–221.
Saccone E. *Commento a Zeno*. Bologna: Il Mulino; 1973.
Salotto E. Frankenstein and Dis(re)membered Identity. *Journal of Narrative Technique*. 1994; 24(3): pp. 190–211.
Sanyal D. *The Violence of Modernity: Baudelaire, Irony, and the Politics of Form*. Baltimore: Johns Hopkins University Press; 2006.
Sartre JP. *Baudelaire*. (Translated by Turnell M.) Paris: New Directions; 1950.
Sartre JP. *Nausea*. (Translated by Alexander L.) New York: New Direction; 2007.
Saxena A, Dixit S. *Hardy's Tess of the D'Urbervilles*. New Delhi: Atlantic Publishers & Distributors; 2001.
Schimmel A. *Islamic Names*. Edinburgh: Edinburgh University Press; 1989.
Schneider G. *What Happens When Nothing Happens: Boredom and Everyday Life in Contemporary Comics*. Leuven: Leuven University Press; 2016.
Schopenhauer A. *The World as Will and Representation, Volume 2*. (Translated by Payne EFJ.) New York: Dover Publications; 1966.
Scott MC. *Baudelaire's Le Spleen de Paris: Shifting Perspectives*. London; New York: Routledge; 2017.
Scott N. Introduction. In: Scott N (Ed.) *Monsters and the Monstrous: Myths and Metaphors of Enduring Evil*. Amsterdam; New York: Rodopi; 2007. pp. 1–6.

Shelley M. *Frankenstein; or, The Modern Prometheus*. Penguin; 2003.
Shelley M. *Frankenstein; or, The Modern Prometheus, 2nd Ed: The Original 1818 Text*. Broadview Press; 1999.
Shelley M. *Valperga: Or, The Life and Adventures of Castruccio, Prince of Lucca*. New York; Oxord: Oxford University Press; 1997.
Shildrick M. *Embodying the Monster: Encounters with the Vulnerable Self*. London: Sage; 2002.
Shteyngart G. *Super Sad True Love Story: A Novel*. New York: Random House; 2010.
Shukla N. *Meatspace*. London: HarperCollins UK; 2014.
Simmel G. *The Sociology of Georg Simmel*. (Translated by Wolff KH.) New York: Free Press; 1964.
Smith NR. Potent Lore and Medieval Popular Culture. In: Campbell JP (Ed.) *Popular Culture in the Middle Ages*. Bowling Green: Popular Press; 1986. pp. 16–28.
Smith SR. 'When it All Changed': Cyberpunk and the Baby Boom's Rejection of Religious Institutions." In: Epstein J (Ed.) *Youth Culture: Identity in a Postmodern World*. Oxford: Blackwell Publishers; 1998. pp. 232–262.
Söderquist AS. *Kierkegaard on Dialogical Education: Vulnerable Freedom*. London: Lexington; 2016.
Sokel WH. *Writer in Extremis Expressionism in Twentieth-Century German Literature*. Standord CA: Stanford University Press; 1959.
Sondhaus L. *World War One: The Global Revolution*. Cambridge: Cambridge University Press; 2011.
Snyder T. *Black Earth: The Holocaust as History and Warning*. New York: Tim Duggan Books; 2015.
Spacks PM. *Boredom: The Literary History of a State of Mind*. Chicago; London: University of Chicago Press; 1996.
Spender D. *Man-Made Language*. Kitchener, ON: Pandora Press; 1998
Stableford B. *Frankenstein* and the Origins of Science Fiction. In: Seed D (Ed.) *Anticipations: Essays on Early Science Fiction and its Precursors*. Syracuse University Press; 1995. pp. 46–57.
Stephens S. *Baudelaire's Prose Poems: The Practice and Politics of Irony*. Oxford: Oxford University Press; 1999.
Sterrenburg L. Mary Shelley's Monster: Politics and Psyche in Frankenstein. In: Levine G, Knoepflmacher UC (Eds.) *The Endurance of Frankenstein: Essays on Mary Shelley's Novel*. Berkeley: University of California Press; 1979. pp. 143–171.
Stiles A. *Popular Fiction and Brain Science in the Late Nineteenth Century*. Cambridge: Cambridge University Press; 2011.
Stryker S. My Words to Victor Frankenstein above the Village of *Chamounix*: Performing Transgender Rage. In: Stryker S, Whittle S (Eds.) *The Transgender Studies Reader*. New York; London: Taylor & Francis; 2006. pp. 244–256.

Summers-Bremner E. *Insomnia: A Cultural History*. London: Reaktion Books; 2008.
Svendsen L. *A Philosophy of Boredom*. (Translated by Irons J.) London: Reaktion Books; 2005.
Svevo I. *La Coscienza di Zeno*. Segrate: Bur; 2015.
Svevo I. *Zeno's Conscience*. (Translated by Weaver W.) Vintage Books; 2003.
Swanwick M. *Vacuum Flowers*. New York: Open Road Media; 2016.
Szakolczai A. *Reflective Historical Sociology*. London: Routledge; 2000.
Tartar M. *Lustmord: Sexual Murder in Weimar Germany*. Princeton NJ: Princeton University Press; 1995.
Taylor C. *A Secular Age*. Cambridge; London: Belknap Press of Harvard University Press; 2007.
Taylor C. Modes of Secularism. In: Bhargava R (Ed.) *Secularism and Its Critics*. Delhi; New York: Oxford University Press; 1998. pp. 31–53.
Taylor E. *The Mystery of Personality: A History of Psychodynamic Theories*. London; New York: Springer Science & Business Media; 2009.
Terdiman R. *Present Past: Modernity and the Memory Crisis*. Ithaca; London: Cornell University Press; 1993.
The Gospel According to Mark. *The New Oxford Annotated Bible*, 3rd ed. Oxford University Press; 2001. pp. 56–92.
The Gospel According to Matthew. *The New Oxford Annotated Bible*, 3rd ed. Oxford University Press; 2001. pp. 7–55.
The Man Without a Map (1968). Directed by **Teshigahara H**. Katsu Production.
The Red Desert (1964). Directed by **Antonioni M**. Criterion Collection: 2010.
Thomassen B. *Liminality and the Modern: Living Through the In-Between*. London; New York: Routledge; 2016.
Thornburg MKP. *The Monster in the Mirror: Gender and the Sentimental/Gothic Myth in Frankenstein*. Ann Arbor: UMI Research Press; 1987.
Thwaites R. *Changing Names and Gendering Identity: Social Organisation in Contemporary Britain*. London; New York: Taylor & Francis; 2017.
Thweatt-Bates J. *Cyborg Selves: A Theological Anthropology of the Posthuman*. London; New York: Routledge; 2016.
Tichelaar TR. *The Gothic Wanderer: From Transgression to Redemption: Literature from 1794–Present*. Ann Arbor: Modern History Press; 2012.
Tillich P. *On Art and Architecture*. Edited by Dillenberger J. New York: Crossroad; 1987.
Tillich P. *On the Boundary: An Autobiographical Sketch*. Eugene OR: Wipf and Stock Publishers; 2012.
Tillich P. *The Essential Tillich: An Anthology of the Writings of Paul Tillich*. Edited by Church FF. New York: Collier Books; 1988.
Toohey P. *Boredom: A Lively History*. New Haven; London: Yale University Press; 2011.
Tuan YF. *Escapism*. Baltimore: Johns Hopkins University Press; 1998.

Turner VW. *Dramas, Fields, and Metaphors: Symbolic Action in Human Society*. Ithaca; London: Cornell University Press; 1975.

Turner VW. *The Forest of Symbols: Aspects of Ndembu Ritual*. Transaction Publishers; 2011.

Turner VW. *The Ritual Process: Structure and Anti-Structure*. New York: Aldine de Gruyter; 1995.

Turner VW, Turner E. *Image and Pilgrimage in Christian Culture: Anthropological Perspectives*. New York: Columbia University Press; 1978.

Turney J. *Frankenstein's Footsteps: Science, Genetics and Popular Culture*. New Haven: Yale University Press; 1998.

Ulanov AB. *Spirit in Jung*. Einsiedeln: Daimon; 2005.

van Gennep A. *Rites of Passage*. (Translated by Vizedom MB, Caffe GL.) Chicago; London: University of Chicago Press; 1960.

van Tilburg WAP, Igou ER. On Boredom and Social Identity: A Pragmatic Meaning-Regulation Approach. *Personality and Social Psychology Bulletin*. 2011; 37(12): pp. 1679–1691.

Vance J. *Secrets: Humanism, Mysticism, and Evangelism in Erasmus of Rotterdam, Bishop Guillaume Briçonnet, and Marguerite de Navarre*. Leiden; Boston: Brill; 2014.

Vidler A. *The Architectural Uncanny: Essays in the Modern Unhomely*. Cambridge MA; London: MIT Press; 1992.

Vietta S, Kemper HG. *Expressionismus*, 6th ed. Munich: Wilhelm Fink; 1997.

Waldby C. The Instruments of Life: Frankenstein and Cyberculture. In: Tofts D, Jonson A, Cavallaro A (Eds.) *Prefiguring Cyberculture: An Intellectual History*. Cambridge MA; London: MIT Press; 2004. pp. 28–37.

Walker J. Through the Looking Glass: Beyond "User' Interfaces. *CADalyst*. 1989 (Dec): pp, 40–43.

Wallace DF. Certainly the End of *Something* or Other, One Would Sort of Have to Think (Re John Updike's *Toward the End of Time*). In: Hallman JC (Ed.) *The Story About the Story II: Great Writers Explore Great Literature*. Portland OR; Brooklyn: Tin House Books; 2013. pp. 215–222.

Walser R. On the Road to Cyberia: A Few Thoughts on Autodesk's Cyberspace Initiative. *CADalyst*. 1989 (Dec): pp. 43–45.

Webster A. Queer to be Religious: Lesbian Adventures beyond the Christian/Post-Christian Dichotomy. *Theology & Sexuality*. 1998; (8): pp. 27–39.

Weisberg RH. *The Failure of the Word: The Protagonist as Lawyer in Modern Fiction*. New Haven; London: Yale University Press; 1984.

White DE. 'The God Undeified': Mary Shelley's Valperga, Italy, and the Aesthetic of Desire. *Romanticism on the Net*. 1997; (6): pp. 1–34. DOI: https://doi.org/10.7202/005750ar

Willems B. Hospitality and Risk Society in Tao Lin's *Taipei*. In: Claff J, Ridge E (Eds.) *Security and Hospitality in Literature and Culture: Modern and Contemporary Perspectives*. New York: Routledge; 2015. pp. 227–242.

Wilson E. *Adorned in Dreams: Fashion and Modernity*. London: I.B. Tauris; 2003.
Wolff J. The Invisible Flaneuse: Women and the Literature of Modernity. In: *Feminine Sentences: Essays on Women and Culture*. Berkeley; Los Angeles: University of California Press; 1990. pp. 34–50.
Wood RC. Lest the World's Amnesia Be Complete: A Reading of Walter Miller's *A Canticle for Leibowitz*. *Religion & Literature*. 2001; 33(1): pp. 23–41.
Worthington M. Posthumous Posturing: The Subversive Power of Death in Contemporary Women's Fiction. *Studies in the Novel*. 2000; 32(2): pp. 243–263.
Wunrow ZB. Power and Presence in Fritz Lang's *M* (1931). *Inquiries*. 2013; 5(06): p. 1. http://www.inquiriesjournal.com/articles/740/power-and-presence-in-fritz-langs-m-1931. Accessed: 20-08-2018.
Yang G. Liminality and Internet Protests in China. Annual Meeting of the American Sociological Association, Montreal, August 11–14, 2006.
Young E. *Black Frankenstein: The Making of an American Metaphor*. New York; London: NYU Press; 2008.
Yousef N. The Monster in a Dark Room: *Frankenstein*, Feminism, and Philosophy. *Modern Language Quarterly*. 2002; 63(2): pp. 197–226.
Zerilli LMG. *Feminism and the Abyss of Freedom*. Chicago: University of Chicago Press; 2005.
Ziolkowski JM. *Fairy Tales from Before Fairy Tales: The Medieval Latin Past of Wonderful Lies*. Ann Arbor: University of Michigan Press; 2010.
Ziolkowski, SE. Svevo's Uomo Senza Qualità: Musil and Modernism in Italy. In: Schwartz A (Ed.) *Gender and Modernity in Central Europe: The Austro-Hungarian Monarchy and Its Legacy*. Ottawa: University of Ottawa Press; 2010. pp. 83–102.
Zipes J. *When Dreams Came True: Classical Fairy Tales and Their Tradition*. New York; London: Routledge; 2013.
Žižek S. *Against the Double Blackmail: Refugees, Terror and Other Troubles with the Neighbours*. London: Penguin; 2016.
Žižek S. *In Defense of Lost Causes*. London; New York: Verso Books; 2009.
Žižek S. *On Belief*. London; New York: Psychology Press; 2001.
Žižek S. *Tarrying with the Negative: Kant, Hegel, and the Critique of Ideology*. Durham: Duke University Press; 1993.
Žižek S. *Welcome to the Desert of the Real!: Five Essays On September 11 and Related Dates*. London; New York: Verso; 2002.
Zonana J. "They Will Prove the Truth of My Tale": Safie's Letters as the Feminist Core of Mary Shelley's Frankenstein. *Journal of Narrative Technique*. 1991; 21(2): pp. 170–184.

Index

A

abject   16, 41, 42, 150, 159, 160
Abraham, N.
  "Notes on the Phantom"   173
  The Shell and the Kernel   173
absurdity   10, 18, 33, 66, 79, 84, 97
abyss   59, 148, 153, 160, 165, 174, 175
Acker, K.
  Don Quixote   145, 148, 149, 157, 160, 163
  Empire of the Senseless   159
  resacralization of the symbolic   165
actuality   17, 61, 66, 89, 91
afterlife   37, 52, 135
Agamben   81
Ahmed
  "Not In the Mood"   121
  concept of the stranger   121
  Happiness   121
alienation   3, 5, 13, 15, 55, 59, 60, 61, 63, 105, 109, 110, 112, 129, 137, 138, 176, 177

ambiguity   10, 12, 22, 23, 80, 82, 105, 110
ambivalence   13, 17, 22, 94, 146
Antonioni, Michelangelo
  action and plot concepts   109
  expressions of modern malaise   117
  films   109, 110, 112, 117, 118, 119
  portrayal of female protagonists   118
  Red Desert, The   118
anxiety   2, 12, 31, 35, 37, 59, 87, 109
apocalypse   27, 99
attunement   106
autonomy   21, 129, 155, 156, 160
avant-garde art movements   77, 84

B

Baudelaire, Charles
  "L'Albatros"   98
  meaning of *modernité*   9
  on boredom   104, 106

Baudelaire, Charles *(continued)*
  on *ennui* 53, 54, 57, 59, 104, 105, 107, 108, 113, 176
  on modern stranger 47, 75, 93, 125, 137
  poetry and philosophical writings 17, 131
beauty 15, 32, 48, 53, 69, 70, 93, 97, 110, 159, 163
belief 4, 8, 19, 66
Benjamin, Walter 2, 50, 54, 56, 59, 67, 69, 77, 80, 99, 103, 137, 172
Bible 134, 141
binaries 3, 5, 7, 18, 19, 38, 42, 104, 107, 124, 129, 151, 160, 162
bisexuality 12, 145
Bloch, Ernst 15, 18, 77, 79, 97, 101, 156, 172, 175
Bloch, Maurice 18, 98
blurring 25, 27, 110, 127, 146, 160, 164, 172
boredom 3, 5, 11, 15, 17, 52, 56, 69, 103, 110, 117
  challenges of defining 105
  digital 113
  modern stranger 49, 69, 105
boundaries 10, 13, 16, 130, 133, 134, 137, 146, 148, 153
Brave New World 140
Buddhism 134
Burke, Edmund 24
Butler, Judith 81, 82, 145, 154, 160

C

capitalism 60, 69, 83
Caputo, John D. "Hospitality and the Trouble With God" 14
Catholicism 28, 30
Cervantes' tale 158, 161
chaos 13, 16, 23, 29, 33, 76, 77, 83, 91, 92, 94
Christ, Jesus 41, 131, 159
Christianity 4, 7, 9, 14, 26, 28, 30, 64, 131, 132
Christology 17, 132, 154
city space 86, 91, 133
city streets 86, 88, 91, 93, 101, 119, 137
civilization 3, 34, 62, 63, 66, 90, 150
Cixous, Hélène 18, 139, 145, 146, 148, 159, 164
  "The Laugh of Medusa" 145, 148, 159
communication 24, 105, 112, 115, 124, 157
communities 5, 40, 90, 108, 125, 132, 140
computers 114, 117, 123, 134
conflict 2, 5, 59, 84, 87, 133, 152, 176
consciousness 21, 57, 78, 86, 104, 112, 128, 132, 136
Count Zero 126, 132, 135
Covid-22 pandemic 177
creation 2, 5, 26, 28, 32, 35, 40, 42, 147, 149, 151
creator 22, 25, 28, 32, 37, 78, 149, 152, 153, 172
creature 22, 23, 25, 29, 31, 35, 145, 147
crime 25, 39, 91, 110, 126, 130, 150, 162
critique 9, 13, 23, 31, 69, 94, 115, 129, 130, 146, 147
culture 3, 128, 133, 150, 153, 154, 155, 162, 164, 169
cyberculture 139
cyberpunk 125, 126, 127, 129, 130. *see also* Liminality
  hybrid religions in 130
cyberspace 18, 113, 124, 133
  expression of individuality 139
  Gods in 134
  strangers in 137
cyborg 124, 133, 134, 135, 136, 141, 145, 146, 150, 156, 161

D

dangers   2, 12, 15, 34, 65, 137, 150, 157, 176
Dante, *Divine Comedy*   55, 128
darkness   12, 15, 35, 38, 47, 75, 79, 97, 101
death   8, 25, 27, 30, 40, 65, 85, 90, 163
deBeauvoir, Simone   76, 132
  Le Deuxième Sexe (The Second Sex)   145
demons   21, 32, 54, 86, 97
depictions   54, 87, 91, 125, 127
depression   100, 107
Derrida, Jacques   13, 16, 21, 34, 82, 169, 170, 173
  deconstruction theory   174
  use of Hamlet quote   172
  Wolf Man's Magic Word: A Cryptonymy   174
despair   15, 58, 61, 67, 78, 97, 103
destruction   25, 69, 78, 79, 81, 83, 94, 99, 151, 155, 175
devil   52, 147
dichotomies   7, 27, 28, 32, 148, 152, 157
Digital God: How Technology Will Reshape Spirituality (Indick)   124
diseases   36, 37, 51, 78, 92, 96, 162
disenchantment   7, 13, 36, 49, 54, 60, 62, 64
disillusionment   5, 7, 15, 63, 100
displacement   104, 116, 130, 173
disruption   2, 14, 62, 156
divine   78, 80, 81, 97, 99, 100, 124, 154, 175
divine violence   77, 80, 98
domination   152, 157, 162
doppelgänger   2, 27, 42
dream   32, 34, 37, 62, 65, 69, 90, 91, 136, 145, 148, 156, 158, 161
drug addicts   68, 126, 137
Durkheim, Emile   7, 119

E

Eggers, Dave, *The Circle*   18, 125, 140
Eksteins, Modris   85
  Rites of Spring: The Great War and the Birth of the Modern Age   78
embodiment   78, 153
emptiness   37, 58, 60, 106, 118, 161
enemy   56, 75, 82, 83, 86
Enlightenment   8, 12, 13, 21, 27, 30, 36, 64, 66
essentialism   154, 164
Europe   2, 3, 21, 83, 87, 124, 129
  and American societies   4
  civil war   75
  contemporary/modern   64
  culture   2
  divided   88
  Eastern   129
  history   30
  postwar   91
  20th-century   13
  22th-century   5
Evangelical secularism   128
excitement   11, 83, 111, 113, 114, 116
exhaustion   96, 104, 108, 110
exile   68, 120, 162, 165
existential boredom   49, 57, 106, 111, 113, 117
existentialism   9, 37, 42, 105, 107

F

failure   3, 9, 32, 41, 69, 70, 77, 83, 100, 161
faith   6, 8, 66, 78, 100, 133
fascination   22, 27, 33, 38, 89, 91, 93, 152
fear   12, 23, 25, 30, 32, 33, 62, 64, 91, 113, 115, 116, 140
female characters   147, 149, 158
feminine   155, 158
feminism   18, 155

Feminism and the Abyss of Freedom   156
fiction   23, 29, 30, 31, 126, 127, 129, 138, 149, 157
films   91, 103, 105, 109, 116, 118, 119, 125, 132
freedom   2, 4, 15, 17, 23, 25, 39, 61, 62, 118, 119, 155, 158, 160, 164
French Revolution   2, 22, 23, 24, 31, 49, 55, 62, 66, 84, 173
Freud, Sigmund   12, 29, 35, 38, 57
  "Das Unheimliche" ("The Uncanny")   12
futurism   77, 87

G

gaze   59, 62, 67, 68, 98, 111, 155, 156, 157, 158, 159, 160
gender   2, 16, 18, 130, 147, 148, 154, 156, 159, 164
  binaries   18, 84, 157
  female   148, 149, 153
  studies   24, 146
generation   64, 105, 139
genesis   26, 158
genre   129, 149, 172
Gibson, William
  Count Zero   126, 132, 135
  cyberpunk novels   114, 137
  idea of transcendence in cyberspace   136, 138
  Mona Lisa Overdrive   126, 135, 136
  Neuromancer   123, 125, 126, 128, 129, 130, 135, 136, 138
  Sprawl trilogy   125, 126, 130, 136
  universal cityscape concept   126
  use of multiplicity   133
  vision of the urban streets   132
God   7, 14, 22, 24, 33, 36, 37, 38, 51, 64, 80, 125, 131, 132, 133, 141, 149, 159. *see also* omnipotence; omnipresence; omnipresent
goddess   69, 150, 153
gothic   26, 30, 41
  fiction   30
  genre   26, 27, 31, 42
  literature   27, 30
  tradition   17
guilt   69, 80, 88

H

Habermas, Jürgen   9
hackers   126, 129, 134, 135, 137
happiness   15, 57, 64, 112, 116, 120
Haraway, Donna   18, 39, 145, 146, 147, 148, 149
  "A Manifesto for Cyborgs"   146
  techno-feminist cyborg   153
heaven   25, 36, 54, 55, 61, 136, 138, 141
Heidegger, Martin   104, 106
hell   17, 25, 49, 52, 54, 55, 60, 61, 79, 139
hero   27, 30, 42, 158
heterotopia   126
history   2, 3, 6, 7, 8, 26, 28, 60, 63, 78, 145, 150, 172
  human   23, 29, 64, 67, 81, 130
Hitchcock, Alfred   110
Hitler, Adolf   82
Holy Grail   145, 158
homo sacer   82, 101
horrors   2, 42, 43, 48, 56, 63, 76, 83, 100, 105, 175
human agency   33, 37, 135
human beings   37, 39, 65, 98, 112, 146, 162
human body   37, 87, 132, 134, 136, 138, 146, 150, 154
hybridity   131, 132, 141, 147, 148, 149, 151, 159, 165
hybridization   2, 151, 153, 171, 172

I

idealism   38, 163
illusions   50, 52, 54, 56, 58, 61, 62, 64, 70, 88, 92, 95, 104, 148
illusory   8, 33, 121, 133, 139, 152, 158
image   41, 51, 52, 60, 68, 69, 150, 153, 155, 163, 171
imagination   26, 32, 37, 48, 53, 56, 65, 170, 171, 176
immortality   130, 135
impasse   13, 82, 90
impossibility   10, 35, 57, 150, 158, 171
inability   30, 34, 39, 49, 57, 64, 70, 112, 160
inaction   95, 102, 109, 116, 120
innocence   25, 129, 132, 136
intellectuals   2, 146, 156
internet   18, 113, 114, 116, 121
invisible religion (Luckmann)   124
Irigaray, Luce   104, 146, 148
irony   77, 95, 97, 102
isolation   39, 84, 170, 173

J

Joyce, James   55, 125
Judeo-Christian   3, 7, 128, 154
judgment   42, 92, 107, 141
Jung, Carl   86

K

Kant, Immanuel   80, 172
Kierkegaard, Soren   60, 78, 104
Klee, Paul   67
knowledge   2, 22, 23, 26, 28, 32, 33, 39, 63, 99, 129, 134
Kristeva, Julia   8, 14, 15, 16, 41, 42, 76, 146, 160
  Strangers to Ourselves   14
Kusanagi, Motoko   132, 136

L

L'Étranger (Camus)   39
Lacan, Jacques   15, 57
Latour, B.   151
  concept of hybridization   152
Le Loyer, Pierre   170
Leopardi, Giacomo
  "La Ginestra O, Il Fiore Del Deserto"   66
  concept of noia   58
  notion of the monstrous   17
  on modern stranger   50, 75
  on pleasure and desire   57
  on secularized hell   61
  return to barbarism   84
  spiritual evolution   66
  view of history   63
Levy, Amy   118
Lewis, Matthew Gregory   61
  The Monk   31
Liminality. *see also* Leopardi, Giacomo; Shelly, Mary, *Frankenstein*
  Agamben's stranger   82
  boredom   3, 5, 11, 15, 17, 18
  Elam, Diane's definition   148
  essential characteristics   76
  Gennep's introduction of   10
  Manifestation   125
  modern culture and society   7
  modern stranger   2, 13, 113, 115, 163, 169
  negative state   99
  secularized modernity   5, 11
Lin, Tao
  EeeeeEeeEeee   113
  Shoplifting from American Apparel   113
  Taipei   113
  Treatise of Specters   170
  trilogy of *L'Avventura, La Notte* and *L'Eclisse*   105

literature 2, 6, 7, 19, 28, 30, 42, 68, 76, 78, 104, 111, 118, 139, 140
Lo and Behold, Reveries of the Connected World (Herzog's documentary) 123
love 38, 47, 63, 70, 93, 100, 109, 157, 161, 163

M

machines 18, 37, 39, 87, 100, 123, 130, 146
madness 90, 158, 163
Marx, Karl 21, 33, 60, 80
Medusa, myth of 18, 145, 148, 159
messianic mission 5, 15, 17, 22, 25, 77, 81, 92, 93, 98, 159, 172, 174
metaphor 87, 95, 118, 119, 124
Middle Ages 16, 30, 106
Miller Jr, Walter M. 98, 126
  A Canticle for Leibowitz 75, 77, 99
Milton, John 41
modern society 11, 17, 39, 76, 90, 97, 107, 152, 176
modern stranger
  adaptation and future 175
  boredom 49, 52, 56, 69, 105
  cyberspace 137
  spectral-monster or spect-actor 175
modernism 10, 24, 28, 55, 77, 93
modernity
  women strangers 119
moderns 25, 34, 55, 56, 62, 95, 146, 151
monsters
  hybridization of 171
  spectres and 169
monstrosity. *see also* Shelly, Mary, *Frankenstein*
  Baudelaire on 53
  Catholicism and 30
  concept of 16
  hybridization of 24
  Leopardi on 51
notion of the spectre 16, 169
un-evil 42
mood 18, 68, 104, 105
morality 30, 48, 56, 79, 112, 164
Mr. Robot 140
myth 23, 27, 34, 36, 48, 60, 148

N

narratives 77, 109, 113, 133, 154, 158, 163
nation states 84, 127
Nietzsche, F 15, 62, 63, 104
nothingness 56, 58, 93, 159

O

objects 14, 38, 40, 110, 158, 159
Old Testament 7
omnipotence 26, 124, 135, 136
omnipresence 124, 131, 163
omnipresent 114, 138
omniscience 124, 135, 136
online 114, 124, 139
optimism 25, 49, 62, 66, 84, 112, 118
Oshii 129, 131, 132, 136, 138
  Ghost in the Shell series 125, 130
otherness 14, 22, 29, 129, 155, 162, 171

P

pain 49, 56, 75, 93, 163
paradoxical 10, 14, 23, 24, 28, 41, 48, 61, 63, 77, 92, 97
patriarchal society 18, 119, 146, 150, 159
patriarchy 101, 146, 150, 156
perfection 36, 51, 75, 95, 132, 153
pessimist 11, 23, 48, 49, 61
phantoms 139, 169, 172
  spectres and 172
philosophy 2, 6, 17, 50, 54, 66, 76, 80, 129, 131
physical body 125, 134, 135, 136, 137, 138, 139, 150, 162

Plato 74
poems 50, 52, 54, 56, 62, 98
poetry 17, 52, 54, 63, 176
poets 48, 54, 59, 62, 76
posthumanism 6, 18, 147, 148, 154
power 27, 28, 43, 127, 128, 135, 145, 153, 157, 158, 159, 161
profane 3, 7, 8, 10, 16, 28, 29, 79, 127, 148, 154
protagonists 42, 82, 94, 113, 157, 158
Protestantism 8, 27, 119
psyches 23, 30, 55, 86, 110
psychoanalysis 6, 24, 50, 78, 94

Q

quantum theory 118

R

religion 7, 134. *see also* God
resacralization 2, 5, 7, 9, 92, 97, 98, 124, 125, 136, 146, 148, 152. *see also* Acker, K
ritual 7, 98, 154
Roman Catholicism 133
Romantic movements 26, 27, 30
ruins 2, 17, 62, 101, 169, 173, 175

S

sacredness 26, 30, 53, 80, 83, 93, 97, 105, 108, 119, 153
salvation 101, 130, 132
science 24, 28, 33, 36, 38, 41, 94, 96, 138, 139
  fiction 28, 77, 126, 138, 139, 140
secrets 12, 24, 26, 28, 29, 42, 50, 80, 140, 141, 169
secularism 2, 4, 13, 14, 27, 57, 60, 128
secularization 5, 7, 8, 12, 15, 27, 36, 48, 61
secularized modernity. *see also* Shelley, Mary, *Frankenstein*

concept of monstrosity 16
liminality 5, 10
modern stranger's role 2
sensations 9, 17, 69, 91, 105
sentiment 10, 33, 83, 85, 87, 106, 141
sexes 150, 163
sexuality 147, 148, 151, 155
shadows 17, 22, 23, 30, 36, 41, 91
Shelley, Mary 24, 25, 26, 27, 28, 31, 32, 33, 34, 35, 36, 38, 39, 40, 41, 42, 43, 48, 54, 79, 87, 131, 147, 148, 153, 169, 170
  Frankenstein 17, 29, 31, 43, 90, 124, 135
sickness 18, 78, 90, 92, 164
social media 5, 18, 105, 113, 115, 121, 140
soul 21, 32, 34, 69, 80, 106, 123, 135, 141, 169
spectres
  modern stranger 174
  monsters and 169
spirituality 12, 16, 97, 153, 154
Stand Alone Complex series 136
suffering 36, 39, 58, 76, 83, 90, 100, 162, 163
supernatural 28, 30, 35, 64, 91
Svevo, Italo 18
  Zeno's Conscience 75, 94
symbolism 7, 98, 128, 131
symbols 12, 16, 28, 29, 42, 87, 90, 165, 173

T

technology 105, 114, 115, 121, 126, 127, 128, 129, 130, 134, 137, 138, 145, 155
terror 13, 31, 33, 54, 65, 76, 91, 92, 110
1987 (novel) 140
Torok, A. 173
  The Shell and the Kernel 173

transcendence   10, 126, 130, 132, 134, 136, 138, 148, 154, 156, 160, 163
truth   4, 6, 32, 34, 42, 64, 95, 115, 164

U

uncanniness   14, 43, 141, 151
uncertainty   12, 13, 31, 37, 43, 49, 82, 84, 88, 120, 124
unhappiness   15, 49, 58, 79, 113, 120
universe   27, 33, 54, 56, 97, 107, 114, 126, 129
utopia/utopian   5, 15, 17, 70, 77, 78, 87, 98, 101, 103, 146, 156
  spirit   25, 79, 80, 98, 142, 162, 164, 175

V

victim   25, 33, 43, 75, 76, 89, 90, 91, 92, 95, 102, 158

violence   18, 70, 77, 83, 84, 92, 93, 94, 97, 98, 102, 158, 159, 161

W

Wallace, David Foster   22
wanderers   42, 55, 99
warfare   83, 87
  modern   78, 87, 88, 92
women   53, 118, 121, 147, 153, 155, 157, 159, 162
WWI   79, 83, 84, 87, 88, 91, 93, 95, 100, 101, 175
WWII   76, 83, 87, 98, 105, 145

Z

Zerilli LMG.
  Feminism and the Abyss of Freedom   156
Žižek, S.   100
  On Belief (Thinking In Action)   134